Seal Wars

TWENTY-FIVE YEARS ON
THE FRONT LINES
WITH THE HARP SEALS

Captain Paul Watson

To Chris,

In appreciation
for your
support for
Sea Shepherd

Captain
Paul Watson

FIREFLY BOOKS

A FIREFLY BOOK

Published by Firefly Books (U.S.) Inc. 2003

First Printing

Publisher Cataloging-in-Publication Data (U.S.)

Watson, Paul.
     Seal wars: twenty-five years on the front lines with the harp seal / Paul Watson ; foreword by Martin Sheen. – 1st ed.

[256] p. : ill. , photos. ; cm.
Includes index.

Summary: Memoir of environmentalist Paul Watson who recounts his 25 years on the front lines in the war to stop the slaughter of the Canadian harp seal.

ISBN 1-55297-751-X (pbk.)

1. Harp seal. 2. Seals (Animals). 3. Watson, Paul. 4. Wildlife conservation. 5. Conservationists—Canada—Biography. I. Title.

639.9/ 795 B 21   QL31.W38 2003

Published in the United States in 2003 by
Firefly Books (U.S.) Inc.
P.O. Box 1338, Ellicott Station
Buffalo, New York, USA
14205

Published in Canada in 2002 by Key Porter Books Limited.

Cover design: Peter Maher
Cover photograph: Peter Brown
Electronic formatting: Heidi Palfrey

Printed and bound in Canada

To my wife, Allison,
who loves the seals
as much as I do.

Contents

Foreword

There are many environmental scientists today who believe we may have already reached the point of no return in our failure to restore the earth and its wildlife to its original health, and that we must begin now to protect that which remains if we ourselves are to survive as a species.

Despite astonishing evidence of catastrophic deterioration already well under way since the mid-1940s, and widely documented as early as 1962 with the publication of Rachael Carson's *Silent Spring,* we have done precious little to restore the damage or stem the tide of environmental decline. Although we now possess the certain knowledge of "things to come" and the means to alter them, we simply do not possess the collective will to do so, accepting instead a delusional mindset that eventually "a miracle cure" will arrive in time to save the planet. Fortunately, such is not the mindset of a handful of dedicated environmental activists who combine limited resources with unlimited imagination and a dearly paid-for personal commitment to the earth's stewardship, and chief among them is Paul Watson.

Watson has been a personal hero of mine ever since I first learned of his heroic efforts to draw the world's attention to the brutal slaughter of the harp seal pups by literally placing himself between the club-swinging sealers and their helpless prey, time and time again, at great personal risk.

A native-born Canadian, Watson grew up a natural-born environmentalist who understood from his early childhood experiences in the wilderness the supreme value of nature and the absolute necessity of preserving it. Forced to confront his fear of death at an early age, and with repeated struggle and challenge, he seems to have reached that level of spiritual freedom, "devoutly to be wished," where courage is commonplace.

Our paths first crossed in 1989 aboard *Sea Shepherd II* at San Pedro harbour, off the coast of Southern California, when I hosted a pilot for a new TV series on the environment called "EcoSpies," for which he granted an interview. The series never went beyond the pilot, but, fortunately, our friendship did.

In the spring of 1995, while I was on a break from filming *The American President* in Los Angeles, Paul invited me to join him and his crew on yet another of his adventuresome efforts to halt the seal hunt in the Magdalen Islands. Although I was naturally apprehensive for my own safety, I borrowed some of his courage and accepted the invitation.

It was a harrowing experience, to say the least! Our efforts were violently thwarted by an angry and drunken mob of sealers. The ensuing riot was widely reported in the press and is accurately recorded by Paul in the first chapter of this book. While I was not harmed personally, Paul was severely beaten, and barely escaped with his life. Still, the incident served to underscore the heavy price he has had to pay for his activism since he began his crusade in the early 1970s. Since that first adventure, my admiration for him has only grown stronger.

The sealers of the Magdalen Islands live isolated lives in a community largely cut off from the mainstream of Canadian culture. Since the hunt is seasonal, there is high unemployment, and many families must depend on government subsidies to survive. This situation is coupled with few opportunities for higher education, limited resources, and widespread alcohol abuse, and yet the sealers remain extremely defensive about their way of life, viewing any outside interference in the hunt as an intolerable threat to their "rightful heritage." Thus, the hands-on slaughter of baby seal pups on the offshore ice pods continues every spring unabated, despite the fact that, with the rapidly declining demand for seal pup products and the alarming decline of the seal population itself, it is no longer lucrative. Nevertheless, any serious consideration of an alternative livelihood or lifestyle remains out of the question. Despite a clear understanding that such arrogance is only ignorance matured, or perhaps even nurtured by it, year after year, Watson returns to the hunt and continues to risk his life confronting it.

In this memoir, Paul Watson records his story of twenty-five years at the helm, confronting an equal measure of government bureaucracy and sealer brutality. Though it may read, from time to time, like the personal exploits of a fearless adventurer, it is in fact the extraordinary history of one man's perilous battle to save a harmless species from extinction. Watson also happens to be a daring sea captain, who along the way co-founded Greenpeace, and eventually formed the Sea Shepherd Conservation Society. Watson's chronicle of the Herculean efforts he and his crew have applied to halt the killings, while enduring subfreezing weather conditions, death threats, vulgar confrontations, beatings, fines, and jail, begs the question, why continue? Why, indeed, is the point of the entire book, and Watson's powerful, elegant, and deeply moving response is saved for the final chapter.

Like a true prophet never honoured in his own land, Paul Watson has won considerable acclaim elsewhere, including, perhaps, no honour more enviable than the long-promised blessing for "those who hunger and thirst for justice"— and the hunt goes on.

MARTIN SHEEN
JULY 2002

Introduction

Ever since I was a boy of nine, I have abhorred the killing of seals. That was in 1960, when I first saw evidence of the seal hunt with my own eyes. To this day, forty-two years later, I can still recall the vivid, scarlet-on-white images that so disturbed me as a child. In my nightmares, newborn seal pups were bludgeoned by men whose cold, savage eyes held a ruthlessness I had never before encountered or imagined. In some dreams, I was the seal pup, shivering defenselessly in the shadow of a huge hairy creature who brutally wielded a spiked club dripping with blood. I remember feeling frustrated, angry, and extremely helpless.

Until I saw those pictures, I had felt that the world was a friendly, peaceful, and gentle place. But my illusions were shattered. To overcome my nightmares, I fantasized raising an army of seal defenders and leading them to the ice floes. These fantasies gave me the strength to accept a reality that my more sensitive side sought to reject.

As I grew older, I refused to put my childhood ideals behind me. The memories of those images remained hauntingly lucid.

Finally, at the age of twenty-five, my childhood fantasies were partially realized when I organized the first Greenpeace campaign to oppose the Canadian seal hunt. Today, at the age of fifty-one, I continue to fight for the harp seals. For me, they have been a passion, a lifetime commitment, and a calling. My allegiance to this species has never faltered, and my passion is renewed with every visit to the harp seal nurseries.

I first set foot on the ice off the Labrador Front in 1976, leading a small crew of Greenpeace campaigners. I returned in 1977 with a larger Greenpeace crew and the French actress Brigitte Bardot. In 1979, my third expedition brought the first seal protection ship to the seal nurseries of the Gulf of St. Lawrence. In 1981, I led the first independent *Sea Shepherd* expedition using ocean kayaks. In my fifth campaign, my ship, the formidable *Sea Shepherd II*, blockaded the harbour of St. John's, the capital of Newfoundland, and then escorted the sealing fleet from the Gulf of St. Lawrence. The kill that year fell 76,000 pups below the quota.

In 1983, the European Economic Community announced that harp seal pelts would be banned from the European markets. The Canadian commercial sealing industry crashed. It was a major victory for the anti-sealing movement.

Unfortunately the killing continued, though the numbers fell from over 200,000 to the still unacceptably high figure of some 60,000 seal casualties per year. We could not stop the so-called landsman hunt, which consisted of thousands of hunters each taking a few seals over thousands of miles of Canadian coastline. Tactically, we were forced, for the time being, to settle for the victory over the big commercial ships.

But in 1992, grumbling from Newfoundland, Norway, and Ottawa indicated that the Canadian government was once again contemplating a return to commercial sealing. I went back to the ice a sixth time in 1994, this time to promote a cruelty-free, non-lethal form of sealing. On the seventh expedition, in 1995, my alternative approach was met with mob violence on the Magdalen Islands. My crew and I barely escaped with our lives.

With the announcement in 1995 of a Canadian quota of 250,000 seals, Canada fired the first shot of the reopening of the seal wars. In 1996, in my eighth campaign, I further explored the possibility of alternative employment for the sealers, only to realize that the Canadian government was not interested.

My ninth campaign was with the *Sea Shepherd III* in 1998, in the ice fields of the Gulf of St. Lawrence. The seal wars had been renewed, and the animosity and the cruelties had returned with a ferociousness more intense than ever. In 1999, Newfoundland Fisheries Minister John Efford called for an end to the "seal problem"—total extermination.

On my last campaign, my tenth expedition to the ice, in 1999, my crew were armed with movie cameras to bring this slaughter, with all its drama and tragedy, to the big screen. On March 15, 1999, as I sat on a chunk of jagged drift ice with baby seals at my feet and inquisitive mothers all around me, I reflected on my many years of struggle opposing this bloody slaughter.

My initial yearning as a child to help the seals molded my development, and as I grew older, it led me to work to protect whales, fish, elephants, rainforests, wolves, bison, frogs, seabirds, and numerous other species. Because my commitment was born out of passion, I swore back in 1976, when I first led a Greenpeace crew to the ice floes off Labrador, that I would never accept a single dollar for myself from charitable donations for the seals. I have kept that vow. Instead, I have supported myself by teaching college and lecturing at universities around the world on ecology and activism.

Despite this, government, industry, and media critics who accuse all seal protectors of being involved for the money have tarred me with the same libelous brush. Nothing could be further from the truth. My passion for the seals from Greenland has cost me dearly—financially, emotionally, and physically.

At the same time, I have reaped one great benefit. I am a happy man for living my dreams, fulfilling my passions, and doing something that has made a difference in this world.

I am a man who loves the wild and all its citizens, and it is this love that sustains me. In the innocent eye of a baby seal, in the mournful eye of a dying whale, in the whispering of redwoods and pines, in the ingenuity of spiders and the free flight of birds I see the salvation of the Earth and even of our own species.

In this book, I will attempt to shed some insight into my passion for the seals. I also hope to illustrate the conflict between people of compassion and big governments, big business, and that dark side of humanity that seeks to destroy the beauty of the natural world.

I came very close to death in 1995 at the hands of a mob of angry sealers. If by chance I should fall before my opposition, this book will serve as my testament. If just one child with a yearning to protect nature is inspired to act in the future because of this story, then it will have been worth the effort.

This book is many things: It is a history of the great campaigns to end the Canadian seal hunt. It is also an adventure tale that illustrates that any of us can

achieve great things through passionate compassion and a dedicated commitment to an ideal. It also documents some of the petty politics and scandals that
underscore conservation and animal rights efforts. This story is not all black
and white; corruption does indeed lurk behind the mask of moral righteousness.
Some have said that the highest-paid sealers are the ones supposedly saving
seals. This criticism has some merit, and I intend to address it.

Most important, I believe the seal wars have involved vicious propaganda campaigns fought by seal killers and seal protectors, and the truth has been a major
casualty of these wars. In this book, I have also given myself the task of present-
ing events as fairly and truthfully as I can. Of course, one cannot avoid subjective
observation when one is a participating combatant in any conflict. I report what *I*
see, what *I* hear, and what *I* experience. In other words, I call it like I see it.
However, I do acknowledge that truth is perception and all truths are biased.

Therefore, I do not pretend to be unbiased about the sealers and the bureaucrats of the Canadian and Norwegian governments. They have beaten me, jailed
me, violated my civil and human rights, and committed crimes against nature
that it has been my burden to witness.

Over the years, though, I have kept logs and journals, and the events that I
describe all occurred as written. However, I'm not writing this to impress you,
the reader. Quite frankly, I do not care a fig for your opinion of my actions or
point of view. This is simply an autobiographical account of my legacy and an
attempt to contribute to the historical record of a cause that has endured for a
generation and will endure until the anthropocentric barbarism of the human
race is forever vanquished.

The validity of our acts today will be judged by people who will not be born
for hundreds of years. I am confident that history will absolve us—the conservationists, the animal welfare workers, and the animal rights movement—of the
accusations and the libels of the spin doctors and the public relations companies
representing industry and government.

The fate of seals, whales, and dolphins being killed in the wild will be
resolved in one of two ways: They will either be saved and allowed to live in
peace with humanity, or we will exterminate them. Our ballooning population,
our greed, our pollution, and our destruction of habitats will never allow the
perpetuation of the myth of "sustainable harvest."

It is my fervent desire to see the slaughter of seals ended forever. If this is an
unreasonable attitude, then I would rather be considered unreasonable than to
compromise the life of another living creature, or the right of a species to survive.

Seals are a part of the natural cycle of life in the seas. They have earned their territorial birthright by virtue of millions of years of evolution. We, the interloper primates from the land, have no right to exploit them for sport or for luxury items like fur, cosmetics, exotic foods, or hocus pocus sex potions.

The seals brought me to the ice and allowed me the opportunity to be their shepherd. As a shepherd I have protected them, and I will fight for them against the forces of hell if need be, and I will never abandon them.

So this book is also the story of a shepherd. I hope it entertains, educates, and provokes an emotional as well as an intellectual response.

But most of all, I hope this book transports you to another world. It is a hostile world, with waters so cold a human can survive only minutes in them. It is an alien world of heaving masses of ice, where hundreds of men have died and millions of seal pups and their mothers have been massacred. It is a world that has attracted the glamour of movie stars, the curiosity of scientists, the courage of conservationists, and the passion of the animal rights movement. It is the world of one of the most beautiful creatures on the planet, the baby harp seal.

This book is about that world and the struggle that is waged upon its unstable, frigid surface every spring.

It Was a Good Day to Die!

The Magdalen Islands, Québec, March 16, 1995

Hoka hey!

—The war cry of the Lakota

T he barbarians were at the gate. The stench of stale tobacco and spilt beer seeped down the hallways into our rooms. The low, nasal snarl of the local French patois was punctuated with bastardized English obscenities. The snarl rose to an ugly growl as a swarm of sealers surged through the hotel hallway, piss-drunk on cheap booze and fuelled by a rabid malevolence born of a history of ethnic feuding and the frustrations of the uneducated and the institutionally unemployed.

Viciously kicking and pounding at doors, terrorizing guests, they screamed for my head.

"Where is dis fokking Watson? Where are dose fokking seal-loving peecees of merde?"

In room 213 we were not feeling very secure. I had a sense of déjà vu as I listened to the angry rumble outside the door. I had been in this same uncomfortable situation before. This time Marc Gaede, our photographer, was with me, along with two plainclothes officers from the Sûreté du Québec. The chaotic roar in the hallway visibly shook Gaede, a former U.S. Marine.

"What do you intend to do when this mob breaks down that door?" I asked the police.

"We can do nothing." The ranking officer, Pierre Dufort, shrugged. "We cannot defend you."

"That's just fucking great!" I yelled at him. I was—much to my surprise—shocked. Not that I had ever had much faith in the abilities of Canadian police to uphold justice, but it was incredible to think that these officers, armed as they were, would actually allow a lynch mob to take us.

My crew was scattered throughout the second floor of the hotel. Actor Martin Sheen was in room 205 with Chuck Swift and a German film crew. Bob Hunter and his Toronto Citytv videographer Todd Southgate were in another room. Outside, the hallway was bursting with large men dressed in black mud-encrusted snowmobile outfits, bellowing threats and obscenities.

Angrily, I turned to Dufort. "I told you an hour ago to call for reinforcements from the mainland. This mob is completely out of control."

Again Dufort shrugged like he hadn't a care in the world. "For what purpose? They would not reach here in time anyway."

I telephoned Dr. Hedy Fry, my member of Parliament for Vancouver Centre. Her staff told me that there was nothing she could do—it was a matter for the police. When I insisted that the police were refusing to defend us, the staff member put me on hold and came back ten minutes later to say that she was sorry but that Fry was unable to help.

Marc said, "You mean your member of Parliament refuses to help us?"

"She won't do a thing," I answered. "You know, she used to be my damn doctor, even helped to deliver my daughter fifteen years ago, and she couldn't give a sweet goddamn about us. I shouldn't be surprised, she's a bloody Liberal, one of Prime Minister Jean 'Crouton's' little ass-kissers."

Suddenly a vicious blow shook the door. An iniquitous roar indicated that the mob had found what they believed was my location.

"Jesus Christ, Dufort," I said anxiously. "What the hell do you intend to do?"

"I cannot shoot them, I live with these people, eh?"

"Dufort, I am here with a federal government research permit. I have not broken any law. That mob out there has already damaged property and they intend to break down that door and attack us. Yet you'll do nothing?"

"Well, they are angry for what you did in 1983," Dufort protested meekly.

"But 1983, damn it, that was twelve goddamn years ago!"

"These people have long memories. Have you not seen our licence plates, monsieur? The motto is '*Je me souviens.*'"

"Well, one of my ancestors was in the Scottish Highlanders under Wolfe at the battle of Québec in 1759. I suppose they won't forgive me for that either. It's all in the past, for Christ's sake."

Dufort smiled. "I wouldn't let them know that if I was you. We have not forgotten Wolfe either."

Marc looked incredulous. "Oh shit, this country is loony tunes."

The door cracked. An ax blade burst through and shattered the top hinge.

I was tempted to tackle Dufort and grab his gun but then quickly dismissed that idea as over the top. Madness could be met with madness, I suppose, but I wasn't feeling particularly suicidal.

Instead, I bolted for the adjoining bedroom and pushed the bed against the door. Pulling a stun gun from my pocket, I positioned myself between the bed and the wall opposite the door, braced my shoulders against the bed and locked my legs straight against the wall. In the next room, the door was ripped off its hinges and the mob burst in with a victorious roar.

Spying Marc, they surged aggressively toward him.

Two of the sealers shoved him hard against the wall. One sealer pushed his fingers into Marc's face and attempted to gouge out his eyes. The man backed off when someone yelled out that Marc was not Watson. None of the sealers was aware that the closed bedroom door was part of the suite. It simply looked like a door to an adjoining room. For a few moments, the mob murmured in confusion. Then Dufort helpfully inclined his head, nodding toward the bedroom door.[1] The room erupted in another roar of rage as a half dozen shoulders slammed into the locked and barricaded door. Braced for the onslaught, I felt my heels driven into the drywall by the pressure.

I had not expected this attack. We had arrived in the Magdalens to offer an alternative. In a few days, Tobias Kirchoff of Kirchoff Bedding Fabrics of Germany would be arriving to make an official offer of employment to the sealers. He would be prepared to pay cash on the spot for collected harp seal pup hair.

The traditional sealers would have no part of such plans. "Seals are meant to be clubbed, not coddled," screeched Gilles Theriault of the Magdalen Islands Sealing Association. "Who the fuck does Watson think he is? Does he think we will trade the club for a hairbrush? We are men! Sealing men! *Tabernac*, does he think we are women?"

Organized by a few old sealers who remembered me from twelve years before, a meeting had been convened at the town hall. Reporters were ousted from the meeting and warned not to interfere. By late afternoon, fired up on alcohol, the sealers had occupied the lobby of our hotel and refused to allow anybody to enter or leave. We called the police and that was when Dufort refused my request to order backup from the mainland.

Six officers had arrived at the hotel, but made no attempt to disperse the crowd.

In the lobby, the sealers snarled that they wanted "no part of a faggoty idea like seal brushing."

Martin Sheen had gone to the lobby and requested that the sealers come with him across the street to the Catholic Church to discuss things. In response, they threatened to lynch him if he didn't leave. Martin was then warned by a Sûreté officer to return to his room because his safety could not be guaranteed.

Martin was no stranger to confrontation. He had submitted to arrest on numerous occasions in protests against nuclear weapons and in defence of environmental issues. He had seen plenty of anger on the picket lines and had seen protesters clubbed and beaten by police.

But he had called me from his room to say, "I am really in fear for all our lives. This is the ugliest, most violent mob that I have ever witnessed."

As I continued to brace myself against the wall, I knew that I could not hold on much longer. The pressure was becoming increasingly unbearable.

The phone rang and I grabbed the cord, knocking down the bedside table. The phone bounced off the floor and I reeled in the line to reach the receiver. It was a reporter from Prince Edward Island. Apparently I had an interview scheduled. "I can't talk right now," I said. "I'm holding back a mob. My room is barricaded. I need you to call the authorities in Québec City. We need help."

In hindsight, I should have kept her on the line to listen in. The phone rang again. This time it was Al McKay, an English sealer from the Magdalens, whom we had taken to the ice the year before to introduce him to the idea of seal brushing instead of seal clubbing.

I told him what was happening as quickly as I could.

"Those fucking idiots," he said. However, there wasn't much he could do.

I dropped the phone as an ax split the door. My mouth was dry. Was this it? After all these years, could it be now and here? With flat resignation, I knew I could be dead within a few minutes.

The ax repeatedly shattered the door, splinters flying, the fibreboard ripping and splitting. Looking over my shoulder, I could begin to make out the movement of bodies behind the rents in the door.

I had no intention of whimpering before those baby-killing sons of bitches—no sir. Clutching the stun gun in my hand, I suddenly jumped up. The bed slammed against the wall, the lamp crashed to the floor. The door sprang violently open and the sealers surged over the threshold, their screaming faces contorted with loathing.

I faced them. At least thirty had forced their way into the room, with another thirty in the room behind, and two hundred more filling the hallways and lobby of the hotel. I will never forget the madness in their eyes. I knew I was a dead man.

But if this was it, I had no intention of giving them the satisfaction of seeing me afraid. I held the stun gun tightly—a joke, really. How far could a stun gun get me with this mob? I cursed the damn Canadian laws that had prevented me from bringing pepper spray to defend myself. "Come and get me, you bastards," I mumbled. "I'm not going to die without a fight."

The mob stopped about six feet from me as if I had erected some force field. They just stared and muttered through clenched lips. I stared right back. They became quiet for a few seconds and I could almost feel embarrassment ripple through their ranks.

Three hundred to one were absurdly unfair odds. Even this unruly rabble realized how cowardly they appeared. Suddenly one of the men, a big, ugly bastard named Langford, stepped forward and swung a blow, connecting with the left side of my head. The stun gun leapt up instinctively and the brute crashed to the floor, eyes wide with surprise. A second sealer rushed in, crashing to the deck at my feet.

The sealers looked confused and a few even looked frightened. A third sealer fell to my stun gun. The others had no idea why their comrades were falling.

Langford struggled to his feet. "The fokking anglais son of a bitch burned me," he roared.

They surged forward, slamming me back against the window. The glass shattered. One of the men yanked the curtains down, and I could see angry faces in the parking lot looking up at the room. A fist came at my head and I ducked. The fist whooshed over me and I heard another windowpane shatter. The man swore painfully, blood spurting from his hand. Another spat full in my face, then retreated. A punch got me in the stomach, another in the side of the head again. Grabbing a man's hand, I jammed the stun gun into him, recoiling in shock as the current ran through his body and back into my hand.

A kick to my wrist forced me to drop the stun gun, and I lost it in the chaos. I was a goner. Looking into those hate-filled faces, I roared, "Hoka hey!"

It was the Lakota war cry that I had learned so many years before while under fire from U.S. forces at Wounded Knee. I had been a medic for the American

Indian Movement in 1973. I faced death then, and I would do so here with the same resolve as any true warrior before me. "Hoka hey, it is a good day to die."

Amidst the tumult, a snatch of poetry surfaced in my thoughts.

Then out spake brave Horatius, the Captain of the gate.
'To every man upon this Earth, Death cometh soon or late,
Yet how can man die better, than facing fearful odds,
For the ashes of his fathers, and the temples of his Gods.'[2]

I smiled to myself, proud that in the midst of terror I could calm my mind with an inspiring verse.

"Hoka hey, you bastards!"

My foot stomped down hard on one attacker's foot and I kneed a second in the crotch.

They roared in rage and pressed harder, furious that I was fighting back.

Suddenly one of the men positioned himself between me and the others. The guy stood a head and a half above me. His broad back obscured the rest of the room from my view.

"Enough," he shouted in French. "The likes of him ain't worth going to jail for!"

"Fokk you," said a voice. "Ain't nobody going to find his body. Stuff 'im under the ice!"

Another yelled, "Dufort ain't going to do anything to us if we kill him. Fokking government will give us medals!"

Over the shoulders of the big man, some of the men struggled to punch me. One of them grabbed my hair and pulled. I viciously bit his hand, drawing blood. Yelping, he retreated.

Two young cops—not that coward Dufort and his partner in the next room—forced their way into the room.

"They want you off our island, English," one of them shouted. "Agree to leave and we can get you out of here alive!"

"Like hell I will. I have a legal right to be here."

I recognized the cop, Jacques Bouchard. I had talked with him a day earlier.

"You leave now, or you're a fokking dead man in five minutes! Do you understand, Anglais?"

He was right, of course. It was the only reasonable thing to do. The big sealer who had blocked for me shouted to the others that I had agreed to leave the island. They muttered but began to retreat.

"You will leave now, with us!"

"Now look here, I'm not about to go out into that mob of drunken jackals."

One of the sealers heard me. The comment crackled through their ranks like a string of Chinese firecrackers. With a roar of indignation, they turned. I would be leaving now.

The two officers each grabbed an arm and hauled me bodily from the room. Dufort and his craven comrade were sitting on the sofa in the next room. A slight smile crossed Dufort's face.

The officers dragged me into the hallway and out the side exit to the stairwell, which was lined with shouting sealers who kicked at me.

Out in the parking lot, the mob milled around me. I felt a sharp pain, then another. They were stabbing me with car keys, stabbing and twisting them into my sides.

I saw Stephen Douglass of the London *Sunday Times* running out of the lobby with his camera. Kicking and punching him, the mob dashed his camera to the ground.

This distraction allowed the officers to throw me into the back seat of a police car. The one called Gilbert took the wheel, with Bouchard beside him up front. Suddenly a sealer jumped in beside me and began punching me.

As Gilbert started the engine, a brick tossed by another sealer exploded through the back window. Gilbert, like an idiot, jumped out and—amazingly—began to chase the culprit. Meanwhile, the big sealer who had tried to calm the mob jumped behind the wheel and nudged the car through the rabble onto the road to the airport.

Great. I was now in a car with one young officer and two sealers. The big guy seemed stable, but the little weasel beside me was a nutcase. The bastard continued to punch me. Without thinking, I walloped him in the jaw, and heard a satisfying crack. Dazed, he retreated to the far side of the back seat.

We now had a convoy of nearly a hundred cars tailing us. Shards of glass from the broken window had embedded themselves near my right temple, and as I picked them out, I felt warm blood trickle down my cheek. I was exhausted and just wanted to sleep.

At the airport, Bouchard escorted me to a room behind a Plexiglass barricade. Two other officers were there, waiting. Screaming, red-faced sealers pressed up to the Plexiglass, banging on it with their fists. They were out of control. The officers were visibly frightened.

"What are you going to do?" I asked Bouchard.

"I don't know," he stammered.

One small consolation was that if the mob was here at the airport, the rest of the crew was relatively safe. Finally quieting down, the sealers sent a spokesperson to the door to talk with Bouchard.

Bouchard came back with a wet paper towel and told me to clean the blood from my face. The sealers wanted to take a photograph of me to prove that I wasn't hurt.

"No bloody way. They cut my head open. I have no intention of providing phony evidence for their side."

"Look, Watson," Bouchard said, "this is not a game. If they come through that barricade, I can't guarantee your safety or ours."

"You're right, it's not a game," I snarled angrily. "I don't take my orders from a mob, and as a police officer, you shouldn't either."

Exasperated, Bouchard walked back to the door. Langford, the big bastard who had hit me first back in the hotel room, was there.

Bouchard came back and asked, "What was it you used to burn Langford's hand like that?"

"A stun gun," I answered. "We have them to defend ourselves from rogue hood seals." I lied, of course. I'd never met a seal that I needed to defend myself against.

"Stun guns are illegal in Canada," he said sternly.

Laughing, I answered, "Well, arrest me then. From what I can see, the damn thing saved my life."

Bouchard smiled. "Under the circumstances, we'll forget it."

"Thanks a lot. Christ, it's good to know you have your priorities straight."

I looked out at the crowd and saw three women; two were reporters, one for the CBC and the other for the local station. Both were red-faced and screaming for my attention. The other woman was Annemieke Roell, the representative for the International Fund for Animal Welfare (IFAW). Flashing me an evil grin, she gave me the finger. Later I learned that she had been advising the sealers to have me kicked off the island.

Annemieke had been sent to the Magdalens as an employee of IFAW. Unfortunately she had "gone native." Some locals had told me she had gone soft on the sealers and I had seen her getting very cozy with a particular sealer at the hotel bar the night before.

One of our few informants in the community had called me up the previous night to warn me that we might be assaulted.

"I would watch that IFAW bitch if I were you," he added. "She's in the sealers' camp."

I had not believed him, but the proof was in front of me now.

I reported her to IFAW, but they did not believe me. Not long afterwards, they found out for themselves she was a turncoat. Since then she has been on a crusade to discredit IFAW, and, in an April 27, 1996, interview with the *Financial Times Magazine*, was quoted as saying: "There's a guy on the Magdalen Islands who owns a restaurant who is every year inventing new [seal] recipes," she said. "I had it in paté, I had it in stew. I had salami and pepperoni. I had some of their garlic sausages. They were absolutely delicious."

What a strange confederacy, I thought, looking at the crowd: sealers, supposed seal savers, and media. I found out later that an off-duty Mountie was in the crowd. Not much had changed since 1983. The seal hunt controversy was boiling up again inside a pressure cooker of hatred, frustration, ethnic rivalry, political manipulation, and greed.

"Bouchard?" I yelled. "What in hell's name are we doing here? There's no plane out of here until tomorrow."

"We have sent for a plane for you," the cop replied. "It should be here soon."

I heard the distant whine of an engine.

"OK, Watson," Bouchard said, "out the door!"

I stood up, smiled at the mob and shook my head to mock their posturing, then darted out toward the plane. The cops followed. The rabble howled and pressed hard against the barricades. It was all déjà vu. I had done this exact same thing twelve years before at this same airport, escaping from the same barbarians. Some people never learn.

The plane wasted no time getting airborne, bound for where? I had no idea. The two pilots weren't talking. Staring out the window at the blackness, I could just make out the ghostly ice floes far below. The seals were down there, those wonderful, innocent creatures. I wished them well for another year.

An hour and a half later, the plane landed at Moncton airport in New Brunswick. I walked into the terminal. I did not have a coat, my shirt was torn, and my face was caked in dry blood. Inside a posse of heavily armed Québec Provincial Police (QPP) officers waited, dressed in paramilitary gear.

Walking up to the ranking officer, I asked him if they were going to the Magdalens.

He sneered at me. "Now that you are here, there is no need."

"Of course there is. I have a crew over there. There are media people over there. That mob is out of control."

He just looked at me and walked away. Having just been flown down from Québec City, the QPP tactical squad was now preparing to return.

Meanwhile, back at the hotel, the crew was slowly recovering from the shock of the attack. Most of the mob had moved on to the airport but a few of the sealers missed getting rides and stood milling around the hotel lobby and parking lot.

Finding a pay phone, I called the hotel and, disguising my voice, asked for Chuck Swift.

"Paul!"

"Yeah. It's me."

"We thought they killed you. The police here wouldn't tell us anything."

"Is it safe there? I'm in Moncton."

"It's hell. The sealers are drunk and prowling the halls. Hunter and some of the German media people have moved to the hospital for protection. Martin, Marc, and I are here. Martin got through to his agent. The agent called the White House. The White House called the U.S. Consul in Montreal, Howie Muir. He was very helpful. Apparently a SWAT team is on the way from Québec City."

"Well," I answered, "Get back to the U.S. Consul and tell them these guys are sitting in Moncton waiting for a flight back to Québec City."

"What? They can't do that!"

"They are doing that. Get on the phone to Howie."

I then called Steve Hurlbutz, the news producer at Citytv in Toronto, who told me to go to the Holiday Inn. Arriving at the hotel, I had only a few moments to catch my breath when two Moncton city police officers knocked at my door.

"Mr. Watson, Citytv in Toronto called us and requested that we arrange for an ambulance to take you to the hospital."

I quickly called Chuck. He told me the U.S. Consul was outraged, and that the SWAT team would be in the Magdalens within the hour.

In the hospital, staff found that I had bruised kidneys, some major bruising to the back and arms, and a cracked rib. They cleaned up my head wound and kept me for observation until the morning. My body ached horribly. I needed to sleep, but I was worried about the crew on the island. About two in the morning I put in another call to Chuck.

He reported that the tactical team had arrived, along with Tom Kennedy from CBC News.

"What a jerk," he said. "He's reporting that there was a minor disturbance and that the sealers requested that you leave, and you agreed to, and nobody was hurt."

Frustrated, I said, "Didn't anybody talk to him?"

"He wasn't interested in talking to us. He only spoke to the police, the sealers, and that bitch from IFAW. We did speak with CNN in Atlanta, but they called the police here and the cops told them that no one was hurt and the sealers were just having a little fun."

"How's everybody else?" I inquired.

"Okay. André from German RTL did get some footage, but Dufort ordered him to turn his tape over to the sealers. Fortunately he hid it in a snowbank. He gave them a blank and they destroyed it, apparently satisfied that no one got any evidence on them."

"How did André get it into a snowbank?"

Chuck laughed. "One of his crew jumped out of the second-floor window into the snow while they were banging on his door."

"This Dufort certainly is a piece of work." I said. "Tell everyone that I'll head back there tomorrow."

"You can't. The police have ordered us to leave the island tomorrow morning for our own protection."

"So much for the true north strong and free. If Martin hadn't been there, the Québec and Canadian governments would have thrown us to those mangy Maggoty Island dogs."

Chuck laughed again. "Maggoty is right, good name for this hellhole. Martin says he'll talk to the media when we get out of here. Kennedy and his Controlled By Canada network may not believe us, but the American networks will sure as hell believe Martin Sheen. Here he is."

Martin's voice came over the line sounding very concerned. "How are you, Captain?"

"What can I say, Martin? Moncton. Shit. I'm still in Moncton."

I was mimicking his famous line from *Apocalypse Now*. He laughed heartily. "It can't be worse than here. On the whole I would rather be in Saigon. But don't worry about the spin these guys are putting on this story. We'll get the truth out tomorrow."

"Thanks, Martin. I meet very few really sincere Catholics and you are one of those few. You know, a Newfoundland missionary named Dr. Wilfred Grenfell once wrote that the Inuit word for the baby harp seal is *kotik*. He used the word to convey to the Eskimo the idea of the Lamb of God. The natives understood the symbolism immediately."

Martin answered, "I can see that. As a Catholic, I also saw something else very symbolic. Last night was the celebration of Mass commemorating the Stations of the Cross. A Mass recalling the persecution of Christ. As the priest held the Mass across the street from us, that mob was dragging you across the parking lot and persecuting you for believing in life. Our Lord was persecuted for the same thing. Seeing that contrast made me realize that a true Catholic fights for justice and for innocence against the might of the State. Roman tyranny or Canadian tyranny, they're the same thing. I'm proud to be on your team, Paul."

Chuck came back on and told me that Bob Hunter had called from another hotel on the island and was doing fine. Apparently Bob, Todd, his videographer, and the Germans had emptied three full mini-bars so far. Knowing that everyone was all right was a great relief.

As I drifted painfully off to sleep, images of angry, hateful, and ugly faces danced before me. How could I ever overcome this legacy of ignorance and blood, hate and propaganda? Perhaps it was all for naught, just another story in a chronicle of savagery going back centuries before my time.

Kotik, the Lamb of God, brought us all to this conflict, killers and saviours alike, united by passions as powerful as they are contradictory.

The Sacrifice of the Lamb of God

(1759–1936)

It has not been easy to convey to the Eskimo mind the meaning of
the Oriental similies of the Bible. Thus the Lamb of God had to be
translated *kotik*, or young seal. This animal, with its perfect whiteness
as it lies in its cradle of ice, its gentle, helpless nature, and its pathetic
innocent eyes, is probably as apt a substitute, however, as nature offers.

—Dr. Wilfred T. Grenfell, 1909

T he rocky, icebound coastline, from the northern tip of Labrador down to Cape Race on the lower tip of the great island of Newfoundland, is a forbidding place at first sight. Desolate, damned, and with a documented history of dreary despair, the northeastern shores of Canada have long resisted the relentless advances of European civilization.

For hundreds of thousands of years, the great seal nations have navigated the offshore waters, adapting to the hostile movements of the annual southerly flow of the ice packs of the Labrador Front. The largest of these pinniped nations is that of the harp seal, known by the translation of its Latin name as the ice lover from Greenland (*pagophilus groenlandica*). These incredibly beautiful animals are born onto a bed of ice, nurtured on the ice, live and move with the ice, and die on or beneath the ice. From time immemorial, the harp seal was the undisputed ruler of its frigid domain, threatened only by the occasional orca and the unpredictable onslaught of storms. With their cousins the hood seals, the great herds of harps travelled through the Straits of Belle Isle and into the calmer land-cradled ice fields of the Gulf of St. Lawrence.

Other herds of harps thrived off the coasts of Greenland, the northern coasts of Norway, and in the White Sea north of the lands of the Russians.

Within the last 10,000 years, nomadic man, hardened by the ordeal of the last great ice age, journeyed into the realm of the ice lovers and partook of the rich bounty of the seals. This was a natural predator–prey relationship, and northern peoples would not have survived but for the existence of the seal. The clothing they wore, the sleds they rode on, the kayaks and boats they plied the chilly waters with, the sewing needles, fish hooks, and a hundred other essential tools they needed for survival came from the seals. Seals inspired their art, their sagas, their myths and legends. Humans killed seals respectfully, for the justified purpose of survival.

The Paleo-inhabitants were followed by the peoples of the Dorset culture, whose habitation extends back to about 1,500 years ago. Their archaeological sites reveal a culture that relied heavily on seal hunting. In relatively recent times, the ancestors of the Naskapi and Montagnais Indians arrived and pushed the Dorset northward, giving the seals a brief respite, because the newcomers did not spend much time on the coast and preferred to hunt caribou and moose in the interior. Around the fourteenth century, the Thule people, or Inuit (meaning "people"), began to migrate down from the Arctic. By the seventeenth century, they had started trading with the Europeans, which led to their rapid population expansion into Labrador. The Thule, whose way of life also revolved around seals, either absorbed or destroyed the last remnants of the Dorset culture.

Trade with the Europeans transformed seals from being a means of survival into a commodity. By the eighteenth century, even the Inuit were regarded as competitors by the advancing Europeans, who pushed them northward, where they were ruthlessly attacked by the interior Naskapi. In Newfoundland, the Beothuk, a coastal people, were driven to extinction by the brutal policies of colonization, which forced them inland, away from the seals they had traditionally hunted.

The arrival of the Europeans opened a sad new chapter in the history of humankind's relationship to the seals. Gaelic fishermen were the first to realize that seals could supplement their income from cod, and in 1689, two seigneuries pivoting around the sealing industry were established to include the whole of Labrador and the coasts of Newfoundland. The sealery became so lucrative that the French used their Indian contacts to wage a successful war of extermination against the Inuit people in order to control the northern shores of the Gulf of St. Lawrence.

By the mid-eighteenth century, the sealing industry of New France was exporting more than 500 tons of seal oil per year, an amount that required the slaughter of about 20,000 adult seals. Even then, more than 200 years ago, one visitor to the New World wrote:

> It is questionable whether it would be in the interests of the Colony to multiply the seal fisheries. . . . They only produce one pup a year; the fishing takes place in springtime which is the season of breeding, or in the autumn at which time the females are pregnant and, in consequence a large number could not be caught without destroying the species and risking the exhaustion of this fishery.[1]

This statement—unusually enlightened for the time—was, of course, ignored. It would not be long before the English got wind of the sealing profits enjoyed by the French.

It was common practice in the seventeenth century for fishing captains to leave some of their crew to winter on the shores of Newfoundland, particularly disreputable men whose nefarious activities made them unwelcome back in their native ports. These men were able to witness the annual migrations of the seals and used this discovery to turn their exile into a profitable venture.

Since it was easier to reach the seals from Newfoundland than to attempt to reach the ice from Britain, and with cod in the summer and seals in the early spring, the inhospitable climes of Newfoundland could now beckon the hardier of His Majesty's colonists.

The first outports bred a unique brand of men: stubborn, tough, resourceful, proud, and because of the nature of their work, a trifle cruel. Cruel, that is, with regard to the Indians and the creatures whose lands they were determined to wrest violently into their possession. Among their own kind, they could be wonderfully kind and charitable. But hunters and fishermen they were, and killing was their bread and butter. To them, the Indian peoples were a nuisance and competition for meat, and they were not Christians. They were to be exterminated, and in the case of the Beothuk of Newfoundland, this was realized with their extinction in the nineteenth century.

In 1760, a French sealer reported seeing a herd of seals passing by the northern tip of Newfoundland. The seals filled the sea from the coast to the horizon and took ten days to pass by him. Sealing was a much simpler task then. Coming close to shore in such numbers, the creatures were easy prey for the nets, some of them 500 feet in length, used to catch them. Late in the eighteenth century, the inhabitants of the Newfoundland coast were using more than 2,000 of these nets and realizing great profits from the seal pelts and oil they obtained. With no quota in those days, and no limit on the killing, seals were being slaughtered in incredible numbers. We don't know how many, but if only 100 seals were caught in each net, 2,000 nets would yield 200,000 seals. It would be safe to venture that each net yielded more than 100 seals; the kill figure could have topped 300,000 per year. The systematic modern sealery had begun.

In the early years, the older seals were the victims. By 1780, sealers were using shallops, thirty-foot-long sailing boats with which they could cruise the bays for a week at a time, hunting down the seals and shooting them with muzzle-loading guns. For a time, the great seal nurseries offshore eluded exploitation. Rarely, probably no more than two or three times in a generation, nature betrayed the seals and the ice pans upon which the whitecoats were born would be driven by northeastern gales to the very shores of Newfoundland. When this happened, the seals were exposed to unparalleled cruelty. Men, women, children, and dogs rushed out onto the ice. The seals were killed with clubs, knives, spears, and the boots of their assailants while dogs ripped the newly born seal pups to pieces. The screams of seal pups being skinned alive and the blood dripping from the hands of adults and children alike turned the panoramic ice floes into a crimson Dantean landscape.

These landfalls were dubbed "whitecoat springs," and each such event is chronicled in Newfoundland history. In 1773, for example, 50,000 newborn seals were slain in Notre Dame Bay. The year 1861 gave the landsmen 60,000 victims in Hamilton Sound and a further 150,000 in Bonavista Bay. The "townies," as the city folk of St. John's were called, took part in the 1872 slaughter of 100,000 seal pups just beyond the harbour mouth known as the Narrows. Such hunts, involving inexperienced seal killers, were the cruellest of all. In 1981, a modern revival of amateur sealing saw thousands of seals fall victim to the inhumanity of hastily recruited, first-time "sealers" on the shores of Cavendish Beach in Prince Edward Island. This orgy of blood and slaughter was recorded in vivid colour by film crews, some of who were promptly arrested by a government hell-bent on stifling protest.

Such landfalls motivated the men of Newfoundland to attempt to reach the nursery floes, which normally lay from thirty to 200 miles off shore. Though early attempts were sometimes lucky, more often than not the hapless shallops were crushed by the ice and lost along with their crews. Building larger, stronger vessels was the answer. In 1793, a St. John's merchant commissioned two forty-five-ton schooners to venture onto the ice in pursuit of seals. By 1795, these stout-timbered ships were being routinely launched and the pelagic sealing industry had begun.

Built by the same men who manned them, the schooners would be gone for a month or more, most of the time drifting helplessly in the ice pack. The crew lived in continual fear of sudden storms, which would ground and crush them in the ice. Every year ships were lost; occasionally a quarter of the fleet would venture forth, never to return. Yet tragedy did not dissuade sealers from sacrificing their ships, the lives of their crews, and even their own lives in pursuit of this bloody but profitable business.

When the Napoleonic Wars (1793–1815) opened up the north to English residents of Newfoundland, they began to move into areas vacated by the French. The range of Newfoundland sealing activities quickly increased.

By 1804, the English sealing fleet numbered 140 vessels, all under thirty tons. By 1840, it had 631 small vessels. With the entry of the large barques, brigantines, and brigs, 1853 witnessed the return of 14,931 men from the ice with 455,000 pelts. Practically every able-bodied man in Newfoundland found himself employed in the seal hunt of that year.

As early as 1840, the cruelty of the seal hunt had not gone unnoticed. In his book *Sea of Slaughter*, Farley Mowat related the observations of Professor J. B. Jukes, who sailed to the ice in the brigantine *Topaz*.

We passed through some loose ice on which the young seals were scattered, and nearly all hands went overboard, slaying, skinning and hauling. We then got into a lake of open water and sent out five punts. [The men of] these joined those already on the ice, the crews dragging either the whole seals or their sculpts to the punts which brought them on board. In this way, when it became too dark to do any more, we found we had got 300 seals on board and the deck was one great shambles.

When piled in a heap together, the young seals looked like so many lambs and when from out of the bloody and dirty mass of carcasses one poor wretch, still alive, would lift up its face and begin to flounder about, I could stand it no longer and, arming myself with a handspike, I proceeded to knock on the head and put out of their misery all in whom

I saw signs of life . . . . One of the men hooked up a young seal with his gaff. Its cries were precisely like those of a young child in the extremity of agony and distress, something between shrieks and convulsive sobbings . . . . I saw one poor wretch skinned while yet alive, and the body writhing in blood after being stripped of its pelt. The vision of [another] writhing its snow-white woolly body with its head bathed in blood, through which it was vainly endeavouring to see and breathe, really haunted my dreams.

The next day, as soon as it was light, all hands went overboard on the ice and were employed in slaughtering young seals in all directions. . .

I stayed on board to help the captain and cook hoist in the pelts as they were brought alongside. By twelve o'clock, we stood more than knee deep in warm sealskins, all blood and fat. By night the decks were covered in many places the full height of the rail.

As the men came aboard they snatched a hasty moment to drink a bowl of tea or eat a piece of biscuit and butter . . . the[ir] hands and bodies were reeking with blood and fat . . . and after this hearty refresh-ment the men would hurry off in search of new victims: besides every pelt was worth a dollar!

During this time hundreds of old seals were popping up their heads in the leads and holes among the ice, anxiously looking for their young. Occasionally one would hurry across a pan in search of the snow-white darling she had left, and which she could no longer recognize in the bloody and broken carcass that alone remained of it . . .[2]

Between 1810 and 1870, more than 400 sealing ships were lost in the ice. The callousness of the sealing merchants is evident in the fact that nobody ever recorded the number of men lost on these doomed ships. Still, it is generally estimated that more than a thousand men and boys were either drowned, crushed in the ice, or frozen on the floes. In return for this incredible waste of human life and ships, the merchants benefited from the slaying of over twelve million seals between 1838 and 1870. In 1843 alone, more than one million seals were killed.

European consumers were developing an insatiable appetite for seal oil. Tasteless and odourless when refined, the oil from seal fat was used for cooking and for lighting. Because of its use in lubricating machinery, it came to be called train oil. As a byproduct, the skins were made into leather and provided an additional source of revenue.

With the discovery and use of electricity and petroleum, the demand for both seal and whale oil fell dramatically, but quickly recovered with the use of seal oil in industry, especially for the manufacture of explosives and margarine.

In 1863, the first steam-driven ship went to the ice. Of the fifty steamships that went sealing between 1863 and 1900, forty-one of them were lost at sea. But despite their power, their manoeuvrability, and the blind ambition of their masters, the steamships could not equal the half-million annual kills of their weaker wind-driven counterparts of two decades before. The once mighty seal herds were already in decline.

By the mid-nineteenth century, every outport of Newfoundland was involved in sealing. At first, it was a communal effort in every respect, from building the ships to rendering the blubber. Soon after, the industry became more centralized, with the community still doing most of the work but the lion's share of the profit going to only a few families. Thus emerged the great Newfoundland sealing families, the Bowrings, the Harveys, the Crosbies, and others. A new aristocracy forever shattered Newfoundland's previously egalitarian society. The seals, the foundation of Newfoundland's common wealth, now became the single greatest factor in impoverishing its people. During the mid-1800s, the average Newfoundlander became little more than a willing slave whose only real task in life was to fatten the wallets of the sealing tycoons. What little he made often went back to the company. For example, to get a job on a sealing ship, the sealer had to pay the company a berth fee for the privilege.

Back then, the physical act of clubbing and skinning a seal was considered the easy part of a sealer's job. It was also the only thing he got paid for. He received no money for the weeks of work involved in the voyage: cutting trees, hauling firewood, loading logs for extra spars, and boarding tons of salt, plus the ship's stores. When all was ready for the ship's departure, it was not unusual to put the crew to work cutting a path through the ice from the dock to the sea. Sometimes it took 1,500 men more than ten days to carve out a channel to release fifty to seventy ships.

In the middle of the nineteenth century, the fishermen who slaved away at sealing were a breed of hard-driven men, desperate and uneducated, fully dependent upon the poor wages to be had in a land where a meagre fare was far better than no fare at all. Through ruthless ambition, the smarter ones rose to the ranks of skippers. A sealing captain in those times was a devil of a human being, a bullying tyrant hell-bent on the pursuit of profit. If he demonstrated any weakness, he would be swiftly struck down by an even more ruthless boss and replaced from the ranks of those below.

In the 1860s, a St. John's clergyman delivered a sermon that bitterly denounced the sealing industry:

> Even when death at its most fearful puts not a sudden period to the sufferings of the sealer, the toils and hardships and perils of the voyage are indescribable; while he has naught to sustain him but the fond hope of being able to realize a temporary provision for an affectionate wife and children. The seal fishery is a lottery where all is risk and uncertainty, but the risk, we must confess, is not equally distributed. Take, for instance, a vessel of 120 tons. Her merchant-owner may gain a thousand pounds or more if the voyage prospers. But also involved in her success are some thirty fishermen—they may each gain twenty pounds. The merchant, to gain a thousand, has risked a capital of perhaps two thousand. The sealer, to gain twenty, has risked his all—his life. If the voyage fails, the owner still has his ship, but the poor man returns penniless with the loss of his labour and his time. If the vessel founder or be dashed to pieces in the ice, insurance relieves the merchant, but if thirty lives are lost, then thirty widows and perhaps a hundred orphans shriek their curses on a fishery that gave them no compensation and was the grave of all their hopes.[3]

Harold Horwood, whose great-uncle was a sealer and a fishing master, wrote of the sealer's way of life:

> The hardships they endured were compounded by the greed of the shipowners, who refused to provide clothing or safety equipment. The men had no meals to cook or any way to cook them: for weeks and months they lived on sea biscuit and tea. Even their drinking water was polluted with blood and seal fat until it stank. They slept like cattle in ships' holds without bedding. As the pelts and fat piled up, they simply lived on top of the cargo in utter filth. Injured men recovered as best they could, or died without medical help.[4]

Farley Mowat rightly characterized the seal hunt as "an organized exploitation of both men and seals."[5]

With the dawn of the new century, St. John's merchant Alick J. Harvey commissioned the building of the *Adventure*, the first steel ship. She was in fact the first icebreaker: Her design enabled her to ride up onto the ice and crush it with her weight. By 1914, Newfoundland had a fleet of icebreakers and the scales were tipped further against the seals.

Also, by 1914, the merchants had developed into an aristocracy. From their base on St. John's Water Street, founded on fish and seal oil, they had expanded to owning steamship lines and had gained control of the import and export trade in their island fiefdom. By controlling the coastal communities through outport merchants, they turned the entire island into a company town, keeping the fishermen in economic bondage through perpetual debt on the company books.

These same merchants lived in mansions in St. John's and shipped their children overseas to the best British schools. The children of the fishermen, on the other hand, rarely, if ever, saw a school. Born into hardship, at ten, if they were boys, they became fishermen, and if they were girls, choregirls and fish cleaners. They held no illusions of a better life and they saw their future reflected in the hardened, miserable faces of their parents. Sealing was the only adventure open to them. The frustrations, the boredom, and the unhappiness of their lives could be vented through the swing of a club and the satisfying thud felt when crushing the skull of an innocent creature.

Most of all, these youths desperately wanted to be a part of something that was a great Newfoundland tradition. To become a sealer was to become a man. Boys as young as ten were enraptured with this primitive rite of passage like nothing else they had ever, or would ever, experience in their lives.

Skippers were the heroes of the sealing industry. Equivalent to hockey, football, or basketball stars today, these sealing masters were idolized, and on rare occasions became cult figures.

Captain Abraham Kean, with his long and lucrative career, was the epitome of the sealing captain. He earned the distinction of killing more seals than any other skipper, his tally passing the one-million mark during his sixty-seven voyages. He also carries the lesser distinction of losing more crew members than any other skipper. This is not surprising—he was careless with life from an early age. At the age of ten, he mishandled a gun, shot himself in the hand and killed his three-year-old nephew.

Born of Devonshire stock on a lonely island in Bonavista Bay, Kean was the son of an illiterate fisherman. A strict Methodist with a total of three years' schooling, he rose to become a politician and a cabinet minister. His enemies, none of whom dared face him with their accusations, denounced him for his intolerance, harshness, and ruthless lack of respect for human life.

Kean married at seventeen, the same year he first sailed to the seal hunt. Ten years later he became a sealing skipper with his first barque, losing two ships before launching his own vessel.

Seven years later, in 1897, he lost another ship, but because he delivered profits, the loss was justified on the books and thus satisfied the owners. The same year, he became Newfoundland Minister of Fisheries, the first fisherman ever to hold the position in the colony. Kean fathered three sealing captains and two doctors and remained a hero throughout his life, despite being involved in two of the most famous disasters in the history of Newfoundland sealing.

The first tragedy occurred in 1898 when forty-eight crew members of the *Greenland*, skippered by Kean, perished in a blizzard. The ship's physician, Dr. Melendy, wrote on the return to St. John's: "Somehow, we limped into St. John's with a cargo of dead seals under hatches and a cargo of dead men roped in a heap on the foredeck. I never went sealing again. Nor ever wanted to."[6]

In March 1914, Captain Kean was in command of the Bowring steamer, the *Stephano*, when the *Newfoundland* disaster occurred. Kean had entered the ice fields along with numerous ships of the Newfoundland fleet. Although the disaster did not befall the crew of the *Stefano*, Kean was the man directly responsible for the decision that led to the death of so many men and boys from the crew of the *Newfoundland*. The skipper of the ill-fated *Newfoundland* was Abraham's youngest son, Westbury Kean, a man of twenty-nine and a chap not entirely happy with his commission to a forty-two-year-old, underpowered wooden steamer that was, simply put, a sea disaster waiting to happen. But that was of little concern in the eyes of her owners; she still had a few years of profit in her.

Reaching the ice floes a hundred miles north of St. John's on the last day of March, the *Newfoundland* was unable to push forward to where the *Stephano* and another ship, the *Florizel*, were operating. Westbury Kean decided to send his men ahead six miles over the ice to reach the seals. He knew that they could not kill seals all day and still have the strength to return to the ship, so he instructed them to go on board the other two ships for the night. George Tuff, an experienced hand and veteran of the *Greenland* disaster, led the crew of sealers.

After four miles of trudging over the worst ice in George Tuff's memory, the crew became agitated over the increasing easterly wind. A few turned back, with taunts of "cowards" directed at their backsides. The few increased to thirty-four.

By the time the remaining sealers realized that the weather was turning for the worst, they were closer to the *Stephano* than the *Newfoundland*. They decided to seek safety with old man Kean's ship.

Kean took the men on board the *Stephano* for tea and then informed them that they had to return to the ice. They could return to the *Newfoundland* after they were done killing. Tuff was appalled by the idea but lacked the courage to argue with Abraham Kean.

One hundred and thirty-two members of the *Newfoundland*'s crew stood sullenly on the ice and watched the stern of the *Stephano* disappear into the murky whiteness. At that moment, the older members of the crew realized that the ship would not be coming back for them.

They found the whitecoats in less than a mile, which caused some consternation because Abraham Kean had said they were two miles off. This meant that they were probably a further mile beyond the *Newfoundland*, a greater distance than they thought when they left the *Stephano*.

Meanwhile, on the *Newfoundland*, Wes Kean was busy denouncing the "cowards" who had returned to his ship, while confident that the rest of his crew were now on board the *Stephano*. The stage had been set for a tragedy of epic proportions.

When the storm hit, the crew were still on the ice. Many died the first night in the gale force winds. More died the next night, overcome with fatigue, hunger, thirst, and exposure. Some simply stepped into the sea and disappeared. One man slashed his own arm with his knife, drank the warm liquid and died.

It was the worst sealing disaster in history. The bodies were collected and laid upon the decks: fifty-eight on the sealer *Bellaventure*, five on the *Florizel*, and one on the *Stephano*. The rest were missing. But even a disaster of such magnitude failed to sway the passion old man Kean had for killing. He ordered the surviving crew to prepare to continue the hunt. They were appalled. For them, the hunt was over.

The clubs continued their bloody work until noon. In a wire sent from the *Bellaventure* to Job Brothers in St. John's, the owners of the ship appealed to allow the vessel to return with her morbid cargo. She left in the late afternoon, followed a few hours later by the *Newfoundland*.

Kean had no intention of returning without a full cargo of pelts. The companies wired back that they supported Kean's decision.

The men were angry. On the *Diana*, seven men simply refused to work. On the *Eagle* and the *Bloodhound*, men mutinied. Even on the *Stephano*, Captain

Kean's formidable power was finally challenged when Mark Sheppard, a common seaman, led a group of men in refusing to obey the captain's orders.

At a court of inquiry convened in St. John's, Abraham Kean took the stand and righteously defended his position, contradicting the views and experience of his accusers. He denied all accusations and declared that his actions throughout had been generous and noble.

The tragedy for Newfoundland was greater still with the announcement that the *Southern Cross* had been lost with all hands on March 29, two days before the *Newfoundland* disaster. With the demise of one of the survivors of the *Newfoundland* in the hospital, the death toll totalled a staggering 253 sealers. The *Newfoundland* lost 72 men and the *Southern Cross* lost 181.

Yet not a single penny of damages for liability was ever ordered from the sealing companies. As for Captain Kean, despite public vilification, he returned to the ice for nineteen more years. In 1927, he was appointed to the Legislative Assembly, and in 1934 was awarded the Order of the British Empire for the distinction of slaughtering a million seals.

Any voice that rose in criticism of the slaughter was ignored. Even the voice of the great Labrador missionary, Dr. Wilfred Grenfell, fell on deaf ears.

> The employment of . . . steamships spells nothing less than the extermination of the seal herds . . . we are relentlessly attacking with ever increasing ingenuity a limited species of mammals who have only a single offspring each year; attacking them with huge vessels and deadly modern repeating rifles, and at a time when every other animal alive is protected, viz, when it is having its young . . .
>
> It is a question of hustle and rapid returns, which cannot possibly last; for no class of mammals on earth has ever, or can ever, long withstand such an onslaught.[7]

The voices of cruelty were far more respected. In his 1924 book, *Vikings of the Ice*, George Allan England relates the pep talk Captain Kean shouts from the deck to his killers on the ice:

> From the bridge I hear the Old Man again:
> "I hate to kill these seal, I do, indeed. It fair pains me!"
> Astonishment! Has the Cap'n gone mad or turned tenderhearted?

Neither. For now he adds:

"They're so wonderful small; some of 'em 'ardly worth the bother. If they could only have let grow another week."

Then England adds, "I understand and mentally apologize to the excellent Cap'n for having misjudged him."

The history of the seal hunt and the history of injustice in Newfoundland have gone hand in hand for more than two centuries. The numbers are astounding. In 1843, 652,370 pelts were landed. The year 1831 witnessed the landing of a record 686,836 pelts. From 1805 until 1936, the total number of seals recorded as killed amounted to a staggering 35,753,188 animals. Only twelve times in the years between 1870 and 1914 did the slaughter of seals dip below the 200,000 mark. The numbers were taking a toll.

In 1928, an editorial in the *Canadian Fisherman* called for a moratorium on sealing to allow the herd to recover. It was ignored.

The seals enjoyed a brief recovery during the Second World War, when many sealers traded their clubs for rifles and few sealing crews dared face the threat of German submarines. The slaughter resumed after 1945, when the Norwegians entered the fray with their modern ships, refrigerated storage, and efficient killing techniques. Barred from the White Sea by the Russians, they bullied their way into the Newfoundland waters.

By 1943, foreign ships outnumbered Newfoundland ships. "Foreign" also meant Canadian ships from Nova Scotia backed by Norwegian investors. The foreign fleets appeased the Newfoundlanders by sailing to St. John's to hire Newfound anders, whose token wages stayed on the island as the profits went to Norway The Norwegians now tapped into the Gulf of St. Lawrence herd, until then the scavenging grounds for the bedraggled, French-speaking inhabitants of the Magdalen Islands.

In 1949, Newfoundland became a part of Canada. The federal government would henceforth oversee and regulate all aspects of sealing, and Newfoundlanders no longer had any direct control over the seal or any other fishery off their coasts.

Newfoundland and Canada were now handmaidens to the cruellest of nations—Norway.

Throughout the fifties, sixties, and seventies, the Canadians heartlessly slaughtered seals for the benefit of Norwegian masters like Rieber and Karlsen.

Only in the eighties was there a relative respite for the seals, thanks to the European Parliament's ban on seal pelts.

As the twenty-first century begins, the sealers have made a comeback. Today, the Chinese and the Koreans are lusting after seal products and investing in the continued tragedy of sealing. With the demand for seal fat long gone and the collapse of the market for seal pelts in 1983, the only product of any real value today is the seal penis, sought in Asia as a quack remedy for impotence.

In truth, the seals continue to be killed, not for the products they yield, but as scapegoats to cover the incompetence of the Canadian Department of Fisheries and Oceans in managing the commercial cod fishery. In the opinion of government scientists and experts, the cod were destroyed by Canadian and Norwegian corporate greed and by government mismanagement. Killing the seals will not bring back the cod. But the governments of Canada and Newfoundland have chosen to blame the seal, and history has demonstrated again and again that the public is always willing to choose a scapegoat over reason, science, or self-criticism.

On the Beach

(1950–1967)

The reason for living is to live.
The reason for dying is to die.
One is not possible without the other.

—Otto Larsen (1870–1963)

From the time I was five, my reality was the bustling New Brunswick fishing town of St. Andrew's-by-the-Sea. My father, Anthony, was an Acadian, born in Restigouche County in the north of the province in 1928. His father, Joseph, was born in Burton, Prince Edward Island, in 1895, and Joseph's father had been born in Nova Scotia in 1867, the year of Confederation. Overall, mine was a Maritime family, whose Scottish roots began with the invasion of Québec in 1759 and whose French roots originated even earlier, with the settling of New France and Acadia.

Although I was raised with an English surname, a legacy from an ancestor in Wolfe's illustrious army, my Acadian ancestry is reflected in the names of my cousins—Maillet, Boudreau, Babineau, Arsenault, Gingras, Dorion.

My mother was Toronto-born, the daughter of an immigrant artist. From her, I inherited my Danish and German roots. I also inherited my rebellious nature. My mother's father, Otto Larsen, had been expelled from Denmark in 1887 for

43

political activities. An artist and a thinker who spoke thirteen languages, he was also an adventurer. He quit the U.S. army as a Rough Rider in Cuba in 1899 to enlist in the Canadian army as a soldier in the Boer War. A decade and a half later, he became an active war resister during the Great War. When my father ran off to join the Canadian army in Korea shortly after I was born, Otto was not very impressed.

During the first five years of my life, I lived with my mother in my grandfather's house in Toronto. I remember this big man in his eighties who carried me on his shoulders and took me on trips to the park and to the nearby Riverdale Zoo. He had long white hair and a long white beard and for years I thought he was Santa Claus.

When my father returned to Canada, he moved my mother, my two sisters, my brother, and me to his home province of New Brunswick. We settled in St. Andrew's-by-the-Sea, within sight of the state of Maine, and home to the Connelly Lobster Company.

It is the Atlantic Ocean I remember most vividly from those years, more than I remember my own parents. Looking across the water, I was always curious about what lay beyond. I spent long hours on the wharf that jutted out into the Passamaquoddy Bay, watching the Grand Manan ferry disembark, sharing sandwiches with the crew of the mail boat.

For an adventurous boy like me, it was a good childhood. I saw whales and harbour seals, and called to some of the multitude of gulls by the names I gave to them. I had two pet lobsters named Flounderface and Bugeye. With Bobby Connelly, my best friend, I explored every inch of the docks, we dug for clams, fished off the end of the wharf, and played in some of the derelict vessels on the beach.

It was as a boy of seven that I first learned to confront fear. While playing pirates at low tide, some older local boys tied me to the lower mast in the hold of the wreck of a schooner. Then they left me.

At first I thought it was fun, until I could no longer hear their voices. The cavernous hold was dank and a little dark, the sun filtering through the fractured ribs of the hull. I struggled, but could not free myself.

A half hour passed and then another, until I noticed something: water, creeping across the deck, oozing up from the boards. The seaweed-covered, rotted deck began to heave and undulate.

The black water rose quickly—Fundy tides are notoriously swift. I had never really thought much about them before, but now, with the brine lapping at my ankles, I was suddenly and horrifically aware that I was at the mercy of the sea. I screamed.

The water rose higher. A few pancake-sized jellyfish moved eerily across the submerged deckboards of the schooner. I screamed again and again, sobbing tearfully for help. With the water at my knees, I continued to cry out until I no longer had the voice for it. I was exhausted.

In a trancelike state, I watched the water rise to my waist. I had never really thought about death. Little boys lived forever, didn't they? But as I felt the water rise up to my belly, I knew that soon there would be no tomorrow for me.

My paralyzing fear was replaced with an anger verging on pure hatred. I screamed again as I struggled against the ropes. I was not going to give in to the sea—the cold, cruel, monstrous sea. I cursed and screamed at it until I was hoarse.

Then, as if in a daze, I realized that it was not the sea that had done this to me. It was other boys. How dare they? I looked across the deepening pool of the crypt-like cargo hold, the sunlight flickering in dancing beads across the black water. Tears rolled down my cheeks. I did not want to die, but I knew with a cold certitude that I would. I laughed in frustration. Laughing and crying, I unconsciously gave myself to the sea and accepted death when I did not even know what death was. My body actually seemed warm beneath the water, shivering cold above it.

Watching the water rise to my chest, I was still angry, but the fear had mysteriously vanished.

Noises on the deck above startled me. "Anyone here?" someone shouted.

I was stunned. Struggling to find my voice. "Yes," I cried. "Down here."

Two young men scrambled down slimy ladder rungs, waded through the water toward me, and cut the ropes. They picked me up and carried me to the topsides, where I shivered and sobbed, feeling strangely ashamed.

Drying my eyes on my sleeve, I looked up. The sun. It was as though I were seeing it for the first time. Too embarrassed to talk to my rescuers, I averted my eyes and wept again. They carried me home, where I went to bed, shivering, and dreamed about drowning under black waters.

In the morning, I knew something had changed. I had come so close to death, had, in fact, accepted it. With this deep new understanding came a vivid appreciation of being alive.

The experience spawned a strengthened courage within me. A few days later, I saw one of the boys who had tied me to the mast. Standing on the end of a dock, he made the mistake of laughing at me. With a flying tackle, I took us both over the side and into the water. As he struggled to reach the surface, I pulled him under until he was coughing up water and pleading for mercy. From that day on, he never laughed at me again, nor did any of his friends mess with me.

A few weeks later, I went trout fishing with my father on the banks of the Wiggedywash. He was catching the fish, ripping the hooks from their mouths, and tossing them beside me on the ground. Watching them struggle to breathe, I was appalled. I now understood their pain and, with this new revelation, I embraced the fish as kindred spirits. Quietly, I picked up each fish as it was tossed. Then I smuggled their gasping little bodies down the stream and released them back into the water, watching in delight as they swam away.

After catching about thirty fish, my father said, "Well, that should do it for today." Turning, he looked for his catch. "Where are my fish?" he said, surprised.

Sheepishly, I stammered, "I let them go. They were drowning."

Surprise gave way to anger. "You what?"

"I let them go, they were drowning."

He hissed, "Fish can't drown, you idiot." He hit me on the side of the head, knocking me to the ground. "Get out of my sight, you moron."

Confused, I ran off into the woods and cried. Something inside told me, however, that I had done the right thing.

My mother was more sympathetic. She signed me up as a member of the Kindness Club, a children's club organized by Aida Flemming, wife of the premier of New Brunswick.

I received a copy of the Kindness Club book from Fredericton and was thrilled to read something that was so akin to my own views and sensitivities. Because of the book, I became more aware of other animals. I released my two pet lobsters into the bay and helped any cat or dog looking hungry or lost. Knowing there were kindred people in the world who shared my understanding of animals, I grew happier and more confident.

Then, in the summer of 1959, a pivotal moment occurred in my life. Spending a few weeks in the woods where my father and uncle were building a hunting camp, I found myself alone and free to explore. I came to a large pond with some domed humps and a trio of very energetic beavers toiling on the top of a complex dam. Seeing me, they dived into the water and disappeared.

I took off my clothes and dived in too. I was swimming around, playing with a pop bottle that I elevated to the status of a U-boat, when I ran face to face into a submerged monster. With a gasp, I stood up, waist-deep in the pond, and watched as my very frightened "monster" scurried toward one of the beaver hutches.

I sat down on the bank and waited for the beaver to return. A young beaver emerged with impatient caution. Within a minute, he was frolicking about the pond, amusing himself. Tossing some small sticks out into the water, I was overjoyed to see him fetch each one and neatly deposit it on the wall of the dam.

Coming back each day, I soon had him taking sticks directly from my hand. Shortly after, we began swimming together, playing tag of sorts and pretending to scare each other by sneaking up unexpectedly.

That little beaver, whom I named Bucky, was my best friend during the summer of 1959. Thankfully, my father ignored me most of the time and allowed me to immerse myself in my own private world, one that he was incapable of comprehending. It was with a very sad heart that I left the summer camp to return to town.

Thoughts of Bucky stayed with me over the following autumn, winter, and spring. I impatiently counted the days until I could return to the hunting camp. When that day arrived, I jumped from the car and ran to the beaver pond.

It was obvious as soon as I reached the muddy shoreline that something was wrong. The beaver huts were in disarray and the dam was in ruins, with no beavers in sight. I waited for hours, but not one beaver raised its head. My friend was no longer there. He was gone, but to where, I had no idea.

Running back to camp, I cried to my father and asked him where the beavers were.

"Oh, them," he said, "Old man Scott probably took 'em out over the winter."

"What do you mean, took them out?"

"Scott's a trapper, son. He trapped them for their fur."

"You mean they're dead?" I was incredulous.

"Yep, trapped means dead, fer' sure."

"That bastard, that dirty rotten . . ."

My father slapped me. "I won't be tolerating any swearing from you."

"But Bucky was my friend, and he's gone and . . ."

"Jesus, boy, he was only a beaver. When are you ever going to grow up?"

It was a horrible summer. I burned with anger and with a blind hatred for old man Scott. By the time winter of 1959 rolled around, I had decided to avenge Bucky. I was on the road to becoming a hit man for the Kindness Club.

I found the bastard's traplines and followed them. Destroying rabbit snares and stealing leghold traps became an obsession with me. On the rare occasions I found a live animal in a trap, I would release it. I gathered up all the traps I could find and threw them off the wharf into to sea. For the first time since losing Bucky, I felt satisfied.

The next spring, I discovered the seal hunt when visiting relatives just north of the Northumberland Straits. I asked my Uncle Phillip to take me to the beach to see the seals. Arriving, we found trails of blood from the white ice to the shoreline. There, on the frozen sand, I saw the little bodies for the first time, split from throat to crotch. I was horrified. Vicious men walked up to the bodies and literally ripped the skins from the small corpses. I stared at one little creature, grotesque and skeletal, his big, glazed eyes reflecting back a dark emptiness. Looking up at the sealers, I saw no compassion, no pity. Sharpening his knife, one brute calmly bent over and severed the flippers from the carcass. I threw up. The men laughed. My uncle, embarrassed, led me away.

That scene on the beach haunted me for years. I never forgot it and I never will.

The following year, I got in trouble for shooting a kid with my BB gun. He was about to shoot a bird. One shot in the kid's rear end saved the bird, but the town constable seized my rifle and my father gave me a vicious strapping.

The die had been cast, however. I was who I was, and neither my father nor the town constable could deter me. I fought with other boys constantly. Lost some battles, won most. Being bigger and stronger for my age had some definite advantages. None of the boys dared harm a creature around me.

I knew I was different, and accepted it. I was a loner, except for my five younger siblings, who all shared my sensitive nature and understood my passion for animals. My mother understood too, but when I was thirteen, she died of complications in childbirth. She had neglected to get help until it was too late because of her shame at being pregnant by a man who was not my father, a man I never knew or knew of. She was only thirty-three. The baby, a boy, was stillborn.

I did not cry at my mother's funeral. Though I knew she was dead, I did not want to believe it. At the same time, I felt resigned that death was unavoidable.

My father, who had deserted us two years earlier, returned and hustled us away to the chaos of the city of Toronto. As the train travelled westward, I felt my roots slipping away forever. One part of me loved the woodlands, the rivers, and the sea. Another part felt relieved to be removed from the cruelty and death. Yet there was little for me in Toronto. My beloved grandfather had been murdered only two months before, at the age of ninety-three, when he was robbed in his own house. Toronto was overwhelming. I found some comfort in books and read everything I could by Grey Owl, Farley Mowat, Jack London, Herman Melville, Joseph Conrad, Romain Gary, and Jules Verne. Especially inspirational were *Twenty Thousand Leagues Under the Sea* by Verne and *Roots of Heaven* by Gary. Nemo was my great hero and Gary's Morel was the runner-up.

Both heroes were romantic, misanthropic defenders of nature. Because of Morel, I went to Africa in 1978 to hunt elephant poachers, but because of Nemo, the creatures of the sea became my first passion.

During the winter of 1965, I stumbled across a book that shook me to the very core of my being. It changed my life and made me angry, has kept me angry every day of my life since.

Published by the New York Zoological Society in 1913, the study by William T. Hornaday was entitled *Our Vanishing Wild Life—Its Extermination and Preservation*. The book documents human atrocities against the natural world and calls for the formation of an army of defence for non-humans. I still have that copy of Hornaday's book and view it as my personal bible.

Another book that impressed me was *Our Plundered Planet* by Fairfield Osborn, published in 1948. It helped me confirm that I pledged allegiance not to Canada, the Church, or humanity, but to nature.

I remained in Toronto for only a few years. I fell in love, for the first time, with Mardi Patterson, the daughter of a friend of my father's. I wanted to finish high school and go on to university to study archaeology. I felt that I had to understand humanity and to do so I needed a proper education in the history of the destruction wrought by our species. My father, though, dismissed my talk of attending university and told me that I was to get a real job after high school. He even forbade me to read *National Geographic*. So, where other boys secretly hoarded comic books or copies of *Playboy*, I had my hidden treasure of *National Geographic* magazines.

Finally, at sixteen, I rebelled against my father for the last time and rode the rails of the Canadian Pacific Railway to the west coast. There I joined the crew of a Norwegian freighter, the *Bris*.

I left Canada behind me on a year-long voyage to the Middle East, Africa, and the Orient, learning to steer a 30,000-ton bulk carrier before I had even learned to drive a car.

My adventures that year were many. I lost my virginity in Singapore. I saw lions and elephants in the wilds of Krueger Park. From the deck of my ship at sea, I watched bombs falling on the coast of Vietnam, and narrowly escaped the clutches of a major typhoon in the South China Sea.

After two years, I returned to Toronto to see my family, but I didn't stay long. The city did not hold the same attraction for me as Vancouver.

Back in Vancouver, I continued to work on ships while studying to complete my high school credits. By 1970, I was working part-time for the Canadian

Coast Guard, writing for the underground newspaper, the *Georgia Straight,* and pursuing my education a semester at a time at Simon Fraser University, majoring in communications, linguistics, and history.

In the summer of 1971, at twenty, I organized my first campaign in environmental activism. The Four Seasons hotel chain was planning to build a complex near the entrance of Vancouver's Stanley Park and intended to bulldoze the nests of Canada geese in the process. We took over the construction site and held the land for six months. As the ringleader, I was the only one arrested. Charged with causing willful damage to public property because the demonstrators had torn down the construction fence, I elected for a trial by judge and jury.

On the stand, the representatives for the property talked in dollars and cents, citing losses and construction setbacks. I spoke of my concern for the Canada geese and the integrity of the Stanley Park entrance. Miraculously, after only fifteen minutes of deliberations, the jury returned a verdict of not guilty.

It was just in time for me to join the crew of the *Greenpeace Too* in November 1971 for the protest voyage to Amchitka to oppose the bomb.

4

Prelude to the Ice Wars

(1964–1975)

A patriot must always be ready to defend
his country against his government.

—Edward Abbey, *Vox Clamantis in Deserto*

Ever since the late twenties, when the *National Geographic* magazine first published an article about the hunt, there had been murmurs of protest. By 1950, the Canadian government was worried enough about the declining seal numbers to set up a research project through the Canadian Fisheries Research Board, based in my own hometown of St. Andrew's-by-the-Sea.

One Canadian Fisheries scientist, Dr. David Sergeant, noted that prior to 1951, the seals were killed primarily for their fat. With fat prices declining, the industry, thanks to refrigeration, was able to concentrate on fur and leather products, from 1952 on.

Sergeant and his colleague Dr. Dean Fisher concluded in their study that the seals "were being exploited at their upper limits of tolerance." They both urged conservation measures.

The change from the fat seal hunt to the fur seal hunt allowed the hunt to begin earlier, as the hunters sought the newborn whitecoats instead of the older, fatter pups.

This was a move that even disgusted many of the veteran sealers. A folk
song written about "Uncle John—The Sealer" in 1951 is proof cf this:

Among the sealers who came home
From the seal fishery
Was stocky wind-tanned Uncle John,
As mad as he could be.

For over forty years and more
A sealer he has been.
He says "That killing infant seals,
He never 'fore has seen.

"Why have our sealing laws been sheared
Is what I want to know.
For March the thirteenth was the date
You first could kill a tow.

"But now as soon as they are pupped,
Before they're any good,
You're forced to murder in cold blood
The baby harp and hood.

"If Mr. St. Laurent could see
What I have seen this spring
'T'would give him nightmares in his sleep.
He'd stop the horrid thing."

And Uncle John will never rest,
Nor will his temper wane,
Until protection for babe seals
Is made the law again.

Even the St. John's newspaper, the *Evening Telegram,* warned in a 1963 editorial that harp seals might be on their way to oblivion. Despite this, not a single piece of legislation was enacted to protect the seals.

The first stirrings of an international protest movement had begun after the 1955 hunt. Dr. Harry Lillie and famed sailor Dr. Joseph Cunningham had travelled to the seal hunt to observe it firsthand and documented it on film.

Both men returned from the hunt angry and disgusted. In lectures to humane organizations throughout North America, Cunningham reported the hunt as "utterly degrading and cruel."

Dr. Lillie published a book in Britain with extracts from the journal he kept in 1949, the first year he'd observed the hunt. "I saw men in a hurry just daze them with a kick," he wrote, "and cut the little bodies out of the pelts while they lay on their backs still crying."

The waste disturbed Lillie as much as the cruelty. "Some seals died at once," he observed, "others . . . writhed on the pans until they flopped . . . into the water to die out of sight. I saw as many as five seals from one single large ice pan disappear, leaving five trails of blood."

The observations of Lillie and Cunningham seeded the beginning of a new awareness of this annual hunt. Newfoundland, Canada, and Norway could no longer keep their vile little secret to themselves. Out on the frozen ice fields, Lillie and Cunningham were able to capture the scarlet horror of the hunt with the Pandora's box of the twentieth century, the movie camera. When the box was opened in the world outside, things, inevitably, would begin to change.

Over the next few decades, the anti-sealing protest would become the largest protest in history for animals, involving millions of people, tens of millions of dollars in policing costs, the jailing and fining of hundreds of people, and a tarnished reputation from which Canada would never recover.

It did not take long before the voice of protest was raised in Newfoundland. In 1960, the great Newfoundland writer and conservationist Harold Horwood wrote an article entitled "Tragedy on the Whelping Ice" for *Canadian Audubon*. In it, he noted that "the hunt has no bag limit, no laws against waste. If you hunt moose in Canada, you are allowed to kill only one animal and must bring all the meat out of the woods. But you may kill an unlimited number of seals and leave all the meat on the ice."

The lack of a quota meant that the unregulated hunt was clearly out of control. Norwegian government tax incentives to sealing companies were increasing the kill numbers more each year. The 1961 kill, for example, came very close to taking every seal pup born that season. To exacerbate matters, modern sealers had radar, wireless radio, airplanes, helicopters, refrigeration, government-subsidized ice-breaking services, weather forecasting, and all the comforts of food, warmth, and entertainment on ships that were ultra-luxury vessels compared to the old wooden-wall sealing ships.

Money was being made and the government was reluctant to interfere. In 1961, Canada proposed that sealing come under the jurisdiction of the Northwest Atlantic Fisheries Organization (NAFO). The fourteen member nations voted the proposal down. With a mere three-mile limit, the Canadian government could only watch as the Norwegians, Russians, Danes, and French took whatever seals or fish they wanted.

The foreign interests were finally causing some concern. The June 24, 1961, issue of *The Financial Post* stated, "It is suspected that some of the foreign vessels decimate the [breeding seals] on their way home . . . . The time may be ripe to impose a few closed seasons."

Still, the Canadian and Norwegian seal hunts were taking place out of sight of the media and out of the mind of a vast proportion of the international public. Dr. Cunningham's film, although it made the rounds of humane societies, had still not reached a mass audience. The move that was to propel the hunt to international infamy was a public relations fiasco financed by the tourism office of the government of Québec in 1961.

The exposure was entirely unintentional. A film company called Artek Films had been commissioned by the Québec government and the French-language network of the Canadian Broadcasting Corporation to produce a documentary film to encourage tourism. In a dramatic example of a public relations nightmare, the company decided to film the seal hunt to dramatize the hardy outdoor livelihood of Québec sealers.

The cameras rolled as the sealers invaded the harp seal nurseries and began their bloody work. They used gaffs—clubs with an ugly spike in the end—to bludgeon the pups. Sometimes the sealers simply kicked the pup in the face. Mothers that attempted to protect their babies were shot. All the while, the hardy macho men of the ice laughed, smoked, drank, and bragged.

The film was entitled *Les Phoques de la Banquise* (The Seals of the Ice Floes) and aired on a series about hunting and fishing. The French-speaking audiences in Québec City and Montreal were outraged. Reaction in Europe was even more hostile.

Canada's Fisheries minister, H. J. Robichaud, was quick to condemn the Artek film as fake before he even saw it. In doing so, he established a pattern for Fisheries ministers for the next four decades: All of them have condemned as fake every film made of the atrocity.

The Artek film crew were not activists. They were all professional documentary filmmakers, commissioned by the Québec government. Yet because of their film, they were victimized by an angry Canadian government, and their personal and professional reputations were damaged.

The film was shown on German television, on a nature program hosted by Dr. Bernard Grzimek, director of the Frankfurt Zoo, and created a huge outcry in Germany. It sparked Grzimek to organize the first-ever protest against the seal hunt. As a result, after the film aired, Europeans sent over a million letters of protest to Canadian embassies and consulates. Another person outraged by the film was Peter Lust, the editor of the German-language Canadian weekly *Montrealer Nachrichten*. Lust had left Germany in 1933, returning in 1945 as a member of the United States Army. One of the first to witness the atrocities of the Nazi death camps at Dachau and Buchenwald, he vowed that if he were ever to confront such injustice again, he would do everything within his power to fight it.

Lust said he saw that evil again when he viewed the Artek film. He managed to secure his own copy of the film, and, armed with his pen, became the first really passionate crusader for the seals. The first of his anti-seal hunt articles was reprinted in over 300 German publications throughout Germany, Austria, Switzerland, and Belgium and provoked the interest of a West German television company. Because they were unable to secure a copy of the Artek film from the CBC or the government of Canada, Lust happily provided them with a copy. Lust was also the first to publish a book dedicated to protesting the hunt. When he gave me a copy of his book in the autumn of 1975, I read it eagerly.

Otto Kertscher of the Hamburg SPCA took up the cause, followed by the Munich-based Gesellschaft gegen Missbrauch der Tiere (Federation Against the Abuse of Animals), which organized the sending of 50,000 letters from Germany to the Canadian government. By 1964, several German members of the Bundestag, the German parliament, had introduced arguments to have the government formally protest the hunt and to ban seal pelts.

In response to this German outcry, some members of the Canadian government retaliated by reminding the Germans that, after the atrocities of World War II, they were in a weak position to criticize. This was not one of Canada's better diplomatic showings, and the comments caused a great deal of resentment among the German public.

The fact is that the Germans were very much involved in the issue, on both sides: In 1967, the German public had purchased 78 percent of Canada's harp sealskins. The German public had every right to protest an atrocity in which they were implicated.

In the face of this international criticism, Canada responded by fanatically "circling the wagons"—an attitude that would last for the next three decades.

Fisheries Minister Robichaud immediately tried to discredit the critics of the hunt and ordered a meeting to be held in Moncton, New Brunswick, on May 20, 1964, between the Ministry of Fisheries and representatives from the sealing industry. That meeting would inadvertently recruit the second major opponent of the seal hunt.

Dr. W. H. Needler, the deputy minister of Fisheries, chaired the meeting. In the back of the room, feeling a little shy among the ship owners, aircraft owners, and fur dealers, stood the secretary of the New Brunswick SPCA, sent by the Canadian Federation of Humane Societies to observe. His name was Brian Davies. Originally from Wales, Davies had served briefly in the Canadian army before joining the SPCA.

What Brian heard that day changed the course of his life. Dr. David Sergeant of the Fisheries Research Board stated clearly that the seals were dramatically declining in number. No one appeared concerned. The attitude was that as many seals should be taken as possible to justify the expense of ships and equipment. As for the cruelty issue—it was not even worth discussing.

Needler, however, had to take some stand to appease the growing criticism. To a chorus of hoots and boos from the industry, he ruled that sealers should be licensed, the size of the club should be regulated by law, and a quota would be put into effect.

Needler also decided to allow three representatives from the humane movement, and one from the conservation movement, to visit the hunt in 1965. One of the men chosen, to Robichaud's lasting regret, was Brian Davies. The others were Tom Hughes of the Ontario Humane Society, Jacques Vallée, the general manager of the Canadian SPCA, and Dr. Douglas H. Pimlott from the Canadian Audubon Society, who later published an article addressing the issue of depletion of numbers of seals.

Robichaud wanted to make a show of delegating humane officials to go to the hunt. He did not actually want them to go there. Hughes did not bother to go. Davies and Vallée were told to report to the ice after the seals had been slain. Nonetheless they arranged their own transportation and, for the first time, Davies was able to see the seals in their natural habitat. He was moved by the beauty and the innocence of these incredible animals and returned from the ice a crusader.

Brian Davies experienced an epiphany when he first saw the killing. He withdrew from teachers' college and started down a new life path dedicated to protecting animals and ending the seal hunt. In his article for the Canadian *Weekend Magazine*, published in the spring of 1966, he publicly declared his opposition to the hunt.

The 1965 hunt had seen the slaughter of 230,000 seals. David Sergeant, writing on behalf of the government to Dr. Grzimek in Germany, said, "We think that the long-term catch has been somewhat too high and that some reduction of the catch would be desirable."[1]

The *Frankfurter Abendpost* called that remark the "understatement of the year."

The Artek film was still circulating in 1966. The Canadian government renewed its accusations that the film had been faked. As its "proof," Robichaud circulated the following affidavit from a Magdalen Islander named Gustave A. Poirier:

> I, the undersigned, Gustave A. Poirier of Magdalen Islands, declare having been employed by a group of photographers, one of whom had a beard, around March 3, 1964, to skin a large seal for a film. I solemnly declare before witnesses that I was asked to torment the said seal and not to use a stick, but just to use a knife to carry out this operation where in a normal practice a stick is used to first kill the seals before skinning them.

The *Victoria Daily Times* commented, "This is absolute unadulterated hogwash. Can you picture a seal hunter attempting to skin alive a 300-pound adult seal? He'd have his hands full!"

In fact the film never shows any such thing, although it does show a sealer prodding a seal with a knife. Somehow the minister had translated this incident into an admission by a sealer that he had been paid by the film crew to skin alive a "large seal."

Robichaud also charged that Brian Davies had a hand in staging the "faked film" despite the fact that Davies did not begin opposing the seal hunt until after the film was shot.

In 1968, Brian headed a delegation of observers to the Gulf hunt that included a photographer and journalist for the *London Daily Mirror*. The *Mirror*'s front-page story, entitled "The Price of a Seal Skin Coat," enraged the British public. The following year, Brian brought a photographer from *Paris Match*, stirring up an equal fervour of protest in France. Also on the ice with Brian that year were Canadian writer Farley Mowat and photographer John De Visser.

Despite the fact that the *Mirror* took its own pictures of the seal killing, the Canadian government responded that the pictures had been faked by fanatical anti-sealing activists. The Department of Fisheries issued a letter accusing Davies of distributing false propaganda and stating that Dr. Grzimek, as an independent observer, had seen no evidence of cruelty or abuse.

Dr. Grzimek immediately responded from Germany that he had not even been on the ice that year and that he had seen nothing to lead him to disagree with Davies' documentation.

People from around the world began to write to the Save the Seals Fund sponsored by the New Brunswick SPCA. Because the seals were beginning to distract from the general animal welfare activities of the society, a decision was made to turn over the assets of the Save the Seals Fund to Brian Davies. With these funds, Brian established the International Fund for Animal Welfare (IFAW) in 1969. Within four years, the IFAW was generating assets in excess of C$500,000.

The next year, 1969, saw a new Minister of Fisheries, Jack Davis, actually visit the hunt to see it for himself. Once again the media documented the cruelty of the hunt, and this time it was *Paris Match* that was accused by the Canadian government of faking pictures. Despite this, the French were outraged and tens of thousands, including Princess Grace of Monaco, protested.

Mr. Davis's visit to the ice, the first for a minister, also injected a little realism and humanity into the government's position. He told the press that "I could not help asking myself whether the hunt in the Gulf of St. Lawrence was really necessary in the first place," and went on to suggest the possibility of limiting the hunt to international waters and establishing a Gulf seal sanctuary.

The minister's visit and the increasing outrage from Europe had had an apparent effect. On October 15, 1969, the Canadian government released a statement on the seal hunt: "Canada will ban the hunting of 'whitecoats' or baby seals in 1970 in the Gulf of St. Lawrence."

It was a lie.

The Department of Fisheries and Oceans had no intention of banning the hunt. By referring to baby seals as whitecoats, they played a public relations gambit and it paid off. The seal pups molt their white fur after two and a half weeks. It is replaced by a mottled brown and greyish white coat. So any animal over twenty-one days old was still fair game for the clubs, but the public and the media believed that the baby seal hunt was over.

Unfortunately for the Canadian government, the seals gave birth later than usual in 1970 due to late formation of the ice. This delayed birth did not result in a change in the opening day of the hunt, and the television cameras and newspaper photographers once again witnessed the mass slaughter of whitecoats in the Gulf. According to Brian Davies, "The 1970 hunt was as bloody, brutal, and sadistic as that of 1969. In spite of all the promises!"

When the New York travel firm Hanns Ebenstein Travel Inc. advertised in the fall of 1972 for a trip to the seals on the icepack, the response was instantaneous. The tour of sixty-five people in three groups was sold out in weeks. The three-day cost for return airfare, food, and hotel was $500 per person. In March 1973, this group of American tourists landed in the Magdalen Islands for a wilderness experience.

The experience was a lot wilder than they had anticipated. They were met at the airport by a screaming mob of sealers brandishing signs that said YANKEES GO HOME and WE KILL SEALS, NOT VIETNAMESE. One woman who waded through the protesters was jostled and slapped before Marcel Hubert, the president of the Magdalen Island Seal Hunters' Association, calmed the rabble down and allowed the tourists to proceed to their hotel.

The following year, IFAW hired the public relations firm of McCann-Erickson to help coordinate its anti-sealing campaign.

Never again would the seals be killed quietly, out of sight of the public eye. The seal wars were going public in a whole new way, and Brian Davies had laid the groundwork. His efforts, however, were not without cost. As early as 1969, he was being hounded for his activities. That year, Davies was ordered to appear in Ottawa before the House Standing Committee on Fisheries and Forestry.

He was interrogated for five bitter hours. In his book, *Savage Luxury*, he described his treatment as an inquisition. Politicians, not jurists, sat in judgment and openly accused him of lying about the seal hunt and being involved only for the money. "Evidence" based on rumour and hearsay was used as if it were fact. Until that day, he said, he had always felt that his rights as a Canadian citizen were protected. He never felt that way again.

The year 1971 saw a number of notable developments in the seal wars. Two other groups joined IFAW in opposing the slaughter: Cleveland Amory's powerful Fund for Animals, and Alice Herrington's organization, the Friends of Animals. Dr. David Sergeant, principal advisor to the Canadian Department of Fisheries and Forestry, warned again that the kill quotas were too high for maintaining the population.[2] Legislation was introduced in the U.S. Senate and House to protect baby seals by banning their pelts. Also in the U.S., Lewis Regenstein, a CIA agent with a love for animals, wrote a scathing indictment of the Canadian hunt and the U.S. hunt in Alaska.

On December 3, 1971, Environment and Fisheries Minister Jack Davis announced that Canada and Norway had set up a joint commission on sealing. In addition to setting a quota of 100,000 seals each for Canada and Norway for the Front, Davis authorized a quota of 60,000 seals for the Gulf. He then made the startling announcement that he would reduce the quota in the Gulf by 25,000 each year until the hunt was ended entirely by 1975. (This had the effect of calming the protest, but by 1975, it was obvious that the government had no intention of delivering on Davis's promise.)

In 1972, Brian Davies came up with an alternative economic plan to replace seal killing with seal watching. Government spokespeople dismissed the scheme, scoffing that no one would visit the Magdalen Islands in winter. Brian went ahead anyway. When a New York travel firm advertised the seal-watching trip, the tour sold out in weeks.

One of the most significant developments that occurred in the early 1970s was the founding of Greenpeace.

In 1970, while I was still a student at Simon Fraser University, I had helped organize a demonstration against nuclear testing in Alaska. Months before, I had started to attend meetings with other opponents of the bomb testing. Out of these meetings we formed a group called the Don't Make a Wave Committee, so named because of the possibility that the tests would cause a tidal wave to strike Vancouver Island. We went on to organize a plan to protest underground nuclear testing by the United States under the Aleutian island of Amchitka. Most of the members of the committee were Quakers or Sierra Club members worried about the bomb. I was there because I had heard that Amchitka was a wildlife refuge and previous tests had already killed thousands of sea otters, seals, and sea birds.

In November 1971, the group's two ships, the *Phyllis Cormack*, renamed *Greenpeace*, and the *Edgewater Fortune*, renamed *Greenpeace Too*, sailed on an expedition to oppose the bomb. On the *Greenpeace Too*, some 500 miles from Amchitka, I heard that the bomb had been detonated ahead of schedule to prevent us being on site. We had failed, or so we thought at the time. In fact, it was the last test in the Aleutians. In large part because of the controversy we had stirred up with our voyage, subsequent tests were cancelled.

In 1972, we changed the name of our group to the Greenpeace Foundation. I was one of the founding directors, along with Bob and Bobbi Hunter, David Garrick, Rod Marining, Pat Moore, and others.

By 1975, we had succeeded in expanding the focus of Greenpeace to encompass wildlife conservation issues and had launched the world's first sea-going expedition to protect the whales. I was the first officer under Captain John Cormack on the *Greenpeace V* (the name was changed with each campaign), the very same boat that had accompanied my ship, the *Greenpeace Too,* to the Aleutians a few years before.

It was in the galley of the *Greenpeace V* that David Garrick and I talked about the possibility of a Greenpeace campaign to protect the harp seals.

I remember the excitement that rippled through me as we talked and I realized that my childhood dreams about protecting seals might indeed become a reality.

5

Shepherds of the Labrador Front

(1975–1976)

Whom when I asked from what place he came,
And how he hight, himselfe he did ycleepe,
The Shepheard of the Ocean by Name,
And said he came from the main-sea deepe.

—Edmund Spenser, "Colin Clouts Come Home Againe"

The Greenpeace Foundation officially entered the seal wars on October 20, 1975. With the success of the first Save the Whale campaign, David Garrick and I were determined to apply a little of the new Greenpeace media muscle to helping the seals on the east coast of Canada. It would not be easy. The board of directors of the Vancouver-based Greenpeace organization, except for David (nicknamed Walrus) and I, were very reluctant to get involved. They felt that Greenpeace should stick to anti-nuclear testing and whale-saving campaigns. We rebelled and insisted that there should and would be a seal campaign.

Greenpeace vice-president Patrick Moore made a board motion that funding would not be provided for a seal campaign. It passed. Walrus and I set up a separate account at the Gulf and Fraser Fisherman's Credit Union and borrowed $500 from the same institution to get the campaign rolling.

On October 20, in Seattle, we fired our opening shot. The occasion was the visit of King Olaf V, the seventy-four-year-old King of Norway. Scattered among the 350 Norwegian-American greeters were a handful of Greenpeacers and a few members of Defenders of Wildlife.

As the king stepped from his plane, he could see the protest banners and the large photos of baby harp seals. With the media focusing on the protest rather than the greeting, we were able to announce that Greenpeace intended to not only protest the 1976 hunt, but—and this had never happened before—to physically interfere with the planned seal kill. I informed the media that a Greenpeace crew would travel to the ice and spray a green vegetable dye onto the snowy pups so as to destroy the commercial value of the pelt without harming the seal itself. We were also prepared to place our bodies on the line by standing between the seals and their killers.

Back in Vancouver, Walrus and I set up an organizing committee. We were the only Greenpeace veterans excited about a seal campaign. To recruit a crew, we placed a small ad in the Vancouver alternative weekly, the *Georgia Straight*. The ad borrowed copy from famed Antarctic explorer Ernest Shackleton's historic recruitment poster and read:

WANTED

Twelve crew members needed for hazardous environmental protest expedition. No wages, bitter cold, three weeks of constant danger living upon the moving ice fields of the Labrador Front.

The task: To shepherd the baby harp seals and protect them from the brutal clubs of Canadian and Norwegian sealers.

The reward: The saving of a species from biological extinction.

The response was overwhelming. Many who crowded into the Greenpeace office that first night remained with Greenpeace for the next decade or two.

With a roomful of volunteers, and no budget from the board, we began to organize button, shirt, and bumper sticker sales to raise funds. The new crew included Al "Jet" Johnson, an American Airlines captain and former fighter pilot with the Royal Canadian Air Force. Jet also spoke fluent Norwegian. We also had veterinarian assistant Carl Rising-Moore; registered nurse Marilyn Kaga; bank teller Bonnie McLeod; writer Alan Thornton; and New Brunswick fisherman Paul Morse. Artist Barry Lavender was put to work as artwork coordinator for the shirts and buttons, while Bonnie McLeod began work on a fund-raising art auction.

David Garrick, also known as the Walrus and Walrus Oakenbough, became the spiritual advisor to the seal campaign. Wanting us to understand the Native perspective on our plans, he consulted with a West Coast medicine man, who suggested a healing ceremony. In a darkened house, David and eight Native people sat in a circle on the floor. As they meditated on the harp seal campaign, a dark, diffuse shape ran across the floor. The medicine man interpreted the shape to mean that any effort to protect the harp seals would be long and strenuous. Impeccable warriors would be needed. They would have to be clearly focused, pure of heart, and ritually clean.

David made a strenuous effort to recruit a Native crew and the board of directors humoured him until departure. In the end, the board, led by Patrick Moore, vetoed the Native members.

Events began to pick up. On November 3, Jean Haché, executive assistant to federal Fisheries Minister Romeo LeBlanc, announced that seal hunting in Canada needed to be banned or drastically reduced on account of decreasing numbers and that the decision would be made by Christmas.

The unexpected announcement was the result of a meeting between the minister and his advisory committee two weeks earlier. Dr. Dean Fisher, a member of the Committee on Seals and Sealing (COSS), attended the meeting. The minister, he said, "was aghast when he heard our new information about the seal population." A new ultraviolet photography technique had vastly increased the accuracy of the annual seal census and showed that if sealing continued at its current rate, the harp seals would be extinct in ten to fifteen years.

"Now it will be decades and decades before an exploitable population is built up again," he said, adding that Canadian scientists, from both government and the academic community, had agreed that all commercial sealing on ice by ships and landsmen should stop for ten years.

Fisher had been most encouraged by the sympathetic attitude of the civil servants at the October 23 meeting.

"As I sat at that meeting, I looked at this new generation of young men who are now moving into executive positions of decision in government," he said. "They are the first product of the age of the environment to be in such positions. They are concerned and I feel we are going to see some action now."

I responded to the possibility of a seal hunt ban in a statement to the media on November 4:

"We are not calling off our expedition unless there is a complete ban. Roughly 200 people have already volunteered to join us. No one is thinking of quitting yet.

"LeBlanc has an absolutely clear moral duty to impose an immediate ban on the hunting of harp seals, which a University of Guelph study shows are definitely threatened due to over-hunting by Norwegian and Canadian commercial sealers."

In response to the federal Fisheries position that the seal hunt was essential to the livelihood of many Newfoundlanders, I stated, "What small amount of money the Newfoundlanders actually lose could very easily be made up for with a slight change of priorities on the part of the federal government, such as paying the men to tend and promote the growth of the creatures, rather than subsidize their slaughter and extinction."

This could easily be done, I said, by turning the harp seal population into a tourist industry for the millions of people who had seen pictures of the harp seal babies and would love to see one up close.

The bait that I had set in Seattle in late October got a nibble from the Newfoundland sealers and then a bite. From a small news item announcing plans to interfere with the seal hunt, buried in the paper, the story escalated to the front page and won national exposure with the Newfoundland reaction.

We were delighted at the *Vancouver Province* headlines of November 5, 1975, "Greenpeace Seal Crusade Takes Clubbing." Both Newfoundland government and opposition spokesmen described the plan to spray the seals with dye as "hare-brained, dangerous, and an unwarranted interference in Newfoundland affairs."

The St. John's *News* attacked our suggestion that the economic loss to sealers could be offset through tourism and warned that the Greenpeace expedition might end up as an expensive search and rescue operation.

On the political side, Newfoundland Fisheries Minister Walter Carter announced that he would contact the government of British Columbia about the Greenpeace plan and advised Greenpeace "to mind its own business."

In reply, I said protecting seals *was* the foundation's business. We then announced that Greenpeace would be working in cooperation with Brian Davies of the International Fund for Animal Welfare, who had offered to lend us $7,000 to assist our seal campaign.

From St. John's to Ottawa to the corridors of academia, the Greenpeace announcement of intended interference set off a chain reaction of response. In the House of Commons, a Newfoundland member of Parliament called on the government to stop the Greenpeace Foundation from disrupting the seal hunt.

At the University of Guelph, Dr. Keith Ronald, dean of biological science, announced that he was astounded by the plan to spray harp seals with a green dye.

"There are other ways of conserving the herd," said Dr. Ronald, who was also the chairman of the federal advisory Committee on Seals and Sealing. Ronald said that the dye would make seal pups more evident to predators during the whelping period near the end of February.

I countered that we had contacted Dr. Dean Fisher about the safety of the dye. Dr. Fisher felt it was safe and pointed out that scientists, including Dr. Ronald, had used dye on seals for population and migratory research. Dr. Ronald admitted to the press that this was true.

As for the claim that the pups would be found by predators, I expressed surprise that Dr. Ronald would be so unscientific. The only predator is man, I argued, and the dye would serve to dissuade the human predator.

In November 1975, David Garrick, Alan Thornton, Marilyn Kaga, and I drove to Bloomington, Indiana, for the National Whale Symposium. There I engaged in a debate with Dr. David Sergeant of the Canadian Fisheries Ministry and succeeded in having the symposium resolve to send the Canadian government a telegram urging the immediate banning of the seal hunt. In Indiana, we recruited Dan Willens for our ice crew.

By December 8, Greenpeace had raised $7,543.55; with the loan from the IFAW, we had $14,543.55. Added to this were donations of survival suits, Arctic boots, sleeping bags, and tents from sympathetic merchants.

I had already travelled back to Québec to negotiate the charter of two Bell Jet Ranger helicopters from a company based in Sept-Îles. Volunteer Paul Morse, whom we called Pablo, left Vancouver in January to arrange for the rental of a van in Cape Breton, Nova Scotia, and to book accommodations in St. Anthony, on the northernmost tip of Newfoundland.

Pablo was a big man but as gentle and jovial as a tamed circus bear. It was a mystery why this practical, salt-of-the-earth Maritime fisherman was on our crew, because fishermen are notoriously anti-seal. Pablo had experienced his own redefinition of values a few years before when an Israeli freighter had run down and sunk his boat, drowning two of his shipmates. The big freighter did not stop to rescue anyone, and Pablo had watched in anger and horror as the killer ship slipped into the darkness and left him struggling for his life in the frigid Atlantic.

In February, David Garrick travelled to the Rocky Mountains to hold a ceremony near Chief Smallboy's camp. Chief Robert Smallboy was a renegade "back to the land" Cree who refused to live on a reserve and had returned with some of his people to the natural world.

Things were going well. We had the funding, the equipment, and, most importantly, the media were following our every move.

On March 1, 1976, we had a fund-raising send-off party at the Commodore Ballroom on Granville Street. A crowd of about 800 people were dancing and the crew were enjoying the band when two police officers entered, seemingly intent on finding someone. Suddenly, a young man bolted from the dance floor and ran past us, the cops in hot pursuit. Foolishly, perhaps instinctively, Greenpeace ice crew member Carl Rising-Moore put out his foot and tripped the first officer, sending the second cop sprawling over his downed comrade. As the two police officers struggled to their feet, the youth escaped.

The officer that Carl tripped grabbed him and searched him. With a look of triumph, he pulled a plastic bag of marijuana out of Carl's back pocket.

"It's not mine," Carl stammered. "I don't know how you found that."

The cop shoved Carl. "You're busted."

As they led Carl away, I spoke with the second officer.

"Officer, unfortunately, he's one of our crew members, and, yes, I know he was an asshole to trip your partner, but this will really set us back for getting out of here tomorrow to save the seals."

Surprisingly, the police officer was sympathetic. Walrus, Rod Marining, and I followed him out to the street, where Carl was handcuffed. The second officer had some words with the arresting officer, who then called me over.

"What are you doing with an asshole like this on the crew?" he asked.

"Volunteers are hard to come by," I answered.

Dangling the plastic bag in front of his partner, the arresting officer said, "And what are we supposed to do with this?"

The cop with a soft spot for seals took the bag, smelled it, and dumped it on the pavement, where it scattered in the breeze. "Oregano," he said calmly.

The arresting officer released Carl. I shook hands with both officers and thanked them. Later I warned my crew that I would not tolerate any use of drugs or alcohol on the campaign. I didn't want to lose this fight because of something as frivolous as grass or even beer.

On March 2, our train pulled away from the Canadian National Railways terminal in Vancouver. Due to the internal politics of Greenpeace, I was forced to include Patrick Moore and his girlfriend, Eileen Chivers, as excess baggage. The board had approved a budget for their expenses, so Pat and Eileen would not be riding the train with us. They would be taking a plane and would meet us in Ottawa.

The train trip became a whistle stop media event and allowed us to hold press conferences right across Canada. At every stop, we taunted Fisheries Minister Romeo LeBlanc and we demonstrated our portable spray dye bottles.

In Calgary, I refuted the minister's asinine accusation that if we dyed seals, their mothers would reject them.

"Expert biologists have advised us that there will be absolutely no rejection. Canadian Fisheries scientists have been dying seals for years for research, and the dye they use is not organic." To hammer the point home and to emotionally appeal to the public, I passed out photos of a seal mother refusing to leave the skinned body of her baby. "Does that look like a mother that would abandon her pup because of some vegetable dye? I don't think so."

We arrived in Winnipeg to a retort from Romeo that our plan to dye the seals would make them more vulnerable to their natural predators, polar bears and orcas.

"Please," I said patiently to reporters, "I dealt with this ridiculous charge months ago. The only natural predator is man."

A reporter spoke up. "Well then, why does the pup have the camouflage of a white coat if there are no predators?"

"Because it does not have a camouflaged white coat," I responded. "In fact, the hairs are individually hollow and transparent and appear white. The purpose of the seal pup's fur is to absorb heat from the sun. The 'whitecoat' is in reality a living solar blanket."

Romeo was still firing off press responses from the hip as our train chugged into Ottawa. The only glitch at the press conference was a statement delivered by Patrick Moore. There was nothing wrong with what he said—it was the usual anti-seal hunt rhetoric given additional "credibility" by Pat's doctorate in ecology. The problem was that Pat was wearing a leather jacket as he made his statement on national television, and the leather jacket was deerhide.

When questioned about the inappropriateness of wearing a deerskin jacket at a press conference condemning the trade in seal fur, Pat, looking shocked that someone would comment, said, "It's okay, I shot it myself."

One little interesting footnote about Pat's degree in ecology: It was actually a degree in forest management. Pat Moore, the son of Bill Moore, a Vancouver Island logging baron, was now attacking the sealers of Newfoundland. Logging profits had sent Pat off to the élite St. George's private school for boys and then on to the University of British Columbia, rather like the sealing profits that had sent John Crosbie off to private schools and a career in the federal government. As I said earlier, Pat's participation was not my idea.

By the time we reached Montreal, we were becoming a real threat to the Fisheries minister. To thwart our plans, he started passing special Order-in-Council regulations, which are laws passed by the cabinet without the vote or approval of Parliament. We suddenly found that it was now illegal to fly under 2,000 feet over a seal or to land an aircraft less then half a nautical mile from the seal hunt without permission from the minister.

Travelling through New Brunswick, I noticed that Carl Rising-Moore was not to be seen anywhere. Searching the train, I found him five cars forward, poaching a ride in the more luxurious first-class carriage.

"Carl," I said, "you should come back to the crew car. It would not be a good reflection on the campaign to get in trouble ripping off the railway company."

Looking extremely annoyed, Carl snapped at me, "Screw off, I can sit where I please."

At Truro, Carl showed up in our car for lunch, then headed forward again to his stolen seat. A few minutes later, he was back, looking pale and angry.

"My car is gone!" he yelled.

"Of course," I told him. "Your car is off to Halifax and our car is bound for Sydney. They shunted your car off in Truro."

Bonnie McLeod laughed. "You'll have to sit with us peasants, Carl."

"But you don't understand," Carl pleaded. "My backpack was in that car."

"Karma," said Hunter, from his corner seat. "Tough break, man."

Walrus looked at me, "Oh shit," he said. "Carl was packing half the dye."

"Christ, Carl, what the hell have you done to us?" I said, glaring at Rising-Moore.

"I'm sorry, man."

"You're going to be more than sorry. When we get to Sydney, you get back on this train to Halifax and you go and retrieve your pack."

"Will you wait for me to get back?" Carl asked timidly.

"Hell no," I said, "we connect to the ferry for Port aux Basques when we arrive. Get the train back, get tomorrow night's ferry and hitch north to St. Anthony. And one more thing—stay out of first class."

The ferry crossing was exhilarating. I spent an hour watching the big ship crush through the thick ice across the Cabot Strait. Seeing the ice heave and buck with the swells, some of the crew were terrified. Floes collided with each other and rafted quickly into pressure ridges, erupting as much as eight feet into the air.

Marilyn looked at me as we stood on the deck. "My God, it's wild out there. Is this the stuff we will be walking on?"

"Yes," I answered. "Although the Front ice is more hostile than this stuff in the Gulf."

Dan Willens just whistled. Walrus calmly said, "Mother Nature will protect us."

We arrived in Port aux Basques to a frigidly cold morning; the air was filled with the musical tinkling of thousands of tons of ice cracking and moving in the harbour. A small band of protestors stood in the freezing air, their signs telling us to go home. One old lady snarled with a toothless lisp, "I'll see ya tonight on tha television with your t'roat slit."

I smiled and answered, "Welcome to Newfoundland."

The crew laughed nervously.

We sent Moore and a few crew ahead by bus to quietly rent a second van in Cornerbrook, because we had not anticipated how much room our supplies would take. Then we headed north into a raging blizzard.

Although people knew we were on the island, no one was on the road to recognize us or give us any trouble. No wonder—black ice, high winds, and drifting snow forced us off the pavement a dozen times. We literally rammed and punched our way through six-foot drifts.

"No worry," I told everyone. "We have the best off-road, all-terrain vehicles there are."

"What?" said Marilyn. "These are Chevy vans."

"True, but a rental van is the best all-terrain vehicle because you don't have to worry about trashing it."

At the end of the day, we had covered three-quarters of the distance to St. Anthony and we were all hungry for a hot meal.

Luck was with us and we found a motel where the management did not know who we were. Though closed for the winter, they agreed to open some rooms for us. All they could make us were some cold sandwiches, but we were thankful even for that.

The place had a small bar and a pool table and things were going well until the news came on the television. We and our hosts watched footage of angry men waving signs as they waited for us on the only road into St. Anthony. They looked like a gang of vigilante thugs, with scarred faces and icicles hanging from their beards.

One of the protestors looked into the camera and muttered, "Those Greenpeacers don't dare show up here."

I smiled at Pablo, Jet Johnson, and Walrus. "Well," I said cheerfully, "we ain't got a choice now. A dare is a dare and we can't let him get away with that, can we?"

They laughed.

Our hosts, however, were not amused. We decided that it would be wise to retire early en masse. What we really wanted was sleep anyway, and despite the near-freezing room temperatures and the fact that there was ice in the toilets, we managed to get a good night's rest.

We got up early and hit the road again. It was a glistening, cold, clear morning. Ron Precious cradled his 16-millimetre camera in his arms and brightly announced, "Looks good."

Whatever happened, we had the light we needed to capture the action.

Knowing what was up ahead was making a few of the crew nervous. Walrus and I were delighted. We wanted—needed—a confrontation. The television cameras would be there and would allow us to send the message that we were not afraid of the big bad sealers.

Eileen Chivers was lobbying to turn around to avoid the roadblock.

"What?" said Bonnie McLeod. "We'd be branded as cowards."

"Better live cowards than dead heroes," she snapped back.

"Speak for yourself, Eileen," retorted Bonnie.

All day long we drove northward, with the jagged jumble of icy floes on our left and the stark whiteness of the treeless land to our right. The wind blew strong and we could feel every frigid blast from the seaside as it slapped the side of our vehicles.

As we drove, CBC radio fed us a steady report of growing numbers and growing tempers on the roadblock up ahead. "They's b'yes ain't fokking gittin' by me, no sirree. I says we string them Greenpissers up to a tree," we heard one protester say in that distinctive Newfoundland accent.

"Hey, Bob," I joked, "you handle that one, OK?"

Finally, around three in the afternoon, we saw them—at least 200 men, most dressed in black snowmobile outfits, and about forty vehicles parked haphazardly along the road. In their midst, we could see television cameras. The protesters waved a collection of crudely manufactured protest signs. A few were holding up ropes in the air, and as we got closer, we could see they were hangmen's nooses.

We were actually relieved to spy a few uniformed Mounties standing to the side of the road.

"Well," said Pat Moore, who was driving. "We seem to be here." He braked, turned off the ignition, and we watched the black-clad mob flow toward us.

Protest signs slapped up against the side windows and blocked them. Men spat on the windshield and cursed us. Eileen was terrified. The crowd began to rock the vans back and forth, threatening to turn them over. I was hoping they would actually turn us over—a visual like that would secure us a spot on the evening news.

When they failed to turn us over, though, we had to go ahead with the plan we'd discussed as we drove up.

I opened my door. Moore opened his at the same time and we both stepped out, followed by Bob Hunter and Walrus.

The sealers were momentarily confused. They had not expected us to step out of the van. They quickly recovered and began to shove us around, focusing on Pat and I because we were wearing bright orange Mustang-brand suits. Bob and Walrus, dressed in navy-coloured coats, were absorbed into the crowd.

As the men got angrier, we got calmer and tried to speak to them as patiently as possible, while keeping an eye out for the Mounties, who were now nowhere to be seen.

As we jostled back and forth in front of the television cameras, Bob had singled out the ringleader of this rabble, a man named Roy Pilgrim, and he learned that this group was a hastily thrown together organization called the Concerned Citizens Committee of St. Anthony Against Greenpeace.

Bob suggested that Pilgrim organize a town meeting so the media could hear both sides of the debate. Pilgrim saw some merit in that idea and yelled for the mob to quiet down.

"Let's string 'em up right here, Roy!"

"Hell, you know we can't do that, George. I've decided to give these b'yes an opportunity to speak to us about how we should run our lives. We'll be having a meeting tonight at nine at the elementary school."

Some of the men booed, others just shrugged and gave us the finger. One of the guys with the noose yelled, "Makes no difference, these b'yes are gonna be on their way back to the mainland by midnight!"

The mob roared with approval and raced to their cars. We found ourselves in a convoy of slow-moving vehicles as we headed on down the road toward Deckers' Boarding House, where Pablo had arranged our accommodations months earlier.

At Deckers', Emily "Ma" Decker herself came out to greet us. She was a Newfoundlander, but she was also our contracted hostess and, by God, she let that rabble know that she did not appreciate them interfering with her business.

But the mob wanted action and a few of the more drunken louts accosted us before we could get to the door. One of them began to shove me.

Suddenly, Walrus rushed over and jabbed his finger into the young sealer's chest, catching the man completely off guard.

"Listen, I haven't heard one of you guys say one word yet about Mother Earth! And that's what this is all about! We're here to protect the seals, the whales, the birds, everything! And you're not going to stop us, because it's the will of Mother Earth that we are here! Those seals are my seals too!"

The sealers backed down. This guy was crazy and not to be messed with. They retreated to their cars.

Once inside the cozy family boarding house, we immediately contacted Rod Marining, who was holding down the fort at our Vancouver office. Rod informed us that the Canadian government had just passed another special Order-in-Council, this one making it illegal to spray living seals with dye.

The prime minister was exercising his power to create laws for specific political purposes. Trudeau himself was defending the sealers, and it was now a showdown between our intrepid little band and the government of the nation.

Bob indignantly dictated a press release implying that Canada was now an authoritarian dictatorship and that democracy had been sacrificed to appease the sealers.

After he hung up the phone, he and Pat had a meeting. Since the dye tactic was now illegal, they decided we could not use it.

Walrus and I were furious. "What the hell do you mean?" I said. "Did Gandhi back down to the British because they declared his tactics illegal? Damn it, the dye is the very backbone of our strategy!"

"Jesus," Walrus added, "I can't believe you guys would capitulate without a fight."

Pat was indignant. "This is a decision of the board and you must abide by it."

Walrus and I looked at each other in amazement. "Pat," I said calmly, "we're both on the board, Walrus and I, and we don't recall a vote being taken on this."

Pat dismissed us contemptuously. "Bob and I, as president and vice-president, respectively, can make decisions in the field for the board without a vote."

"Oh," I retorted. "It's sort of like an Order-in-Council."

"Paul, you've got to learn to be a team player."

Walrus looked at Pat. "Don't tell me," he said. "You own the ball so you get to make the rules. Christ, Pat."

Later that evening, we walked over to the school auditorium. The parking lot was jammed with cars and snowmobiles.

As we opened the door to the building, the low murmur of voices erupted into a cacophony. We entered to the blinding flashes of strobe lights and the intense glare of television floodlights. This was not friendly ground.

"You know, Walrus," I said, "Sun Tzu says you should never let the enemy choose the battlefield. To do so is to lose the battle before it begins."

Walrus shrugged. "A campaign led by bureaucrats also leads to defeat, and if Sun Tzu did not say that, well, he should have."

Predictably, the meeting was a disaster. Hunter and Moore capitulated immediately, surrendering our organic dye and handing the sealers a strategic victory. Hunter then announced that Greenpeace did not oppose the landsmen's hunt, nor did it oppose the Newfoundland hunt. To our surprise, we found out that we now opposed only the Norwegian hunt.

Bonnie McLeod was furious with me. "Are you telling me that I spent months standing outside of liquor stores in the rain, selling buttons and T-shirts, for this? This is total bullshit."

I agreed with her, but neither Walrus nor I could do anything about it. We were now simply subservient to the executive members of the board.

I took Bob Hunter over to the local pub in order to get him away from Moore and talk with him. Bob was sympathetic, but it was clear that he now believed that Pat should be running the show.

"Why, Bob, why him?"

"Well, he's an ecologist," he answered. "Besides Marvin Storrow, our legal advisor, backs us up on surrendering the dye."

"Of course he does, he's a goddamn lawyer."

Bob felt a little sheepish, but he argued that he was trying to build up an organizational structure and that people like Marvin and Pat were essential to that structure. "We have to back off from the exclusively radical and adventurous approach," he said, "and tap into the mainstream now and again."

"I don't think so, Bob. It was our radical and adventurous tactics that made us what we are. We didn't have any lawyers around telling us what we couldn't do, nor do I recall Moore ever being on the front lines. In fact, Moore was adamantly opposed to the seal campaign until we raised the money."

"Well," said Bob, "it comes down to the fact that, fair or not, the use of the dye is illegal, and if we want to maintain our tax-exempt status, we must abide by the law."

"Fuck the law and fuck the tax-exempt status," I answered angrily. "Do you think Thoreau was worried about his tax status? Hell no, he wouldn't pay his taxes to support a corrupt regime. Do you think Gandhi cared a good goddamn about his tax-exempt status?"

Bob listened patiently and a few beers later was once again the eco-warrior, ready to hit the warpath. We agreed that I would take a forward crew to Belle Isle to set up a base camp. I would bring Moore along to keep him from further interference with the media. Bob would stay behind and handle the media himself, and I knew that, freed of Moore's conservative influence, he could spin a story brilliantly. I was happy. I just wanted to get away from this enemy camp, where we had been forced to surrender our most powerful tactic.

We had one last beer to toast our resolve for a new approach, and it was out the door for the short quarter-mile walk back to Deckers' boarding house.

Or so we thought. We stepped out into a raging blizzard, a whiteout of swirling snow and wind. Within minutes, we were hopelessly lost. We could not tell if we were on the road or if we had stumbled onto the shore-fast ice bordering the road.

"This is just great, Bob. Can you imagine the headlines if they find us both frozen stiff in the morning?"

"Paul, you have a very strange sense of humour." He laughed anyway.

"OK, let's get our bearings here. We are both slightly tipsy. We are both very tired. We know that Decker's is down the road from here and we can't see a goddamn thing. So let's start walking in widening circles until we bump into some sort of landmark."

After a few minutes of this, we found a telephone pole.

"Eureka!" I shouted.

From there, we were able to make our way down the road, moving from pole to pole. Having measured the distance between two poles, we calculated an approximate quarter mile. After investigating three nearby houses, we found Deckers'. It had taken an hour.

When we walked through the door, most of the crew were there, worried. Their expressions of relief changed to disbelief as they stared at us. I looked at Bob clearly for the first time and he at me. Our beards and hair were dripping with icicles. We both laughed. If ever two men looked like polar explorers, we sure did.

With the arrival that same night of Brian Davies and his crew, the ranks of our anti-sealing movement increased. Moore was concerned about being associated with Davies and his animal welfare approach. I wished he had been as concerned about being associated with the seal killers, whom he seemed to prefer over Brian.

The next morning, our helicopters arrived, two sleek, expensive-looking Jet Rangers piloted by Jack Wallace and Bernd Firnung. We immediately put them to work ferrying fuel and supplies out to Belle Isle. It looked like bad weather coming in, but we erected three tents and Walrus, Johnson, Moore and I settled in for two days of a storm that reduced our world to a blinding nightmare of whiteness.

Our camp was atop cliffs towering 400 feet above the jagged ice, which jumbled and crashed below us in a constant roar. Out of touch with St. Anthony and the rest of the world, all we could do was stay in our sleeping bags and wait for the tempest to die down.

The storm abated on March 15, the first day of the seal hunt.

We awoke to an eerie stillness and walked out to a landscape of ice dotted with little outcroppings of white quartz rock. The winds had polished the ice to such brilliance that the reflected sunlight hurt our eyes.

As we walked around in a daze, we heard a distant thunk, thunk. A few moments later, the sky above us was filled with helicopters—first, two Fisheries machines, followed by Brian Davies and his IFAW machines, carrying flight attendants whom he was taking to view the hunt. They swooped low and carried on toward the sea. On their heels, our two machines appeared and landed. Bob Hunter, Ron Precious, Michael Chechik, Eileen Chivers, and a local guide named Art Elliott got out. We didn't really need Elliott. He had about as much experience on the ice as any of us, and that was none, but Hunter thought it would be good politics to bring along a Newfoundlander.

We quickly organized. Our helicopters lifted off from the frozen, lichen-encrusted surface of Belle Isle and headed out toward the sealers.

Davies and his flight attendants had reached the ice first. Near the sealing vessel *Arctic Explorer*, his cameras were recording the reactions of the women to the slaughter. He was in a race with us to get his images back before we did. I wished him good luck. He was still my hero for being the first to really challenge the hunt.

About midday we spotted two sealing ships on the horizon, small black specks on a vast canvas of white. As we got closer, we identified them as the *Theron* and the *Martin Karlsen*, both Canadian-registered, but Norwegian-owned. The hulls of both ships were red and scores of men in black, armed with clubs, stormed over the ice.

Now we could see two other ships, the *Melshorn* and the *Arctic Explorer*.

This was really the first time that the full-scale horror of the slaughter struck me. Large red bloody spokes radiated out from the ships where the winch lines had hauled piles of bleeding pelts across the ice. The ice floes were littered with tiny flayed corpses, each lying in a pool of congealing blood.

Stepping onto the ice was surreal. We were immediately greeted by little fluffy balls of soft white fur, whose round, jet-black eyes seemed to glisten with tears. Their crying sounded hauntingly human.

As the rotor blades slowed and stopped, we could hear screams and the thuds of clubs as the sealers carried on their bloody business. Something inside of me raged and I sprang out of the chopper running.

"Let's get them," I yelled.

Moore was horrified to see our small cadre dash over the ice. Suddenly, Jet broke to the right and rushed two Norwegian sealers before they could club a pup. Throwing his body over the baby, Jet told the man in Norwegian—Jet's parents were Norwegian immigrants—to back off.

The sealer did. Jet had saved our first seal.

The sealer headed for another victim, but Walrus beat him to it and covered the little body with his own, saving our second seal. This was something new to the sealers. We were not pretty flight attendants but men as big and tough as they were. Al was an ex-fighter pilot, Walrus a jungle-hiking archaeologist, and I was a seaman. The rules had been changed. The seals now had some new allies.

Both Jet and Walrus followed their men, blocking their every attempt to kill a seal until they both turned and walked back toward the *Melshorn*. I had chosen another sealer and prevented him from killing a seal, saving a third.

Meanwhile, Moore was taking photographs of dead seals—their carcasses. They lay, strewn callously about on the blue-white ice, each one oozing gore into a puddle of congealing blood.

As we struggled to save one seal at a time, I noticed that the sealing ships were constantly moving forward through the ice, unmindful of the helpless pups in their path. I could see a baby seal in front of the *Melshorn*, crying in fright at the advancing mountain of steel.

I ran as fast as I could toward that little pup. Sealers stood on the deck, jeering at me as the space between steel hull and seal pup grew increasingly smaller.

Just as the red hull split the ice beneath the seal, I reached him. I grabbed him under his flippers and was able to pull him up before he dropped through the expanding crack. With the ship's bow only ten feet away, I found myself on a small pan floating in black frigid water. With the pup in my arms, I could not jump to safety, and I did not even think of abandoning the baby.

The bow of the *Melshorn* struck the edge of my pan and twirled it around like a top, almost sending us sliding into the brine. Luckily, the pan, pushed sideways by the advancing wake, crunched up against the solid ice and I jumped.

I led the baby a fair distance and placed him in a depression behind the advancing sealers. The signal had come for us all to return to the helicopters. A storm was coming in.

Reluctantly, I left that little tyke. He looked up at me with wide, moist black eyes and I was touched by his incredible beauty and innocence. Things got kind of personal at that point. He was no longer just *any* seal. I knew him now, and he knew me. We were buddies who had met on a battlefield.

One of the helicopters landed beside me and we headed back to Belle Isle.

I sent Pat Moore back to St. Anthony and replaced him with Paul Morse.

When the replacement crew, including Marilyn Kaga, reached our camp, we discovered that the mainland supply crew had forgotten to load food and camp stove fuel. The helicopters had only just departed when the storm swooped in and grounded us in a white hell.

Eight people in three tents with enough food for one day and no stove fuel. It did not look good.

Jet Johnson solved the fuel problem. He siphoned off some of the helicopter jet fuel from the fuel cache, got it in the little stoves, and worked laboriously to ignite and burn it. The tent he shared with Pablo, Walrus, and Ron Precious quickly became known as Blacklung tent. I shared a tent and a sleeping bag with Marilyn Kaga, with whom a relationship had developed; we didn't need a soot-spewing stove.

Unbeknownst to us, the storm was being described in the media as the worst in a decade. Without radio communications, our support party in St. Anthony could only wait and worry. Also unknown to us, the entire sealing fleet was shut down, unable to dispatch sealers onto the treacherous floes to kill seals.

After three days, a brief respite in the storm allowed the helicopters to retrieve us all and hustle us back to Ma Decker's boarding house. It was a fortunate rescue. The storm returned with renewed fury, and when we returned to Belle Isle, we found our base camp in ruins.

Undaunted, we returned to the sealing grounds, landing over a mile away to avoid being arrested. Under the Canadian Seal Protection Act, no one other than a sealer may land closer than half a mile from a seal. The government claimed that the act protected the seals from being disturbed. In other words, you could only disturb a seal if you intended to kill it. In fact, this Orwellian ruling protected the sealers from being disturbed by those opposing the hunt.

This time the ice was badly broken up. We had to take an organized approach—no mad dash across the unbroken ice like before.

It took us more than an hour before we reached the sealers, who stood around beside piles of steaming scarlet pelts. Blood dripped from their gloved hands and smeared their faces. They smoked and laughed and grinned derisively at us.

"Why don't ya b'yes go the fokk home? We don't want your kind out here, ya goddamn tourists."

Marilyn Kaga responded first. "Perhaps the seals don't want your kind out here either."

One particularly ugly brute eyed her up and down and sneered, "Maybe we should skin your pretty pelt, you yellow bitch."

The others and I bristled. Fortunately, some approaching Mounties and Fisheries officers prevented the situation from getting violent.

We had better luck when we approached another sealer some 300 feet from the others. Marilyn Kaga approached him. "Are you proud of your handiwork?" she asked.

"No, b'ye's," he replied. "Naught proud t'all. It be me furst year a swiling, I hav' na hart fer it." He admitted he would kill no more seals.

Later, a government spokesperson informed the press that it was not unusual for a first-time sealer to lose his stomach for the job on the first day: "It takes a special kind of man to kill a baby seal. Not a soft man, not a girly man, but a tough old salt of a man who knows that killing is a necessity in this here life."

I decided that we should continue where we had left off. The objective would be to stop the ships in the ice, and, we hoped, slow them down.

Once again we saw a sealing ship, the *Arctic Endeavour*, bearing down on a helpless harp seal pup and ran to the rescue. This time Bob Hunter came bounding over the ice beside me. Behind us raced Michael Chechik and Ron Precious, frantically lugging their camera equipment.

We reached the seal in front of the ship. I moved the pup well out in front of us and Bob and I turned our backs to the advancing vessel.

Fifteen feet away, Chechik set up his shotgun microphone and Ron Precious prepared his twelve-pound single mag Éclair. Patrick Moore had talked Hunter into supporting his return and he was hanging back with his stills camera ready.

This was another pivotal moment for both Bob and me. The year before, we had been the first two people to place ourselves between a harpoon and a whale. Now we were the first to place ourselves between a sealing ship and a seal.

The ice was vibrating and beginning to heave under our feet.

A crewman at the starboard side of the bow screamed down at us.

"Y'betta move, b'yes. The ol' man ain't one t'tink twice about running ya into the ice."

Bob Hunter turned and yelled back. "Tell the old bastard to do what he wants! We're not moving."

The ship suddenly stopped and began to back off. For a moment, we felt a surge of elation. But then the big red hull began to move forward again with increasing speed. I looked back and saw her advancing. It was an awesome and frightening sight, but we had absolutely no intention of moving.

The ship's bow lunged forward and a thousand tons of steel connected with a thousand tons of ice.

The crewman on the bow hollered back to the bridge.

"Stop 'er, Cap! Stop 'er! The stupid asses ain't movin'!"

Ron was getting it all on film, and from his point of view it was spectacular. The big ship gave one last shudder as the ice seized and held her fast only five feet behind our backs.

I had picked up the pup to walk it to safety when a Ministry of Fisheries officer blocked my path. He took my picture and began to read from the new "Greenpeace" amendments to the Seal Protection Act.

"Section 21(B) states that it is a federal offence to remove a live seal from one location to another. You are in violation of this regulation."

I was becoming very angry. "The law can go to hell," I snorted and brushed past him with the seal. The surprised officer watched in silence as I walked away to bring the seal to a place of safety. The little seal looked up at me quizzically as I laid him gently down on the ice.

Back at the *Arctic Endeavour*, Bob Hunter was still blocking the ship's path. I returned and stood with him. We stayed there the rest of the afternoon.

We returned again the next day, but this time, despite our pilots taking meticulous care not to land within less than half a nautical mile of a seal, the Fisheries helicopters swooped in and charged both pilots with doing just that.

"Where's the seal?" asked Bernd Firnung.

The officer shrugged. "He was in that lead over there, but you scared him into the water."

We were ordered back to St. Anthony. We thought about staying behind on the floes to protest the arrest of our machines, but both pilots warned that another whiteout was on the way.

It was our last day on the floes. Once we returned to Newfoundland, our helicopters were placed under a twenty-four-hour RCMP guard and our pilots put under house arrest at Ma Decker's. Bond for their release was set at $20,000 each, and it took us a week to raise the funds. By then, the ice nurseries were beyond our reach. We returned to Ottawa. Here we found that we had stirred up a row in both the government and the media. We had not saved the lives of many seals, but we had delivered a protest that was reported around the world.

Before departing Ottawa, we read a statement at the National Press Building demanding the immediate resignation of the Minister of Fisheries on the grounds of negligence. We also demanded that Canada unilaterally declare a 200-mile limit in order to preserve its marine resources, and pressed for the release of a recent report on harp seal populations.

The following year, we would return, with more media and more clout, and we would be on the ice again to protect the ice puppies.

Brigitte Bardot and the Labrador Three-Ring Circus

(1977)

Sauvez les petits bébés phoques. (**Save the little baby seals.**)

—Brigitte Bardot

In September 1976, Jet Johnson and I flew from Vancouver to Bergen, Norway, to attend the Marine Mammal Conference. We used the opportunity to publicize our opposition to Norwegian whaling and sealing. Jet's fluent Norwegian came in handy. We also met most of the influential marine mammal scientists and established close relations with a few, including Dr. Roger Payne, who impressed me enormously when he told a delegation of scientists that, "I would not want to live in a world that had destroyed the great whales."

Nor would I, I thought. To save the whales was to save the seas, and to save the seas was to save humanity. Hell, the same could be said about the seals and the fish.

In Bergen, we checked out whaling and sealing boats and, posing as journalists, arranged for a tour of the Rieber Company warehouse to get a good look at the inventory of seal pelts. After the conference, Al returned home and I stayed on for a week to raise support for the upcoming 1977 campaign.

In a student bar in Bergen, I was introduced to three Norwegian women—Vibeke Arviddsson, Elizabeth Rasmussen, and Kristin Aarflot—who seemed very interested in protecting seals.

They welcomed the chance to talk about Norway's involvement in the hunt and all three practically begged me to include them in our next campaign. I quickly agreed: They were strong, attractive, and, most importantly, they were Norwegian. For the first time, we would have Norwegians saving seals instead of killing them.

I left Bergen reluctantly, because I had fallen for Kristin and we had gotten involved. I also discovered that she would be a natural for the conditions on Belle Isle; she had a particular fondness for making love in the snow. I kissed Kristin goodbye, knowing that I would see her again soon. In the meantime, she, Vibeke, and Elizabeth would stoke the flames of publicity in Norway.

Back in Vancouver, the office politics of Greenpeace had become more heated. Moore and I were no longer talking. Hunter and I were extremely cool with each other. I made it clear that the upcoming seal campaign was my baby.

Since Walrus had left for Japan to help organize an anti-whaling movement, I asked Jet Johnson to be the deputy leader of the seal expedition. Once again we began the tedious struggle to raise funds and organize a crew.

By January 1977, politics, not ecology, had come to dominate our activities. Moore made a move to depose Hunter as president, and because I did not want Hunter to compromise the 1977 expedition, I found myself backing Moore against Hunter, a move that surprised everybody, especially me. An embittered Hunter held on to the office by one vote. The board was also bitterly divided between the financial and legal people that Bob Hunter had brought in and the younger, more radical crowd recruited primarily by me. And I had become the "rebel leader" because of my determination to control the upcoming seal campaign.

To add to the turmoil, Greenpeace offices were spreading like cancer. We now had 80,000 members and offices in a dozen cities. And they all had their own boards and they all wanted to be in on the action. We needed the money they raised for the debts that we had incurred, but we could only get funds from them in return for promises of representation on the expedition crews.

So, although I needed only a dozen people for the seal campaign, my crew swelled to more than thirty-five, with representatives from such diverse cities as San Francisco, London, Montreal and Thunder Bay, plus the three women from Norway. The only seal vets aside from myself were Jet Johnson and Walrus, who would be coming from Japan.

It was a taxing time. I was editing and publishing the *Greenpeace Chronicle*, including arranging for a French-language edition. I was fund-raising, recruiting, organizing a campaign, and fighting internal politics, all as a full-time unpaid volunteer.

My relationship with Marilyn began to falter. She had close ties to the Japanese community and found herself torn between loyalty to Greenpeace and me, and loyalties to people who viewed Greenpeace as anti-Japanese or even racist. Then there was my increasing obsession with the Greenpeace cause, which consumed most of my time and energy. Marilyn felt that I was becoming misanthropic; she couldn't understand my anger. I couldn't understand her compassion for humanity. She chose people and I chose the Earth, and thus we began to drift apart.

As slowly as I parted from Marilyn, I had just as slowly became involved with Starlet Melody Lum, whom Bobbi Hunter had hired to keep the books for Greenpeace. A startlingly attractive Eurasian beauty with an aura of self-confidence and almost haughty intelligence, she captivated me. We became friends first, then lovers much later. In Starlet, I had an ally with a finger on the financial pulse of the neophyte Greenpeace empire.

On returning to Vancouver from my Norway trip, I discovered that Starlet was moving to Montreal to set up a Greenpeace office with Michael Manolson. She was very much committed to my ideas and wanted to work to support the next seal campaign.

Emotionally, I was in a quandary. I loved Marilyn, but we were drifting apart. I was very much infatuated with Kristin's beauty and sensuality although I knew little else about her. With Starlet, I felt both an attraction and an understanding, and it was mutual. I spent time with her before she left for Montreal and I knew that I would miss her.

As a young man of twenty-six, I was working through my biological instincts with women and it was confusing, to say the least. What I was really looking for in a woman was a commitment to the cause of conservation. Thus Marilyn was lost, but Starlet and Kristin both held promise. As for the ice in '77, my companion would be Kristin and I looked forward to her arrival.

The seal campaign earlier that year had left a bitter taste in my mouth. I was frustrated to see our 1976 efforts hijacked by the board of directors. I respected Bob, but we could not break down the defence that his intellectual bodyguard, one Dr. Patrick Moore, Ph.D., put up around him. It is amazing the amount of sway a piece of sheepskin can have. To me, it simply meant that Moore had had the money to attend university, where he could swallow bullshit and regurgitate academic pulp, his tuition paid for with the lifeblood of thousands of trees. But Pat refused to acknowledge the contradiction. Humans have an amazing capacity for self-justification and rationalization.

Moore regarded Walrus and me as his social inferiors and hung around our projects like a vulture, ready to swoop down and claim credit for anything we might be doing that would advance his position within the foundation. The difference between us was simple. Moore viewed Greenpeace as a vehicle for self-advancement. Walrus and I viewed Greenpeace as a tool to further the movement. Bob Hunter, on the other hand, viewed himself as a man with a destiny and Greenpeace as a means of experimenting with the fantastic but possible idea of changing the consciousness of humanity. Thus, in early 1976, the fate of Greenpeace was in the hands of the Corporate Opportunist, the Warrior Brothers, and the Messiah.

The other directors allied themselves behind the three camps. All three views could have been and would have been combined, had it not been for Patrick's egocentric lust for control. His plan was clear: to use Hunter to oust David and me, with Hunter's ouster to follow.

In early January, I flew to Switzerland to meet with Franz Weber, a millionaire animal rights advocate. In a mountaintop restaurant overlooking Montreux, I convinced him and his wife to give us a sizable contribution. He asked me to arrange some helicopters for him so he could bring some European journalists to the ice floes off Newfoundland. I agreed.

Returning to Canada, I landed at Mirabel, Montreal's new and impractical airport, built some fifty miles from the city. Even more inconvenient, however, was the reception that Canadian Immigration gave me when I handed them my Canadian passport. I was ordered into a side room to wait for two senior officials to arrive. I was slightly amused—what could they do? Deny me admittance to my own country?

The two officials, one holding my passport in his right hand as he peered at me intently, approached. He continued to peer and study as his partner spoke.

"Mr. Watson?"

"Yes," I replied.

"How long have you been out of the country?"

"Three days."

"Where did you travel to?"

"Switzerland."

"What was your business?"

"Business," I said.

"What was the nature of your business?"

"My own."

"Pardon me!" He choked.

"My own. In other words it was my business, not your business."

"Mr. Watson, I don't believe you understand. When we ask a question, we expect a straight answer."

"Yes, and I gave you my answer. I'm not smuggling drugs or anything else. You can search my bags. You can search me, but what is in my head is of no concern or business to you or the government of Canada."

"Mr. Watson, you must answer our questions."

I looked at this humourless bureaucrat and sighed. "I am answering your questions, you just don't like my answers."

"We would like the names of people you met with in Switzerland."

I smiled. "I bet you would, but that's my business also."

The other officer, the one holding my passport, spoke up for the first time. "Why do you insist on being difficult?"

"I'm just standing up for my right as a Canadian citizen to protect my privacy."

"You don't have a right to privacy in Canada as a citizen," he stated matter-of-factly. "You've been watching American television."

"Well, I believe I do, and if I don't, then I bloody well should."

I was rewarded with a strip search and the confiscation of my address book, which was photocopied and returned to me an hour later. I was then allowed to enter my own country, with the admonishment that I should be more respectful of government officials in the future. Right!

I stopped off in Montreal to visit the Greenpeace office there and to have dinner with Starlet. She had received the stats from the Canadian Department of Fisheries and Oceans on the seal hunt.

The previous year, the kill quota had been set at 127,000 seal pups. The actual kill was 160,000 pups, yet there were no charges, no reprimands, no fines. Again, the government's own scientific body called for a moratorium. They were ignored. The government finally responded by revising the kill quota at 170,000—some response!

To add insult to injury, the government had commissioned oil-spill studies to determine their effect on seal herds. The experiments included immersing hundreds of seals in oil so the effects could be measured. Any kindergarten graduate could have predicted that the seals would die. Dr. Joseph R. Geraci, on the other hand, defended his experiments on the grounds that "real observation was the only criterion for science."

In 1977, the life of a seal wasn't worth a puddle of spilt oil in Canada. On top of that, an article in the Canadian *Catholic Register* condemned Greenpeace and me for doing Satan's work by risking human souls for soulless creatures. I did not respond. I learned a long time ago that the best way to deal with the Roman Catholic Church was to not deal with it at all. Not that I entirely deplored the Church. After all, my radicalism is firmly rooted in my juvenile rebellion against blatant Catholic hypocrisy.

My contact with Franz Weber paid off. Weber offered to build a factory in Newfoundland to manufacture baby harp seal toys made of fake fur. He promised the government of Canada that he would employ 600 people in his factory, compared to the 150 being seasonally employed for one month of the year by the sealing industry. Additionally, he offered to compensate the sealers in the amount of $2.5 million.

Canadian Fisheries Minister Romeo LeBlanc turned the offer down flat, saying that he would not be "blackmailed."

I wrote in the *Greenpeace Chronicles*:

If the Minister was truly interested in the financial circumstances of the sealers, he would not have turned down the 2.5-million-dollar offer of compensation . . . [or] Mr. Weber's offer to build a fake fur factory . . . . Year-round employment vs. seasonal employment, and the government turned it down! . . .

Canada spends more money policing the hunt than Canadian citizens make from it. There is a very fishy smell clinging to the Ministry of Fisheries and the Environment.

The government retaliated with emotional arguments about the cultural purity of the hunt—the traditions, the colourful history, the destruction of a way of life. We fought back with facts and condemned the hunt as a perversity. Canadian photographer and conservationist Fred Bruemmer described the hunt best:

The hunt of the harp seals has no equal. . . . More than fifty million seals have been killed in the [Labrador] Front and Gulf [of St. Lawrence] herds of Newfoundland alone. If one adds to this the harp seals killed from the other two herds—the one east of Greenland, the other in Russia's

White Sea—the total rises to about seventy million, the greatest, most protracted mass slaughter ever inflicted upon any wild mammal species.

In late February, Kristin and her friends arrived in Vancouver, and the three women, all looking gorgeously Nordic, quickly became the focus of the Canadian media. I took great delight showing Kristin around and sharing my city with her. One evening, she wanted to see the Capilano suspension bridge, which spans the gorge of the Capilano River with a drop of some 400 feet beneath it. I told her that it was closed. She looked at me coyly and asked, "Does that make any difference?"

We drove over to North Vancouver and succeeded in scaling the fence and slipping past the guard. As we walked to the centre of the bridge, it swayed gently in the cool breeze.

Kristin took my hand. "It's a full moon, just like the night in Bergen when we made love in the snow."

My arms encircled the soft warmth of her waist and I kissed her. Her lips were hot, sweet, and eager. She laughed, then stepped back.

"Now!" she said, in a sultry voice. "Right here!"

I was dumbfounded. In the middle of the Capilano suspension bridge, in the winter, under a full moon, with a guard only a few hundred feet away?

She smiled. She was wearing a jacket over a pink ski suit. She took off the jacket and then slowly pulled the zipper down the front of her suit. As the material parted, her breasts and then her firm belly reflected the eerie blue-white of the moon. Underneath she was naked. She stepped out of her suit and kicked it behind her. Her hair shone with silver light.

"Jesus, Kristin, you planned this."

She stood before me like a Nordic Venus and opened her arms.

I shed my clothing in seconds and moved into her arms. As I lowered her gently to the deck of the bridge, I made a move to place the discarded clothing beneath her. She stopped me.

"No, I want to feel the coldness. I want it without clothing, just the two of us, suspended over the wildness of the river in the moonlight, surrounded by the shadows of the fir trees."

Her nails dug into my back, and for a moment I worried that we would break the boards and plunge to the rocky, frigid stream below. She pulled me toward the edge until her head hung over, her silver-blonde locks tumbling free into space. With my cheek against hers, I found myself looking down into the raging rapids, the moon glistening magically on ice-encrusted stones. She kissed my cheeks, my eyes, and bit the lobe of my ear.

"Are you afraid of falling?" she whispered.

"No," I answered. "Are you?"

She looked at me and smiled. "There is nothing that I'm afraid of."

She was definitely the woman I needed on the ice with me.

A few weeks later, our train pulled away from Vancouver. We were a handsome collection of young eco-hawks. Aside from Kristin, Vibeke, and Elizabeth, we had Alan Thornton, who had worked the home front the year before and then set up the Greenpeace office in London. He had brought with him a young woman named Susi Newborn, a most fitting name for a seal defender. The veterans were Jet Johnson and Walrus Oakenbough, and we also had a few of the old whale campaign veterans—Gary Zimmerman, Mike Bailey, and Michael Manolson. From the Portland office, we had Margaret Tilbury, a middle-aged woman married to a lawyer. She had become the guiding energy behind the formation of Greenpeace Oregon, which I had set up a few months before. Also coming from Oregon, against my advice, was Cindy Baker. Cindy was dying of cancer and the board of directors thought it would be good public relations to include her. Ingrid Lustig arrived from Seattle. From Detroit, we had recruited a veterinarian, Dr. Bruce Bunting. Patrick Ranahan, a cameraman, came from San Francisco.

The contingent of new Canadians included Corre Stiller of Winnipeg, Dan McDermott from Toronto, John Frizell from Vancouver, David Drainville from Thunder Bay, George Potter of Kitchener, Marvin Tanasychuk of Toronto, and Andrew Pines of Montreal. From Québec, we had a French Canadian teacher friend of Walrus's and mine, Laurent Trudel. To get us out of legal woes, we also took on a Vancouver lawyer named Peter Ballem. Old-time original Don't Make a Wave Committee founder Bob Cummings would do media liaison work. The remaining crew consisted of a film crew and some advance scouts. And, against my wishes but by order of the board of directors, Patrick Moore would come along to observe and to watchdog me, accompanied by his now wife, Eileen. The plan was to ride the train to Québec City, where we would take a scheduled airline to Sept-Îles, on the north shore of the St. Lawrence River. From there, I had arranged for a DC-3, an Otter, a Cessna 182, and five Jet Ranger helicopters to take us to Blanc Sablon, Québec, just a few miles from the Labrador border. I did not want to deal with Newfies again, and I reasoned that we could play off the traditional hostility between Québecers and

Newfoundlanders. If the Newfies hated us, I was betting that the Québecois would embrace us. I was right.

This campaign was completely different than any other we had mounted. We were the Greenpeace Airborne Assault Squad. I felt more like an air field marshal than a conservationist, but, at the same time, I felt truly alive and in my element. I have a bit of a military bent, tempered with a healthy aversion to slaughter. This campaign allowed me the pleasure of strategy, tactics, and field manoeuvres without the crippling karmic consequences of being responsible for inflicting death and injury.

The potential for danger was real. One of my aircraft could crash. A crew member could fall through the ice, or be shot by a sealer or a Mountie. Many of my crew were inexperienced, and any death or injury would be my fault.

In Sept-Îles, I allotted spaces on the helicopters and the two planes. Most of the crew and some accompanying reporters would travel by DC-3.

I took Kristin with me in Bernd Firnung's helicopter for what would be a ten-hour flight in the Jet Rangers. We stopped many times to refuel and, at each stop, we had to use axes and shovels to retrieve the fuel barrels from under the ice and snow. An hour from Blanc Sablon, we were forced down onto a lake because of an incoming blizzard. Fortunately, some people who lived in cabins on the shore allowed us to lay our sleeping bags out on their floors. They also treated us to a steaming, home-cooked meal.

Early in the morning, we set off and touched down on the snow-covered lawn of the Alexandre Dumas motel in Blanc Sablon. It was a bleak, white, one-storey, twelve-room structure sitting on the bleak, white, ice-locked shores of Belle Isle Strait. Inside, however, it was toasty warm, the rooms were comfortable, the bar was stocked, and the owner, Monsieur Dumas, was more than pleased with such unheard-of business at that time of the year.

Two of my helicopters were intended for Franz Weber, who was in St. Anthony along with Brian Davies and his crew. Bernd and I accompanied Weber's two choppers across the Belle Isle Strait. Upon arrival, I knew that we had been wise in selecting Blanc Sablon. St. Anthony was virtually an occupied zone. The motels were jammed with protesters from the International Fund for Animal Welfare, reporters from around the world, and hordes of government police, Fisheries officers, Newfoundland politicians, and anyone else in the mood to join the circus. The pro-sealing protesters had grounded Brian's helicopters. The two helicopters for Weber were surrounded immediately upon landing, but Franz could sort it out from there. I then sped over to Ma and Pa

Decker's boarding house to pay our respects to our hosts of last year. Ma Decker was delighted to see us; I swear she was the only friendly face in Newfoundland. Bernd and I had a quick cup of tea with her. Through the window, we could see the swilers coming down the road.

"Thanks for the tea, Ma," I said. "We've got to be going or we may not be going anywhere at all."

We got the helicopter off the ground just as the Newfies swarmed in, throwing snowballs and stones at us. I simply smiled and waved as we headed back across the Gulf to the relative peace of the northern shore.

Over the year, we had done our job. The Canadian seal hunt had become a whopper of a media event, and the overflow of journalists from Europe, Australia, the United States, and Canada descended on Blanc Sablon. Every room within 200 miles was sold out. Some reporters were even crashing on the floors of some of our rooms. Sleeping was difficult. Each reporter had a different deadline and portable typewriters were clicking away around the clock.

There was a twenty-four-hour lineup at the two public phones, with reporters bribing their way into the Dumas kitchen to use the family phone.

In the bar, French and country and western songs blared incessantly. Even when the official closing hour came at three a.m. and the last round was legally ordered, the drinking continued. Reporters simply took over the bar and rendered a fair accounting. Hell, this was the Arctic, or the next damn thing to it, and the journalists, most of whom were familiar with Robert Service and Dangerous Dan McGrew, felt this was their chance to live a myth. To add to the circus, the bar suddenly became the most popular hangout in the town (population 800) for the awestruck local youth. A situation like this had never happened in Blanc Sablon before. Local girls were being wined, dined, and romanced by flashy European reporters who spoke their language with the locals. Romance dripped like honey from these "gentlemen adventurers" of the press. The mademoiselles savoured every moment.

Across the strait, the Newfies were raking in more dough than they ever thought they could make in such a short time. Cab drivers were charging outrageous fares and motels had tripled their rates. It suddenly dawned on the St. Anthony Chamber of Commerce that the town could make more from catering to the anti-sealing protesters and the reporters than could be realized from the seal hunt itself. The pro-seal forces no longer wanted the anti-sealing forces to leave. Their protest took on a theatrical quality, as though they were simply playing the role of antagonists. Besides, they were thoroughly enjoying the worldwide attention.

When the journalists found out that the seals were more than 100 miles away on the ice floes off Newfoundland, they were not very happy. They had understood that you could see the seals being killed from the motel windows; some were even hoping that the local bars would come with a panoramic view of the slaughter. Since the protesters had the only helicopters, the journalists began some royal ass-kissing to secure seats on aircrafts. Some exchanged the promise of suitably slanted stories for rides in government helicopters. One West German television crew became so desperate for film that they borrowed a stuffed seal, poured ketchup around on the ice and hired a local man to pose as though getting ready to strike it. This was the only evidence of a staged kill I ever saw. It looked so damn phony they never used it.

My main problem was that I had three times as many crew members as the year before and this was three times more than what we needed. Not everyone could go to the ice, and I became really annoyed when Frizell and Bailey insisted on putting Cindy Baker on the first helicopter.

"Damn it, Friz," I said. "This is not the frigging Make a Wish Foundation. I need people out there who can block the sealers."

"Look, Paul, she wants to see the seals before she dies. How can you deny her that?"

Jet Johnson added, "We'll have to sacrifice another spot for someone to keep an eye on her. I agree with Paul. No way."

"It'll be great media," Bailey argued. "Terminal cancer patient taken by Greenpeace to see the seals."

"I don't think so, Mike," I replied. "It will make us look like we're putting her in harm's way."

"We could take her if she would agree to block a sealing ship," Jet piped in. "Now that's a story. Woman dying of cancer stops sealing ship in the ice and saves seals."

"She won't do that, and I won't see her risking her life for a headline," yelled Friz.

"Why not?" I said. "We're risking our bloody lives. If I had terminal cancer, I would not only risk my life out there, I'd probably sacrifice it out there for the seals. I'd much prefer that to a slow, miserable death in some damn hospital bed. Tell Cindy she can go if she agrees to block a ship like the rest of us."

But Cindy refused, and Jet and I were not very popular for leaving her behind. We also made an enemy out of Cindy Baker, who spent the last few months of her life in the Greenpeace office in San Francisco embroiled in bureaucratic politics. I vowed to myself that if I ever found myself in the same position as Cindy, I would make my death an instrument for change.

The next morning, I began moving many of my crew out to Belle Isle. At the same time, in St. Anthony, Franz Weber arrived at the airport in a Lear jet with a secret weapon—Brigitte Bardot.

She stepped out onto the runway, as glamorous as ever. Dumbstruck by her celebrity, awed by her beauty, and embarrassed by her politics, the sealers were thrown into complete confusion. Not so the Mounted Police. They slapped a $200 fine on her plane as a sort of parking ticket, for what they called a violation of a "customs technicality."

And so began the 1977 save the seals campaign. By the fourteenth of March, the day before the hunt was scheduled to begin, twenty-one of my crew were airlifted to Belle Isle, where they set up a tent town surrounded by a windbreak of blocks of snow and looking like a frontier outpost in Antarctica.

The morning of March 15 opened with the screams of thousands of seal pups as the hakapiks and clubs greeted the rising sun with a blood sacrifice. Our Cessna was already in the air to locate the fleet. The sky was clear and our prospects looked good.

To the cheers of the remaining crew, the first assault squad of choppers swooped down off the cliffs of Belle Isle and sped over the jigsaw landscape toward the bloodthirsty Goliaths of Doom. The battle was about to begin.

With the floe ice, nothing can be taken for granted. Last year's solid sheets of thick ice had been replaced by small, jagged pans of wet, slippery slop ice. To make matters worse, a huge swell had transformed the Front into a heaving mass of undulating hills.

We spotted the eleven mammoth sealing ships, crimson spokes of blood radiating for miles as their draglines hauled in large bundles of steaming sculps. For newcomers Fred Easton, Alan Thornton, Peter Ballem, Mike Bailey, and *Time* photographer Arthur Grace, the amount of blood was a shock. An even greater shock was the realization that because of the laws, we would have to land more than a half mile from the nearest seal, which would put us over a mile from the closest ship. The only way to reach the hunt would be by foot over that dizzying, heaving mess. Our pilots were nervous. Even with floats, the choppers could be ground up between the churning tons of slab ice.

Our first casualty was the *Time* photographer, a former Vietnam veteran. He had bragged that he could go anywhere, so we had agreed to take him. Now, white-faced, he shouted, "Ain't no way I'm crossing that shit!"

I was angry. "I bumped a crew member for you!"

"Only a lunatic would cross that!" He was visibly trembling.

Jet Johnson jumped out and onto the ice and smiled at the photographer. "Talk's cheap, buddy. It takes money to buy whiskey." With that, he approached the edge of the pan and jumped to the next.

I turned to the crew, "Everybody out! Let's go."

As daunting as it looked, we had no intention of surrendering to the elements. The seals needed us. We set off in a running charge across the shattered, writhing landscape, where a slip could mean drowning or being crushed to death between blocks of churning ice.

Jet twisted his ankle and had to limp back to the helicopters. Michael Bailey, confronted by a stretch of open water, decided the scene was just too crazy and turned back. Along the way, I spotted a seal pup just as it spilled off the edge of a floe. Within seconds, it would be crushed. I reached it just in time, grabbed hold of a flipper and hauled the little fellow back up into the middle of the pan. The first life saved, even if only from the sea.

Panting and sweating inside our gear, Peter Ballem and I reached the hunters first. Ahead of us, a sealer had just bashed a pup with his club and was preparing to bludgeon a second. I approached him, momentarily surprising him. He did not hesitate long. Turning to swing his club, he said, "This one's for you, ya bastard."

Grabbing the sealer by the wrist, I intercepted the club before it struck and twisted his wrist until he dropped the club. With a swift kick, I sent it into the open water of a lead.

The sealer was angry, but I was bigger and he backed off. I carried the body of the recently slain seal to the water.

"Rest in peace," I said. "You'll not be adorning some hag in Paris. Back to the sea with you." I dropped the body into the sea.

"I don't think you should do that, Paul," Ballem, the lawyer, warned. "It could be construed as theft under the Criminal Code."

"It ain't my goddamn code," I answered.

We came upon a second sealer, his hands and face plastered with black blood and gore, coldly sculping a pup's corpse with his knife. Behind him, his club lay on the ice. I quickly give it a swift kick, sending it into the water of an open lead.

The crew and I made our way to the nearest sealing ship, the *Martin Karlsen*. Her decks were lined with sealers, their faces smeared with blood and contorted with rage. A helicopter carrying RCMP officers swooped in and landed close by. They made no move to get out.

Beside the ship stood a pile of pelts bundled together and attached to a winch line. The winchman was getting ready to haul it in. Without any warning, I walked up to the winch line, pulled a pair of handcuffs out of my pocket, and slapped one cuff on my wrist and the other to the line.

The objective was to stop the operation of the ship by preventing their crew from bringing in the pelts. It was a classic act of non-violent resistance. The decision to use violence against me would be theirs, and I did not think that likely with the Mounties present. I was wrong.

The sealers stared at me speechlessly at first. Then they began to chant, "Haul da b'ye in," and "Give da b'ye a right cold swim."

Beside me, a grizzled old sealer inspected my cuffs and said, "We's goin' ta haul ya in."

"You're not going to risk killing me," I answered confidently.

He snorted and spat out a plug of tobacco, the brown spittle splattering obscenely against the virgin white of the floe. "Ye be right daft, b'ye," he muttered, "Risk! Dere ain't no risk to it, we's will kill ya fo sure."

When I felt the tug, my heart almost stopped. The wire grew taut, and two dozen shipboard sealers began cheering and urging the winchman on. I felt myself pulled off my feet and dragged across the ice. My wrist throbbed with pain. I sent a pleading look toward the Mounties. They made no move; they just sat in the chopper and looked on without expression. I could hear and feel my parka and pants ripped open on the sharp ice; one piece slashed a jagged cut in my calf. Suddenly, the solid ice gave way beneath me. Cold, freezing cold, unbelievably cold water penetrated my clothing. The shock was merciful; I could no longer feel the throbbing of my wrist nor the pain of my torn leg. I felt myself sinking into the thick slush. The winchman let me sink and then reeled me in again.

With a jerk, the line pulled me from the sea and into the air. I dangled like a water-sogged rag doll, suspended above the bloody pile of pelts. The winchman put on the brake, leaving me hanging. The sealers leaned over the rail only a few feet away, screaming, swearing, laughing, and spitting. I swung around. I could see Peter Ballem on the ice, screaming back at the sealers. In the helicopter, the Mounties continued to observe; one of them even smiled.

The winchman released the brake and I fell. As the slush closed over me, I could no longer feel the cold. I was strangely calm. I had put my life on the line for something I believed in. Hoka hey, at least there was no pain. I knew that I was about to drown and accepted it.

The winchman had other ideas. He hoisted me from the briny slop and into the air. I could no longer see and I felt myself fading.

I came to on the deck of the sealer. A couple of the swilers grabbed my hands and dragged me across the deck through the seal fat and blood while the others kicked and spat at me. Then I was shoved face forward into the blood-drenched pile of fresh seal sculps.

"Suffocate, ya bleedin' no-good do-gooder!"

"Shove a goddamn pelt down his goddamn t'roat!"

More laughing, and then I passed out again.

Peter Ballem had managed to muscle his way on board, and, by virtue of his status as a lawyer, he quickly intimidated the onboard Fisheries officer into intervening.

Peter picked me up and carried me into the ship, and the captain had me brought to his cabin. Peter undressed me and covered me with hot towels.

The door opened and the captain, a large burly Norwegian, entered.

"What the hell are you trying to pull?" he asked. "Trying to get yourself killed? For what? For a damn seal? It ain't worth it, boy."

I tried to explain, although it was hard to talk, that unless people like me take action, there might be no more harp seals. I began to cite statistics, but he was in no mood to listen.

"People like you are a fucking menace," he ranted. "There are more seals now than ever before. Assholes like you put an end to whaling, and now the ocean is overrun with whales, eating all our fish. I used to be a whaler. Now I'm just a sealer and it's your damn fault. To hell with the lot of you." With that, he turned on his heel and walked out.

Slowly, sensation began to return. My chest felt like a furnace, my body wracked with pain and fever. Peter stayed with me through the night, watching and caring for me.

The next morning, I felt weak but better. My leg was cut, but not enough to require stitches. I had severe bruises, a couple of cracked ribs, and the skin was scraped raw around my wrist. The captain gave me some warm clothing and I dressed and went out on deck. The sealers were spread across the ice, their hakapiks rising and falling. The seals were screaming. There was blood everywhere.

The Fisheries officer stood beside me. Frowning, he said, "You godless commie bastards ain't ever going to shut this hunt down."

I shrugged. "So much for objectivity."

As we stood there, a young sealer walked up close to the ship with a writhing pup slung over his shoulder. Tossing the seal onto the ice like a sack of potatoes, he looked up, smiled, gave me a finger and then kicked the pup full in the face. As I watched, he flipped the stunned creature over and slit it from crotch to throat. While the pup continued to thrash about, the swiler placed a foot on its head and tore the skin from its still live and quivering body.

"You fucking bastard!" I yelled.

Turning to the officer, I demanded that the man be arrested under the humane regulations of the Canadian Seal Protection Act.

With an evil smile, the officer said, "I didn't see anything."

"You sons of bitches never do."

"And we never will!" he vehemently hissed back.

Talking with Peter a few minutes later, he told me that he was not surprised. The Mounties claimed not to have seen anything the day before.

I found the political overtones to this issue shocking. The police and representatives of the government were supposed to be objective, their mandate apolitical. That was far from the case in this situation. I was beginning to grasp that our opposition to the seal hunt was in reality a declaration of war against the government of Canada.

The helicopter that picked us up stopped at Belle Isle, where I found that Walrus had organized the second assault team. They were ready and waiting to board.

Kristin, who would be going with Vibeke and Elizabeth, was dressed for the floes. The Norwegian unit would be joined by the Walrus unit, which included Walrus, Laurent Trudel, and Gary Zimmerman. I kissed Kristin briefly as she headed toward the chopper.

"You feel so cold," she said as her hand slid against my cheek. Her palm blazed with fire and her lips were red-hot.

And then they were off, the first all-women's brigade and the first Europeans to interfere with the hunt on the ice.

As I stepped out of the aircraft at Blanc Sablon, I could see cameras and reporters. Suddenly, a bundled-up figure came toward me, threw her arms about me and began to kiss my cheeks.

"You are a hero, Paul."

I could not recognize her, but she was tall and French and had gorgeous eyes and exquisite lips. She kissed me again and then Peter led me into the small regional hospital.

"Who the hell was that?" I asked.

Peter laughed, "That was Mademoiselle Bardot."

"No way!"

Back on the ice, Walrus led his squad across the heaving floes. The women, young, strong, and athletic, were undaunted. They placed themselves between the hunters and their clubs, turning back dozens of attempts to kill individual seals. The sealers were shocked to see women opposing them. The Norwegian sealers were even more shocked when Elizabeth hurled a stream of Norwegian profanity at one of them.

Meanwhile, Laurent Trudel and Gary Zimmerman strode into position before the oncoming bow of the *Theron*. Without even slowing down, the ship smashed through the ice, forcing both men to dive aside at the last second. Laurent ran behind the ship, caught up with it and once more placed himself before the bow. This time, the captain backed off. The sealers were recalled and the area abandoned. The hundreds of seals on that part of the ice were safe, at least for now.

I was released from the hospital with the warning that I was a sure bet for pneumonia and arrived back at the motel in time for Brigitte Bardot's press conference. She welcomed me to her table. The press conference is best described by the actress herself. In her journal, she wrote:

At 5 o'clock I try to pull myself together for a press conference, but my eyes have circles under them and my clothes are crumpled from two days in my bag. . . . Several hunters have slipped in among the journalists. Franz [Weber] tries to speak softly into the microphone, to explain why we are there, but no one listens. At this moment, a strength rises up in me and I stand up. I look them all in the face and order them to shut up. There are some rumblings. I am still looking them straight in the eye, when finally a silence falls over the room. I approach the subject directly. I am not here for fun and I am speaking for the entire world. . . . I am strong-willed and relentless. Insidious questions are hurled at me. They ask me if I will attend the massacre as if they were asking about a premiere at The Lido. I am sick and tired of all this. Since they don't understand anything, I use the strongest means. "In Europe," I say, "you are called Canadian assassins." . . .After a frosty silence, the room again becomes agitated. I am at the edge of my nerves. . .

During this terrible tumult, a voice comes out of the crowd. "Miss Brigitte, would you like to see a baby seal that was freshly killed this afternoon?" This is too much. There is the little body of a still warm baby seal in a plastic bag. I feel like vomiting as tears come to my eyes. I got up, made for my room, my eyes blurred by my tears. I cried for a long time.

The star of the film *And God Created Woman* was vilified in the Canadian media. Romeo LeBlanc remarked from Ottawa that maybe he would see Mlle Bardot, just so long as she took her clothing off. Prime Minister Pierre Trudeau joked that the only people who had a right to protest the seal hunt were nude vegetarians. He would speak to her also if she met all the qualifications.

In Europe, however, things were going differently. The French especially were infuriated with the remarks by Canadian politicians. Brigitte Bardot was the symbol of *la belle France*. *Mon dieu*, but these *Canadiens* were barbarians.

Never ones to miss an opportunity, we quickly talked Brigitte into flying to the ice with us. She told me that she could not bear to see the seals being killed. "You will not have to," I told her. "All that is needed is a picture of you, cheek to cheek with a live and lovely baby seal. Will you do it?"

"*Oui*, of course." She understood and smiled.

The next morning, we helped Brigitte into the helicopter beside our pilot Bernd Firnung. Brigitte was a legend to his generation. The look of complete adoration on his face was almost comical. I just hoped that he could keep his eyes and his mind focused.

Bernd was not the only gaga member of my expedition. Patrick Moore had been drooling over her since she arrived. He now demanded to fly to the ice with Brigitte. I said no.

But Pat retaliated by calling the Vancouver office, which sent me an order from the board of directors to fly Moore out to the ice with Bardot.

I could not defy the board without risking my own removal, so Moore climbed into the seat behind Bernd along with Brigitte's young lover and cameraman, Mirko Brozek. I got in the second helicopter with the photographers. Brigitte described the trip to Belle Isle in her journal:

> After flying across the jagged ice, we reached some high brown cliffs . . . .
> Suddenly, I see about a dozen tents and a flag through the thick fog!
> The Greenpeace people welcome us with open arms . . .
>
> They show me their kitchen—a Bunsen burner and an ice wall protecting it from the snow . . . . They offer me a cup of hot chocolate. Never before has hot chocolate tasted so good to me. I am cold. My feet are freezing and I go over to one of the tents . . . . The wind whistles around, and there is no heat source . . . . At night the temperature dips to –40 degrees.
>
> They make me drink rum from a bottle—their way of keeping warm. The tent breaks, the wind is always strong, but they tell me that today it is warm in comparison to other days. I admire them.

What courage and devotion . . .

The wind has died down a bit outside. The pilots decide that we can afford the risk of going back to Blanc Sablon. It would be unthinkable to go on the ice field. We leave the encampment in an atmosphere of warmth. They are fabulous people. Vive Greenpeace.

The next day, Brigitte returned and made it to the ice, where she posed with the seals. The photos of her appearing cheek to cheek with the wide-eyed, adorable seal pups was a natural; the photo graced the covers of *Paris Match* in France, of *Stern* and of *Bunte* in West Germany, and of tabloids in all the European countries.

In Canada, the sealers and the politicians, smarting from all the adverse publicity, retaliated by saying that Brigitte was lying, that she had never landed on the ice and that the seal pups were fake. At the same time, the helicopter pilot who took her to the floes was charged under the Seal Protection Act.

By March 20, the media circus was drawing to a close. It was clear that our camp would have to be evacuated—the forecast called for winds up to eighty miles an hour, enough to sweep our camp and its occupants across the flat mesa of the island and over the icy cliffs. The evacuation was a near disaster. One helicopter was forced down by a whiteout some five miles from Blanc Sablon. local snowmobilers rescued our crew members and the pilot.

On Belle Isle, the last helicopter rose up and rapidly disappeared into the swirling whiteness. Five of us remained in two tents.

While Jet primed the camp stove and Dan McDermott fiddled with the radio, I crawled into my sleeping bag to nurse the beginnings of pneumonia. How gallantly dumb I had been to insist that Kristin go back on the last helicopter. Her lovely Nordic body would have provided much-needed comfort in this cold.

"We could die in this thing," Dan mumbled.

"Sure could," Jet replied. "But don't worry, I have a deck of cards."

"What's that going to do?" said Dan.

"When I was in the air farce they always issued us a deck of cards with our arctic survival package. If you crashed on the tundra—just find a flat rock and play solitaire."

"How's that supposed to help save you?"

"Guaranteed. Before you know it, some guy is looking over your shoulder telling you to put the red queen on the black king."

I laughed. McDermott was not amused.

Finally the storm abated, and two days later, the helicopters returned to ferry us back to Blanc Sablon.

Brigitte had departed, and with her the reporters. Already we were yesterday's news. Fortunately, the fallout from our story had rained down on the media outlets of the entire world. Brigitte's participation became legend and helped us overcome the hurdle of establishment acceptability. Those who criticized her for her stand had already, like it or not, accepted her as an icon, a modern film goddess. Many of the men in Ottawa who resented her now had once pleasured themselves to her image. Though her defence of the seals belittled them, even humiliated them, they could not easily dismiss her. Romeo LeBlanc's snide remark—that he might listen to her if she strode into the House nude—spoke volumes about his confusion. Like most heterosexual French men of his age, he had probably once lusted for her. Now Brigitte not only opposed his will, she challenged his manhood with her moral superiority. Unfortunately, this would only make LeBlanc a more dangerous opponent.

On the other hand, Brigitte Bardot had accomplished more than a legion of scientists, humane activists, and conservationists ever had—she had converted the Europeans to the cause. She had even influenced the Americans. On March 22, 1977, the U.S. government approved a motion condemning the Canadian seal hunt as "a cruel practice." Newfoundland Premier Brian Peckford quickly attacked the U.S. resolution as a "miscarriage of justice," but, whine and moan as he might, he could not compete with Mlle Bardot for the affections of European and American politicians.

I myself would not soon forget her kiss. To have her call me a hero was, to say the least, morale boosting. In my eyes, she was more than just an actress and a sex symbol. By going to the ice and posing with the seals, she had demonstrated to the world her remarkable courage as well as her proud and passionate beliefs. To me, she was also a warrior.

Most importantly, Ottawa was fuming, raging mad. We had definitely gotten the attention of the big enchiladas in Parliament.

Bruised, battered, and tired, I boarded the Otter for the long flight back to Sept-Îles. It had been an incredibly successful campaign. Sure it had been a media circus, but it wasn't just some dog-and-pony show: we had succeeded in staging a three-ring extravaganza.

Even the Greenpeace bloody board of directors would have to acknowledge that reality.

7
Goodbye to the Big Mean Green Machine

(1977–1978)

We were the discards of the pack, the foreloopers of Unrest,
Reckless spirits of fierce revolt in the ferment of the West.
—Robert Service, "The Ballad of the Northern Lights"

I knew that my refusal to kowtow to Patrick Moore would get me into trouble with the newly expanding and increasingly more "respectable" board of directors. I was prepared for a confrontation and knew that it would come soon.

Upon returning to Vancouver, I delayed the showdown by jumping on a plane to Hawaii. Kristin came with me. I needed a rest and I needed time to recover from pneumonia. Kristin proved to be an excellent nurse and within weeks, thanks to her, the sun, the warm water, and plenty of tropical fruit, I was well on the way to recovery.

After that, there was little rest. I quickly became embroiled in the politics of Greenpeace Hawaii. Since the previous summer, George Korotva and Ross Thornwood had hammered together a loose framework of supporters—a collection of conservationists, feminists, vegetarians, and leftists. They resented Vancouver's centralized control and were determined to run the next whale campaign—their way.

George had been an original crew member on the 1975 whale campaign and had served as captain on the 1976 voyage of the *James Bay* to protect the whales. I had been his first mate. Ross Thornwood had also been a member of the 1975 voyage and it was he who invited George to Hawaii to organize Greenpeace Hawaii.

I liked their attitude. Korotva had located a "new" ship that was in reality a very old World War II sub chaser now named the *Ohana Kai*. It was a rusty, ancient tub and I was not enthusiastic about it. But the Hawaii crowd seemed determined to whip it into shape, and I was not about to dampen their zest. I signed on as first mate again under "Captain Cruel Korotva."

I left Hawaii for a week in April to speak at the University of California at Berkeley's Earth Day celebration. I was thrilled at the turnout of students concerned about the seal hunt in Canada. Since Prime Minister Trudeau was delivering the commencement address the same day, I quickly organized 500 protesters to march with placards against the prime minister.

Gary Zimmerman, as president of the newly formed Greenpeace USA, helped to organize the march. Jet Johnson, after founding Greenpeace in the United States, had appointed Zimmerman its first president. It was not a wise choice. Gary was much too conservative, too establishment, and too much of a technocrat for the position.

During the People's Park riots in Berkeley, in fact, Gary had been in the Army Reserve Training Corps (ROTC) and had been one of the people who had, as he put it, "helped restore order" on campus.

Now the former ROTC recruit was carrying a placard in a demonstration.

We marched across campus just in time to greet the prime minister as he came out of the arts museum. Canadian consular employees and U.S. Secret Service agents flanked him. Instead of avoiding us, Trudeau strode up to me.

"You're nothing but a goddamn hypocrite!" he yelled.

I was slightly stunned. I had never confronted a head of state before, and certainly not my own, and I had most certainly never had a head of state swear at me. I was a little taken aback by how short he was. You sort of expect prime ministers and presidents to be bigger.

He continued, "How can you oppose the seal hunt and stand there in leather shoes. You're a hypocrite and a troublemaker."

I smiled. "Mr. Prime Minister, you're right. I suppose they are leather—technically speaking."

The prime minister looked down at my bare feet, reddened slightly, turned, and quickly got into his limousine and sped off.

The laughter of the students followed him.

The next day, I returned to Hawaii. Kristin told me that she and her friends wanted to travel and that she had plans to join the barefoot doctors in Guatemala. For our last night together, I took her to Hanauma Bay. We made love in the water and on the beach, slept under a palm, and greeted the rising sun. She was so beautiful, this Viking princess, and I did not want to see her go.

Later that morning, I took her to the airport. I placed a thick lei of red carnations around her neck and gave her a locket with a seal pup painted on fossilized ivory.

She kissed me for the last time.

I never heard from her again. A few years later, her friend Vibeke told Jet that she had gone into the jungles of Guatemala and had simply disappeared. I felt her loss deeply.

As Kristin's plane flew eastward, I returned to the battlefield; only this time it was not sealers that I had to deal with, but my brothers and sisters in Greenpeace.

Vancouver began to telex instructions about the organization of the new expedition. Patrick Moore was acting like some sort of colonial overlord, dictating plans to the ship from his desk back at Greenpeace Central. I supported Hawaii in challenging the board. I was ordered back to Vancouver to face the music.

I knew that the end of my career with Greenpeace was at hand. Patrick Moore had just been elected president after Bob had resigned. I was certain he would make good on his threat a few months back to oust me.

I returned by way of St. Louis, Missouri, where I represented Greenpeace at a conference sponsored by Marlin Perkins and the Mutual of Omaha Insurance Company. Delivering an impassioned and radical speech, I told the audience that the key to change was media strategy, and that although many of them had never heard of us, Greenpeace would be a household name within the decade. I received a standing ovation. Mr. Perkins and his wife told me that it was high time that someone lit a fire—figuratively, of course—under the conservation movement.

Back in Vancouver, I refused to pre-lobby any of my fellow Greenpeace directors. If they wanted me out because of Moore, I was not about to beg. I was defiantly and stubbornly indignant that they were putting me on the carpet for defending Hawaii against Vancouver's meddling.

The meeting took place at the home of accountant Bill Gannon in the élite enclave of Point Grey. Bill was a newly appointed director and in charge of making the group financially responsible.

While I was in Hawaii, the board had also taken on conservative publisher Peter Speck and lawyer Marvin Storrow. In addition, we had Gary Zimmerman, John Frizell, Carlie Truman, and Michael Bailey. Of the old crowd, we had Hunter and his new bride, Bobbi, Patrick Moore and his wife, Eileen, Rod Marining, David "Walrus" Garrick, Paul Spong, Captain John Cormack, and me.

Moore began the meeting by attacking me.

"The board demands an explanation for the reason that the seal expedition exceeded its budget."

"You should know the reason, Pat. I had to take three times the number of people that I needed. In addition, you ran up bills that I did not approve."

Pat ignored me. "Going over budget would be excused if you had been successful, but we have determined that the campaign was a failure."

I was angry now. "Damn you, Pat, how can you say that? We've elevated this issue higher than it's ever been before."

"Thanks to Brigitte Bardot," he interrupted.

"That's one reason, yeah, but she was a part of this campaign you say is a failure. The only thing that failed was that I wasn't able to keep you from meddling in the expedition. If you had wanted to protect seals as much as you wanted to cozy up to Bardot, we might have accomplished even more."

Hunter interrupted. "Enough of that!"

Eileen gave me a disgusted look, as if to say her Pat would never entertain such a fantasy.

I continued. "This campaign brought the cause into the U.S. Senate, where it was condemned. We have made this issue more controversial, more international, more political, and more public than it has ever been. How the hell can you call that a failure?"

Raising his voice, Moore yelled, "You didn't end the seal hunt!"

"Yeah, and we didn't end the whale hunt either, but I don't hear that being called a failure."

Moore pressed harder. "We have an even more serious issue. This is a non-violent organization. We cannot allow any of our members to break the law or to commit violence. We have to pay off debts and finance future efforts, and we will not be able to do so if we lose our federal charitable status. We need that number more than we need you. For this reason, I am asking that you resign, because you have flagrantly broken the principle of refraining from violence."

"What the hell are you talking about? What violence? I didn't hurt anybody, nor did I damage any property."

Gary Zimmerman, the former ROTC cadet, interrupted. "On the contrary. You assaulted a sealer and you stole and destroyed his property. You took a seal club and threw it in the water."

"Well, holy shit." I was astounded. "The jerk was about to bash in the brains of a baby seal, for Christ's sake. I was not going to stand there and watch it."

Eileen interjected, "It is our duty to bear witness."

"You bear witness, Eileen. Me, I'm into saving lives."

Storrow, the lawyer, spoke up. "Paul, I don't think you understand what this organization is all about."

"I'm an original founding member of this group. I've been an unpaid volunteer for seven years, and now some high-paid, three-piece-suited barracuda who had never heard of us a year ago is saying that I don't know what this organization is about? Give me a break."

Finally, Bob spoke up. "Paul, I sympathize with your opinions, but it was an act of violence. We're not asking you to leave Greenpeace. We are simply asking you to apologize for your actions and resign from the board. You can rejoin the board again in a few months."

"I'll never be allowed to rejoin the board as long as he's president." I glared at Moore. "He told me that he would oust me and he meant it. I saved a seal's life and I'll never apologize for that. I hurt nobody, and a seal club isn't property, it's an obscenity. I have no intention of resigning."

"Well then," thundered Moore, "if you won't resign, we'll vote you off. I'm calling the vote. Who will second it?"

"I will," said Gary Zimmerman.

"All in favour!" said Moore.

I watched as Moore and the new members of the board raised their hands. Then came Hunter, Rod Marining, and all the rest except for Walrus and John Cormack, the only two to stand by me.

"The ayes have it," Moore announced gleefully.

Hunter said, "Paul, you're welcome to stay and work with us."

"Not me, Bob, I'll start up my own organization. The Second Foundation, Bob." I laughed and added, "To keep you bastards in line."

Bob laughed too, at the reference to Isaac Asimov's *Foundation Trilogy*.

"Get the hell out of here, Watson," Moore said, "we've got a board meeting to run."

"You should learn to be a little more polite, Pat."

I left.

Hunter had risen to shake my hand. Later I learned that, after I left, Hunter looked at the board members and said quietly, "Gentlemen and ladies, I think we just lost our balls."

With Greenpeace, I had foreseen an organization that would grow, prosper, and evolve into a bureaucracy. But that's what it needed to be to spread around the world.

Hunter, Marining, Garrick, and I had already discussed the need for a second foundation, as in Asimov's book, an organization whose purpose was to watch over and positively influence the foundation, aka Greenpeace. My ousting from the board was a perfect opportunity to set the wheels in motion. I also knew that, according to the Asimov plan, Greenpeace would seek to undermine us at every opportunity. I chose the name Earthforce because it contained the same number of letters as Greenpeace but conveyed a more aggressive image.

I was a biocentrist. I found it difficult to cooperate with human systems independent of the overall ecosystem. Let Greenpeace build empires—I found it difficult to work with large groups. My new organization would stay small, with a loose structure that was "individual-friendly." To discourage bureaucracy, I set in place the first rules of the constitution that would guide Earthforce.

Rule One: No Earthforcer would be paid. I wanted dedicated volunteers.

Rule Two: No compromise.

Rule Three: Aggressive non-violence, meaning that damage would be permitted to inanimate objects used to kill sentient creatures.

Rule Four: Leadership within the organization would be based solely on merit and ability.

Rule Five: No person could sit on the board of directors unless he or she had been a veteran of a field campaign.

I took these ideas back to Hawaii, where the Greenpeace voyage to save the whales had been a disaster. After dealing with me, Vancouver sent their own people to Hawaii to run things. The *Ohana Kai* cost a small fortune to prepare. Purchased for $75,000, Greenpeace invested more than $300,000 to make her shipshape. The ship, however, was a World War II vessel that had been riveted together in six weeks and was never meant to be permanently operational.

Greenpeace located the Russian whaling fleet in the summer of 1977. They did not do much more than play Zodiac games with them, but by now the Russians were accustomed to the temporary annoyance. The whales continued to die. The Greenpeace ship broke down repeatedly and finally limped into San Francisco, where it was tied up and never used again. Eventually it was sold at $8,000 for scrap.

Ross Thornwood and I approached the board of directors of Greenpeace Hawaii, supported by director Bobby Baker, with plans for what we called "Operation Asshole."

We offered Greenpeace a dollar for the *Ohana Kai* after the 1977 summer campaign. We would take the ship out, locate the Russian factory ship, the *Dalyni Vostok*, and then ram the old sub chaser at full speed up her stern slipway. The momentum would jam the *Ohana Kai* so far up her ass-end that the fleet would have to return to Vladivostok for a shipyard enema.

Nobody would get hurt. Ross and I would man the ship by ourselves for the final manoeuvre. At the last moment, we would jump over the side into an inflatable and be picked up by a seaplane.

It would have been a glorious, dramatic, high-profile, controversial, and effective campaign. It would also be a fitting end to a ship that had cost the Greenpeace membership so much in contributions.

The board of directors would not and could not justify damage to property. They turned us down. After one campaign, they were becoming as bureaucratic and cautious as their parent group in Vancouver. I was incredibly frustrated. I had the drive, the motivation, the guts, and the skills to carry the fight to the whalers, but I was denied the materials and the money. Meanwhile, Greenpeace directors were wining and dining themselves and flying to convention after convention. Instead of a conservation organization, it was rapidly becoming a conversation organization. I left the meeting with the board in disgust.

I spent the early part of 1978 investigating elephant poaching in East Africa. It was the first and only Earthforce project, and although the campaign was exciting and successful, it is not relevant to this book. Suffice to say that upon my return from Africa, I was ready to pursue the demons on my own continent with renewed energy.

While I was in Africa, Greenpeace had sent a third expedition to Newfoundland, this time under the leadership of none other than Patrick Moore. He brought with him another actress, Pamela Sue Martin, the star of *Nancy Drew*, and a couple of United States congressmen, James Jeffords (D-Vt) and Leo Ryan (D-CA).

By 1978, the sealers were getting organized. The Newfoundland government paid the public relations firm of Quantum Communications in Toronto a fee of $160,000 to promote the sealers' side of the story. Federal government grants went to other pro-hunt groups. A Newfoundland theatre group called the Mummers got money for a cross-country tour of their play, *They Club Seals, Don't They*. Other funds went to a non-government street theatre group called Codpeace to organize an anti-Greenpeace protest.

Codpeace, employing typical Newfoundland humour, had characters dressed up as the Codfather and Captain Jacques Codstew talk about how the harp seal was slaughtering the poor baby cod. And in St. John's, Mayor Dorothy Wyatt kissed dead codfish on the mouth for the national television news cameras.

The Newfoundlanders had discovered something we had realized years ago. The media are not interested in facts. The media want drama, humour, entertainment—in short, little mini-circuses to amuse the public every night. The mayor of St. John's kissing a fish would serve that purpose as easily as a story about Mother Teresa helping children. Content took a back seat to entertainment value.

So the fact that harp seals did not prey upon cod was not mentioned. The fact that the large corporate draggers were responsible for wiping out the cod was not mentioned. It was a better story to say that Greenpeace had spawned Codpeace and both were nothing more than clowns to amuse the masses.

However, for the first time, the sealers were getting their point of view across to the public. In a peculiar Freudian slip of the tongue, Premier Frank Moores said, "We'll get all the bloody exposure we want now." I chuckled when I heard this. That's exactly what we wanted—all the "bloody" exposure they could give us.

Quantum, the PR firm hired by the Newfoundland government, organized a road show to tour the U.S. and Europe. Tom Hughes of the Ontario Humane Society and Dr. Harry Rowsell of the Canadian Council on Animal Care agreed to defend the hunt, for a price, and signed on along with sealing captain Morrissey Johnson, sealer Jim Winters, and a bureaucrat from the Department of Fisheries. We were stunned that Hughes and Rowsell had sold out the seals. What kind of Humane Society would support the seal hunt?

The Newfoundland and Canadian governments handed us a great opportunity with their pro-seal hunt road show. Brian Davies, Cleveland Amory, and representatives of other groups simply followed the jaunt around and held their own press conferences, handing out film and photographs of the hunt. The media would run the gory footage or print the gruesome pictures, and after that the public was no longer interested in "rational" justifications for the slaughter.

Davies was delighted with the road show. He had been found guilty of violating the Seal Protection Act and had been barred from the hunt for the following season. But now the hunters were coming to him—in London, New York, and Paris.

The ban on Davies left the ice field open only to Greenpeace, and it was galling for both Walrus and me to watch Pat Moore announce that he would be leading the Greenpeace effort to the ice in 1978.

Moore sent a crew to Halifax to use Zodiacs to block the departure of the sealing ships *Martin Karlsen* and *Arctic Endeavour*. It was a great plan and I wish I had thought of it.

As the two sealing ships departed, the Greenpeace Zodiacs raced into position before the cameras. They stopped in the path of the *Martin Karlsen* and bravely defied the captain to run them down. But Captain Snarby intended to call their bluff. He did not stop; he did not even slow down. With the cameras running, the Zodiac crew were honour-bound to hold their position. Instead they panicked and quickly moved out of the way of the oncoming bow. The *Martin Karlsen* sped out of the harbour, leaving a frightened and embarrassed Greenpeace in their wake.

On that day, February 27, cowardice temporarily put an end to a tactic that had served us well in the past—putting one's life on the line to prove a point. Hunter and I had done it in front of the Soviet harpoons in the Pacific, and again in 1976 in front of a sealing ship. Our crews had done it too. The tactic worked for one reason only—we held our ground and our courage made the day.

Your opponents must believe that you are willing to die. Only then will they fear the consequences. But now the sealers figured we would flee, and the sealing captains became quite cocky as a result.

"If they want to go through a propeller, fine. I don't give a damn," said Captain Snarby.

The government declared a new policy that year. Only those individuals issued a federal permit would be legally allowed onto the ice. My application for a permit was refused. Pat Moore and Rex Weyler were both issued a permit for a mere two days.

There was only one confrontation, of sorts, with the law. Patrick Moore, with TV cameras carefully placed, walked up to a group of sealers and a Fisheries officer and squatted down over a seal as though he was humping the poor thing. As the cameras rolled, the officer informed Moore that he was under arrest for obstructing a sealer. Patrick dutifully stood up and submitted to the arrest. Behind him, the sealer walked over and clubbed the seal to death.

"The bastard," I said, when I later saw it on film. "He didn't fight for that seal. He turned his back and let that son of a bitch scumbucket kill it—that's unforgivable."

Pat the martyr was given a fine and Greenpeace paid it. He was immensely proud of his deed and went so far as to commission a soapstone Inuit carving of himself squatting over the seal pup. Everyone I knew who saw it always referred to it as the "Pat Moore fucking the seal statuette."

I was gratified, however, that repercussions from our 1977 campaign were still being felt. Leo Ryan came to observe the hunt because of the attention we had brought to the issue the year before.

In one of the most bizarre confrontations on the ice, the U.S. congressmen, Jeffords and Ryan, were verbally abused by a sealer carrying a bloody club. He turned out to be John Lundrigan, the Newfoundland Minister of Rural Affairs. This man, who obviously did not need to kill seals for a living, chastised the congressmen and told them to mind their own business. Lundrigan was living proof that some men kill seals for the thrill of killing them.

Later, Ryan wrote a letter to Prime Minister Trudeau from Washington that said, in part: "The Canadian government was determined, in one way or another, to keep us from seeing the harp seal slaughter. . . . I have never been treated more rudely or with more consistent contempt by every official with whom I came in contact, from Ottawa to the local level."

There were some successes, though, in 1978. France announced a total ban on sealskins. It was the first European nation to do so, and that gave us heart that the rest of Europe would follow.

The French decision prompted Newfoundland member of Parliament John Crosbie to call for the banning of French wine because of the "brutalization of the grapes."

As ludicrous as this sounded, in December 1978, the Canadian government actually ended its 1933 wine-importing agreement with France that prevented Canadian wineries from using the trademark name of champagne.

The message to the world was—mess with Canadian sealers and we'll retaliate.

I knew that I would be at the 1979 seal hunt even if I had to walk across the ice floes to get there.

I flew back to Vancouver. Starlet Lum met me at the airport with some hopeful news. Starlet had moved back to Vancouver and had moved in with me. Cleveland Amory wanted me to meet with him in Los Angeles three days later.

I was still broke from my African trip, so Starlet lent me the fare. I couldn't afford a hotel room, so I took a bus to Hollywood, walked the streets and drank coffee at all-night restaurants until the morning, then walked to the Beverly Hills Hotel to meet with Amory.

Cleveland, the founder and president of the Fund for Animals, had helped us with a large contribution when I was with Greenpeace. I had written to him and offered to take the Fund for Animals banner onto the ice off eastern Canada. He was interested.

"What can you do?" he asked.

"We have to continue to hold the attention of the international public to keep the pressure on Canada. My plan is to go to the ice off Newfoundland and spray indelible organic dye on the seal pelts. This destroys their economic value but it won't harm the seals."

Cleveland didn't beat around the bush. He asked, "How do you get there?"

"Either of two ways," I said. "The least expensive way, for about $25,000, is to fly a crew in and drop them on the ice by parachute. It would be extremely dangerous, but we can do it."

Cleveland looked at me thoughtfully.

"Is there anything that's less dangerous?" he said.

"Yes. The other way to do it—but it's more expensive—is to take a ship in.'

"Do you know where to get a ship?"

"Well, I have an idea. I think it would be less expensive to buy one than to charter one."

"Okay," he said. "Go find us a ship."

On the advice of a friend in Greece, I ended up on the east coast of England, where a London shipbroker found me a veritable grab bag of retired fishing boats. Veterans of the Icelandic "cod wars," they were perfectly seaworthy, just economically redundant.

Of all the ships I looked at, the *Westella* was the most appealing, for practical reasons, such as her solid construction and her record at sea, and for reasons having nothing to do with practicality: She had been launched on March 15, 1960. The Ides of March was the traditional starting date of the Newfoundland seal hunt. Launched for the purpose of plundering the creatures of the seas, the *Westella* would—nineteen years to the day later—sail out to protect those same creatures. Poetic.

Starlet's birthday was also March 15. That was a good sign also. The *Westella* was 206 feet long and displaced 779 tons—a Yorkshire deep-water side-trawler designed for a life of hard work in the frigid and stormy northern seas. She had served her former masters well. Three times she had won the Silver Cod Trophy, a highly coveted prize. Speed, capacity, economy, and efficiency— these were some of the qualities the British looked for in giving the award, and these were the qualities that would serve us best as well.

The *Westella* had spent nearly two decades fishing in the White Sea, the Barents Sea, the North Sea, and the North Atlantic waters around Iceland. She had had a number of skirmishes, once with a Soviet destroyer in the White Sea and, on more than a few occasions, with the Icelandic Coast Guard. She was painted a ghastly yellow, though the years had not been kind to the paint. With rust showing through the bilious ochre, the *Westella*, when I first saw her, looked like a scabrous, dying thing. But rust can be removed. Underneath, after sandblasting, was clean, unpitted metal.

I did a thorough inspection, then had her hauled out of the water and examined from stem to stern. That cost $4,000, but it was worth it. I wanted to make sure that she was seaworthy and tough enough to do the job. And she was. She would have cost more than eight million dollars to build. I purchased her for $120,000. Cleveland Amory, true to his promise, managed to scrape together the money and send it to me. We completed the sale on December 5, 1978. Because she was a British ship, she could not be owned by the U.S.-based Fund for Animals. As a Canadian and thus a subject of Her Majesty, I became the registered owner.

Soon after, we renamed her the *Sea Shepherd*. The name was my idea, based on the vision quest that had directed me toward the ice seals back in 1975. The name was also inspired by the young seaman, Mark Sheppard, who had dared to challenge the authority of Captain Abraham Kean, the most notorious sealer in history.

Starlet had arrived in early December, bringing me a birthday present of a samurai sword. She was invaluable. Organizing the ship for her delivery was a time-consuming and stressful task.

Other volunteers—Joe Goodwin, Mark Sterk, and Erin McMullin—arrived. They manned the needle guns and repainted the ship deep blue and white, and lettered the name SEA SHEPHERD on the bow and stern.

We still needed money for fuel and other expenses. Dr. Bill Jordan, the wildlife director for the prestigious British Royal Society for the Prevention of Cruelty to Animals (RSPCA), came through with a grant of $48,000. With that money, I paid for a marine survey of the ship, fuel, supplies, and the hiring of a delivery crew to help me take the ship to Boston, where we intended to prepare secretly for our run through the ice. We also bought a second-hand Loran C, the precursor to GPS systems for marine navigation—for us, a prize piece of equipment.

Because I was unfamiliar with the Atlantic and had no experience of an Atlantic winter crossing, I hired a certificated master named Leslie Fewster, along with a mate, three engineers, a deckhand, and a radio operator. These six, added to the five volunteers, including Starlet and me, brought the crew to twelve. Just before leaving, we added a thirteenth crew member when Dr. Jordan asked if we could take his son Richard along.

I was not going to apply to Canada for a permit to go to the ice. With a British ship, we could enter from international waters and under international law we could land on the ice outside of the twelve-mile limit without being subject to the laws of Canada. With a ship, we would not be at the mercy of the bureaucrats or the government, and we could stay out with the seals day and night.

I was determined that in 1979 the protest would be more aggressive and more effective than ever. Finally, I had some real muscle—solid steel backed up by a mammoth 1,500-horsepower diesel engine.

As the ship, my first command, departed the Humber River, I stood on the bow, took a deep breath of salty air and smiled. I watched the swell from the North Sea lift her bow and I felt very happy. I had a ship. There will be no stopping us now, I thought.

It would be good to get back to the ice and the seals, and back into the fight.

The Home of the Bean and the Cod

(1979)

Here's to the City of Boston,
The home of the bean and the Cod,
Where the Cabots talk only to the Lodges,
And the Lodges talk only to God.

—Anonymous

e left Hull's Royal Albert dock on a cold and blustery January 3, 1979. To save the cost of pilots' fees, I decided not to go around the south of England by way of the English Channel. Instead, we risked foul weather and went north around Scotland. As chance would have it, a terrible storm struck the southern Channel and sank four fishing boats. On the fourth, we passed within sight of Thurso on the northern Scottish coast, and on the fifth, we headed down south by southwest past the green Irish coastline.

A storm hit Scottish waters a day after we passed, and another blew up off the coast of Ireland the day following our passage there. We felt lucky and vaguely guilty, as if we were a Typhoid Mary of the sea.

The *Sea Shepherd* handled smoothly and proved very economical, burning just over three tons per day. Her total fuel capacity was 200 tons. We could remain at sea for over two months if need be.

Leaving the fog-haunted coast of Ireland in our wake, we sailed westward to Boston. The seas were smooth and the air balmy for the entire crossing. I was a

Pacific sailor; I had never crossed the Atlantic before. I told Captain Leslie Fewster that I thought the tales of the savage Atlantic were exaggerated.

"I don't understand it," he told me. "I have never seen it like this at this time of year, and I've been on the Atlantic for nearly forty years."

South of Newfoundland, we took full advantage of the warm currents of the Gulf of Mexico and worked on deck in T-shirts.

The waters south of Newfoundland had given us an affirmation. For more than an hour, we ran along with six majestic and gargantuan blue whales—all of them longer than seventy feet, which seemed immense enough, although I knew blue whales averaged ninety feet fully grown.

As I stood my daily watch schedule on the bridge, I thought a lot about what we should do this year. First, the ship would be something new, which would attract the fickle media that required novelty to keep their interest. Second, I would be bringing two large, relatively established organizations to the seal hunt—the Fund for Animals and the RSPCA. Third, I intended to use the dye tactic that Greenpeace had taken away from us in 1976. Fourth, we would not stoop to going onto the ice with a permit. The Canadian government had no right to prevent us from seeing and recording the horror of the hunt. Fifth, I knew that this was the year that the government would begin making some serious arrests. I did not intend Cleveland Amory or any representative of the RSPCA to be arrested, so I would have to keep the Canadian government's ire focused on me and the crew members I could count on to take that stand without complaint. This year, we would definitely and defiantly change the course of the anti-sealing protests.

The day before we reached Boston, winter finally hit us.

Six inches of ice armoured every rigging line and mast, and we had to patrol the decks constantly with ice hammers to shatter it before it built up too heavily. Despite this, we were in excellent spirits as we approached the New England shores.

We had hoped to keep our arrival in Boston a secret. But some of our friends on shore had other ideas, and a story appeared in the *Boston Globe* detailing our intention to get out to the sealers by the middle of March. Understandably, the Canadian government was upset. It had passed laws to prevent access by helicopter but was unprepared to deal with a foreign-registered ship in waters that technically did not fall under its legal jurisdiction.

Actually, the media coverage probably made very little difference to our security. We had reason to believe that the Canadian government had had us under surveillance from the moment we acquired the ship.

We sailed into Boston Harbour on January 15, 1979, and, even though the crossing had been idyllic, we were all pretty happy to see it end. Five of the seven rough-hewn Yorkshiremen who were making the trip for pay were at continued odds with us, the six younger volunteers. We were all vegetarians, for one thing; the Yorkshiremen liked their meat.

We also argued over the morality of killing whales and seals versus the necessity of human survival in what some still considered to be a fundamentally hostile world. Captain Leslie Fewster and deckhand Stan Johnson sided with the conservation argument that humans were overtaxing the oceans. On the other hand, Jeff Twidle and chief engineer Leslie Smith were appalled that an honest fishing trawler out of a proud fishing port like Hull would be used to thwart those who made a living off the sea. They regarded Fewster and Johnson as traitors.

Leslie Fewster just smiled at the abuse from his countrymen. "You know," he said, "the sea has been awfully good to us, she has. I think it's only fair that we give back a little when we can."

As soon as we entered Boston Harbour and dropped anchor, we were swamped by bureaucratic harassment, derisive treatment by the media, and sabotage.

Before being allowed to moor in South Boston, we had to undergo a full search by the U.S. Coast Guard. It seemed like undue attention. Apparently they had been tipped off that we might have drugs on board. I knew that tip had originated in Ottawa. Despite ripping up half the cabins, they left without finding a thing and without even a word of apology. Such is the arrogance of bureaucracies!

Cleveland Amory was there to greet us, pleased as punch to inspect the newly acquired Fund for Animals' navy. He turned over the keys to his converted white checker cab to me. I took the crew to Boston's Chinatown for a most welcome Chinese meal. Soon after returning to the ship, Joe Goodwin came to my cabin to report he had just seen Terry Grayson, the radio operator, acting suspiciously. Joe had surprised him on the aftdeck just as Grayson was about to drop a gleaming piece of metal over the side. Goodwin stopped him and asked what it was. Grayson replied that it was a piece of junk. Goodwin, correctly thinking that it was a well-oiled, well-machined piece of junk, took it from him and brought it to my attention.

We took the piece to the chief engineer.

"Where did you find this?" he asked, very much surprised.

"Grayson was about to toss it over the side," said Goodwin.

The engineer's eyes rolled and he looked alarmed.

"What the hell is it?" I demanded.

In answer, Leslie Smith led me below to the steerage compartment. Approaching the hydraulic steering gear, he gently placed the metal piece on to two bolts, like a perfectly fitting jigsaw puzzle piece. It was the connecting rod to the automatic steering gear.

"What would happen," I asked quietly, "if we got under way without this?"

Leslie hesitated, torn between his loyalty to his job and his loyalty to his fellow Yorkshireman, Grayson.

"It would, well, it would, er, you would not have, eh, any steering."

"You're kidding."

I could see from his expression that he was not.

I was seething. That bastard Grayson had attempted to sabotage my ship.

I went up top to confront him. He and Jeff Twidle had locked themselves on the bridge. I banged on the door. The men did not answer.

I began to think about aspects of Grayson's behaviour that had seemed peculiar. None of the other men knew him except Twidle. He had a curious Royal Navy air about him and admitted that he had served in the Navy as a radio operator. He also admitted during the voyage that he was a deep-sea diver and a demolition expert. He shook me up at one point by suddenly saying, "You know, I could finish off one of those sealing ships by placing cordite explosives around the shaft. I could blow her props off. I'll do it for you for $10,000."

I mumbled that we did not condone explosives and quickly changed the subject.

He had also spent quite some time sending and receiving messages in Morse code, but when I asked whom he was talking to, he replied, "Oh, nobody in particular—just getting back into practice." And in Boston, when he met Cleveland Amory, he said, "You look older than your pictures." How had a Yorkshire fisherman come to see pictures of Cleveland Amory?

I left the ship and found a pay phone. I called the Boston Police, who referred me to the Massachusetts State Police, who in turn referred me to the U.S. Coast Guard, who told me to call the Boston Police—a perfect circle of bureaucratic incompetence.

"Look," I said, "one of you should get over here instead of giving me the runaround."

They all came. Police car after police car arrived to disgorge their occupants, each from a different arm of the law. Sixty policeman, some with guns drawn, swarmed on board. "Where's the mutiny?" they shouted. "Who's been shot?"

At the same time, a television crew materialized—so much for a low profile. I stationed a volunteer at the gangplank to keep reporters off the ship.

The cops interrogated the entire crew. Twidle and Grayson cowered on the bridge until the police ordered them to open up. Under interrogation, Grayson twitched constantly and sweated profusely.

"Do you want him locked up?" a detective asked.

"No," I said. "I just want him off the ship."

The Coast Guard inspected the electronics and the machinery, and we had both Twidle and Grayson sign an affidavit saying that nothing else had been tampered with.

They were then escorted to the airport and placed on board a flight to London.

As we put together a crew for the expedition into the ice fields of the Gulf of St. Lawrence, I was concerned that no last-minute trap be sprung to delay our projected departure.

"We're going to leave here on the first of March," I told the U.S. Coast Guard. "I don't want you coming down here on the last day of February to say I need a safety inspection or a fire inspection. Please tell me now, and let's get it over with."

"Oh, no," the Coast Guard replied. "We're satisfied that everything's in order."

That was in January. We went ahead frantically to ready our scheduled departure. On February 28, though, the Coast Guard arrived to hassle us.

Our lawyer was there to meet them.

"What the hell are you guys doing?" Tom Muzyka demanded.

"The Canadian Department of Transport requested that we inspect you," came the frank reply. The ship was inspected for this, and inspected for that, and it was obvious that we were getting the bureaucratic runaround.

Next came the British consul in Boston, with a flurry of inquiries and forms to be filled. Then we were hit by U.S. Customs, who told us they were acting on a request by Canadian Immigration to check us out. Finally, on March 3, two days after our planned departure, the man from Lloyd's arrived to make a survey. He delayed us one more day and cost us $3,000 to strengthen some deck supports. When he tried to hassle us further, we threatened to sue him for harassment. He backed off.

And so, finally, the *Sea Shepherd* was allowed to leave the port of Boston, carrying forty tons of rock ballast and eighteen tons of concrete we'd had poured into her forepeak water ballast hold. We wanted some authority down there when we pushed up against the heavy ice floes in the Gulf of St. Lawrence.

We also carried thirty-two crew members, including six from the crew that had made the transatlantic crossing; my friend Keith Krueger from Honolulu; and my father, Tony, who had volunteered to be the ship's cook. My father had done some soul-searching since I had left home and had renounced hunting. He was now surprisingly very supportive of my conservation work. Frank Milner, an RSPCA inspector from England, and our benefactor himself, Cleveland Amory, were also among us. Matt Herron came on board as first mate. He and I had run a Zodiac inflatable up the slipway of a Soviet whaling factory ship back in 1976.

We also had a dozen news people aboard. (Technically, they were crew members, because the British consul had ordered as a condition of our maintaining our British licence that we carry "no passengers.") The positive press contingent included Sid Moody of the Associated Press and Sunny Lewis of Canada's CHUM radio network. They pitched right in, Sid with his knowledge of navigation and Sunny with her Canadian radio operator's ticket. We had a negative press contingent too: a pessimistic Tom Bevier of the *Detroit Free Press*, a whining Gene Puskar from Associated Press, and a very arrogant Tom Schell of the American Broadcasting Company's radio network. Fortunately, we were to see little of Schell, who spent the entire voyage to the ice in his bunk, seasick.

A small crowd of well-wishers waved us away from the dock, and the Boston Harbour chaplain, Wally Cederleaf, came down to give us his blessing. Reverend Cederleaf was a candle in the dark for us, because most men of the cloth were no friends to *kotik*, the Lamb of God, and the Catholic press was condemning me anew.

The Boston skyline dipped below the western horizon as our ship headed seaward and across the Gulf of Maine. Out on the high seas, we were under constant aerial surveillance by Canadian Coast Guard planes and helicopters, but I was happy. Once again, I was leading a campaign to oppose the baby-killers.

Now that the seals had a navy, the sealers were in for a fight.

9
Caught
Red-Handed

(1979)

I am not what you call a civilized man! I have done with
society entirely, for reasons which I alone have the right of
appreciating. I do not therefore obey its laws, and
I desire you never to alllude to them before me again!

—Captain Nemo

I caught the blow from the cop's club with the edge of my staff and felt pain jolt up my arms. As another mounted police officer jabbed a pole toward my ribs, I deflected his attack too, just in time to spin around and face a third officer coming at me from behind. I swung at him so hard that his pole splintered and broke.

They had me, it was simply a matter of time. I was precariously balanced on a small pan of slop ice, floating insecurely in the middle of an open lead of frigid water. The lead was just ten feet wide. On both sides, along the more solid pack ice, stood a dozen or more Mounties and Fisheries cops. Armed with seal clubs and seven-foot wooden poles, not to mention sidearms, the officers yelled and screamed at me.

"Big goddamn fucking hero!" shouted the head Fisheries officer, and the man responsible for policing the Gulf of St. Lawrence, a large, ugly guy named Stan Dudka. "Standing out there in the middle of the lead! You want a medal, hero?"

"You going to give me one, Dudka?"

"We're going to send you away for the rest of your worthless fucking life!" Dudka lunged at me with his pole, but I brought mine down hard, dislodging the weapon from his hands. It clattered onto the ice and rolled into the inky water

"You make me sick, Dudka, you and these Dudley Do-Right types. You should be ashamed of yourself, defending this perversion."

"You're the criminal here, asshole," he snarled back. "We're the law."

"If you're the law, then I ain't interested in the law. Take your baby-killing laws and shove 'em up your ass, Dudka."

Out of the corner of my eye, I saw a flash of something dark. Instinctively, I dodged. A Fishery fuzz went hurtling by me, only to plunge headfirst into the black water. A flying tackle on loose ice? Rash move!

The fish cop surfaced, gasping with the shock of the freezing water. Two Mounties hauled him onto the ice. At the same time, another Mountie lunged across the lead, tackling me, and we both toppled into the water. The icy brine bit into my neck, numbed my face and hit me with a searing ache behind the eyes. The shock of the cold sea forced him to let go of me. As his buddies hauled him out, I desperately clambered back onto the small floe.

They were all jabbing at me now with their poles. I felt pain in my back, the side of my head, my ribs. Dudka was the closest and I could see him beginning to swing his stick. Holding my pole with both hands, I blocked him. His shaft splintered against mine. Quickly, I pushed away and poled my floe out of their reach.

"You can't escape from us!" said a Mountie. "Give up, you're under arrest."

"It isn't in my nature to give up!" I yelled back.

I was wet, cold, and sore. I knew that they would take me soon. I also knew that they would hurt me when they did. At the same time, I revelled in the excitement of combatting these ogres. My rage against the seal hunt was becoming a rage against Canada, and the Mounties were the ultimate Canadian symbol.

In the water around my little surfboard-sized island, dozens of mother seals popped their heads quizzically out of the sea, their coal-black eyes frightened yet curious. On the ice, a few seal pups cried and scuttled about, seeking their mothers. Around them, bloody corpses glared red on the blue-white ice, their eyes bulging and sightless. My own crew, all seven of them, had already been apprehended and were sitting on the ice, hands cuffed behind their backs. To the north, half a mile away, loomed the Canadian Coast Guard icebreaker, the *Wolfe*. Beyond the icebreaker, three dark sealing ships moved freely among the seals, methodically dispatching their agents of death.

I felt overwhelmingly frustrated. Compared to the government, we had so little power. It had been an ordeal to simply reach the ice, and for what? To fall into the clutches of the Mounties. On the other hand, we had accomplished our mission and humiliated those thugs. We had "painted" the seals.

Only two days earlier, as the *Sea Shepherd*'s hull first split the ice of the Cabot Strait, the Minister of Fisheries had vowed to the press that we would never make it to the hunt. If by some chance we did, though, he promised the sealers that not a single seal would be dyed. The police, he said, would guarantee it.

We had arrived the night before. We had barged, rammed, heaved, and forced our way through 150 miles of ice to reach the hunt. We knew that the authorities were expecting us in the morning. We would not be able to go ten feet with our spray canisters before they would pounce.

I had stood on the bow with Cleveland Amory, the chill wind knifing through our parkas. Cleveland was feeling triumphant. That day, he had stepped on the ice and picked up a baby seal. Cradled gently in his big arms, the seal had snuggled in and affectionately nosed his cheek. The press took his photograph and within twenty-four hours the photo would be wired worldwide. The Fund for Animals' leader was on the ice.

Cleveland looked across the blackness to the lights of the icebreaker and her pack of sealing vessels.

"I don't know, Paul. We got here, but I'm afraid we won't be able to paint the seals."

"Cleveland, we can reach hundreds of seals if we leave now. They won't expect us out there tonight. By morning, the minister's word will be mud."

"It's too dark, too dangerous. I can't allow you to take chances like that."

"Damn it," I said, "taking chances is what I do. If we stick together, we can cross the ice. We'll carry long poles to feel our way across."

"Okay, but if it gets too treacherous, I want you to turn back."

Within fifteen minutes, eight of us were suited up. With spray tanks strapped on our backs, we went over the side of the ship by rope ladder. Only a few hundred feet in front of the bow, I encountered the first seal. The pup lay calmly, looking up at me with that wide-eyed innocence I had grown used to but which never failed to melt my heart.

I knelt down and laid a hand on its back. The pup cried weakly, its eyes as trusting as only the eyes of the newborn can be. Picking it up, I took it back to the *Sea Shepherd* to meet the press. In the glare of the ship's spotlight, Joe

Goodwin sprayed a little red dye on its back and rubbed it in. It would do no physical harm. It was a completely organic, vegetable-based dye, bright blood-red and indelible. Within a week, the dyed hairs would be shed and replaced by a darker coat.

I had chosen red dye so that our action would not be confused with the aborted attempt by Greenpeace to dye the seals green. Red also had the advantage of looking like blood. We hoped that, from a distance at least, the pups might appear to the sealers to be already dead and skinned.

"There!" I said to Cleveland before the cameras. "Romeo LeBlanc failed to stop us. We have just done what he vowed we would not do."

We returned the pup to the ice, and then I led my ice crew out into the darkness. Within the first hour, we had reached, sprayed, and commercially neutralized over 150 seal pups.

We hopped and leaped from ice floe to ice floe, balancing ourselves with our pike poles. We pushed on without respite, spraying as we went. The seals were difficult to spot—white on white in the darkness, shadows against shadows.

As we got closer to the sealing ships, we began to see evidence of the sealers' grisly craft. The live pups scattered among the dead bodies were noticeably frightened. They cringed as we approached; some tried to crawl away, searching desperately for shelter. The injustice of it moved me deeply: the miracle of birth desecrated by such a barbaric and premature death, and for what? A bloody fur coat.

We wanted to spray as many seals as we could. It was methodical work, a slow-motion race against the coming of the dawn. Keith Krueger wrote later in his journal that his eyes teared whenever he let his guard down enough to contemplate the stupidity and cruelty of the hunt. But he had one consolation: By the time the sun surfaced on the icy horizon, we had branded well over 1,000 seals with the mark of the *Sea Shepherd*. Commercially worthless, they were our seals now, ours to return to the teats of their mothers and to the sea.

As the sun began to lighten the sky, Keith wrote that he was close to exhaustion. He was a big man, built like a professional wrestler, but hours of jumping from floe to floe had worn us all down.

But he held in there. The whole crew did. And then the sun was up. From the sky came the increasing cacophony of a full-scale helicopter assault—six of them approaching from out of nowhere. They skimmed madly over the ice toward us, then set down, disgorging officers of the Fisheries Ministry, the Québec Provincial Police (QPP), and the Royal Canadian Mounted Police (RCMP).

Stanley Dudka was in charge. He tore over the ice, his face red and contorted as he hurtled a stream of obscenities at us.

"Come on!" I hollered to Mark Sterk, who was close by. "In here!"

We dove into a natural ice cave formed by the shifting, rafting ice. Out of sight, we could hear the commotion as our colleagues were arrested and marched away.

It took the officials about ten minutes to find us. Flushed from our hiding place, Mark and I ran in opposite directions as the police moved in. Dudka chose to chase me. He almost had me when I jumped from the lead to that small, floating pan of ice. I fought to get my balance, precariously twisting and tilting to keep my equilibrium with my seven-foot-long pole. Standing at the edge of the lead, Dudka pointed to my stick and yelled at a Mountie:

"Shoot that man! He's armed!"

The officer looked at Dudka incredulously and did nothing.

One of the helicopters came over and hovered a few feet above me, the icy blast from its rotor blade threatening to knock me from the floe. The pilot lowered the chopper, intending to push me off my chunk of ice with his machine. Crouching, I pulled my staff back like a javelin and made a motion to drive it between the rotor blades. The pilot's eyes widened and the chopper shot upward and away.

Then came the pole-fencing scuffle with Dudka and his boys, which had left me marooned on my miniature iceberg and surrounded by over a dozen officers. The two soaking-wet Mounties were now making their way to the helicopter. Rivulets of frigid water were still running from my hair down my neck and back. I shivered.

All my crew were in cuffs except for Matt Herron. I took my camera out from inside my suit and made to throw it to him, but Dudka positioned himself to bat the camera down with his stick. I held on to the camera.

Cops were manhandling Mark Sterk as they led him to a helicopter. I took a picture of him.

"You'll never see that photograph," Dudka snarled.

I had kept the police at bay for twenty minutes or so when they finally figured out how to get me. Stretching a rope across the lead and holding it taut, they used it to sweep me off the pan, through the water, and onto the solid ice. I fought, but without a knife, I couldn't get free of the rope.

As the police hauled me up on to the ice, Dudka came over and kicked me hard in the groin. Grinding his boot into my hand, he growled, "Resist me, you fucking son of a bitch, and I'll kill you!"

He was still kicking me as the Mounties struggled to handcuff me. They tied my feet together and tied my manacled hands to my ankles. Then, tossing me like a sodden sack of oysters into a helicopter, they took me to the *Wolfe*. There they dragged me by the handcuffs into a wardroom and removed the ropes that bound my hands to my feet.

In the wardroom, I briefly rejoined the rest of my bedraggled ice crew. Joe Goodwin, who had put up considerable resistance when apprehended, was still in handcuffs.

"You come with me," a Mountie said, grabbing me by the hair.

As I tried to resist, Joe flew out of his chair, handcuffs and all, and dove headlong into the Mountie. Two other officers grabbed him and threw him forcefully across the room.

They dragged me out of the room and out onto the deck, where the arctic air hit my soaking body like a knife. Then they tossed me into an unheated room. I landed on my knees and fell forward, bruising my cheek on the steel deck.

Shivering and aching all over, with my hands and feet growing numb, I knew I had to get up and move. As I struggled to get to my feet, an officer put his boot to my rear and shoved me back onto my knees. Each time I tried to stand, someone would kick or push me down again. Exhausted, I finally stayed down, waiting to see what they intended to do with me.

For the next two and a half hours, according to my crew in the wardroom, I lay face down on that cold steel deck, hands cuffed behind my back. I was so cold and in such pain that I was only dimly aware of the Mounties and Fisheries officers standing around me. They spoke only in French, so I couldn't understand them, but sometimes I'd hear one of them laughing. Each time I moved, they viciously kicked and cursed me. I would pass out for minutes at a time. I just wanted to sleep, but I knew that the sweet sleep that beckons the freezing is dangerous and final. I fought it.

It occurred to me, frighteningly, that in fact they intended to have me freeze to death. He escaped, they would say, and ran across the ice. By the time we found him, *mon dieu*, it was too late. The autopsy would say death by freezing. As always, the media would believe what the government said and, as always, the politicians would believe what the Mounties said.

I remembered a story I had written a few years earlier on the death of Fred Quilt, a Chilcotin Indian in British Columbia, who had been kicked to death by two Mounties. A coroner's jury ruled that death resulted from peritonitis caused by an accidental fall—despite more than a dozen eyewitnesses. I didn't even have one witness.

I began to get angry—very angry. With great effort, I raised my head and then brought it crashing down on the deck. It hurt badly, but the hurt was almost welcome relief from the creeping numbness. Again I raised my head, and again I struck the deck hard. I felt a boot press down on me. I hit the deck again with my head.

Someone grabbed me and shook me roughly.

"What the hell do you think you are doing? Are you crazy?"

Was *I* crazy? What about them?

"You bastards, I know what you're doing. I intend to leave some bruises for the coroner. You've killed Indians like this, you fucking Gestapo pigs."

They pulled me to my feet. "Have you had enough, English?" a Mountie taunted, leaning over me. "Do you think you will return to the ice next year? Do you?"

"No," I managed to groan. I lied.

"Good," he said. "If you return, next time we'll kill you."

They dragged me back across the deck to the wardroom. Matt Herron demanded blankets and hot coffee or tea for me, but the Mounties refused. He asked for the ship's doctor, and they told him there was none. His fury mounting, Matt helped Keith Krueger strip me of my frozen clothing. They rubbed me to restore my circulation. The numbness began to fade, and as it did, my body felt as if it were on fire.

Soon after, the Mounties came back and dragged us into the helicopters for a flight to the Magdalen Islands and jail. Looking down as we flew over the seal pack, I could see the clubs rising and falling, the blood smeared red across the ice. I closed my eyes to shut out the sight and fell into the welcome serenity of sleep.

I awoke to searing pain. A Mountie had grabbed me by the handcuffs, and as he twisted and turned, the cuffs dug in unbearably. My wrists were raw and bleeding, although it was difficult to tell because my hands, I noticed for the first time, were stained red from the dye.

Pulling me out of the helicopter, he pushed me face down onto the ground. I sensed I was in the midst of a jeering crowd of perhaps thirty or forty men. The Mountie struck me across the back three times with what felt like a rubber hose. Each time, the crowd cheered and clapped.

My crew arrived one by one: Keith Krueger, first, followed by Matt Herron and then the others. The Fisheries Ministry was using one helicopter per demonstrator, and each newcomer had to run the gauntlet of abuse set up outside the jail by local sealer sympathizers.

Inside the jail, we met our jailer, a scar-faced, sadistic creep named André whose idea of a joke was to serve us seal meat stew for dinner. The next morning it was seal meat for breakfast. Even though we were famished, there was no question of eating it.

All of us were amused that our hands were stained with the red dye. "Talk about being caught red-handed," said Mark.

As we sat in jail, the media blasted us as foreigners interfering with Canada's sovereign right to kill seals. On March 6, 1979, the *Ottawa Journal* reported that "in the Commons MPs gave unanimous approval to a motion giving full support to the sealers taking part in this year's hunt." The *Journal* cited Hansard, the official record of parliamentary debate, as its source.

So we were heartened when member of Parliament Marke Raines stood up in the House and protested that this could not be because he, for one, did not support the seal hunt. He demanded that the statement be withdrawn.

The Speaker of the House struck down his protest.[1] In other words, Canada was not interested in the truth, and our opposition was not just sealers and seal hunt supporters. How could we ever win? The seal hunt was becoming as patriotic a symbol of the "true north strong and free" as the maple leaf or the beaver.

I knew, though, that if I had to choose between Canada and the seals, I would, without hesitation, choose the seals. Suddenly the reason for the beatings and the abuse became clear. I was not merely being charged with the crime of approaching the seal hunt without a permit. Those men in the bureaucratic cesspool of Ottawa actually looked upon me as a traitor. If they could have charged me with treason, they would have eagerly done so.

For the first time, I realized that I was an enemy to my own country, a traitor to my own people, and that, sitting here in this bleak jail on this godforsaken, windswept island—I was a political prisoner.

10

Escape from the Maganderthals

(1979)

> I've run into one hell of a bunch of cruel bastards in my day,
> slob hunters, elephant-killers, bullfighters, bunny-bashers, horse-whippers,
> all of them thugs and cowards, every one, but that bunch in the
> Magdalen Islands—they take the prize for the most savage, brutal,
> and unforgivable acts of cruelty on God's green Earth!
>
> —Cleveland Amory

The jail was a cold, dreary place in the basement of the courthouse. André continued to smile as he served us seal meat with each meal. The joke was getting a little thin, and we were getting hungry. White bread and peanut butter was our mainstay. Boredom was another problem. There were eight of us to keep each other company, but not much to do. All the available books and magazines were in French. The one deck of playing cards lacked thirteen cards, and the one jigsaw puzzle, a picture of a deer hunter about to destroy a magnificent buck, was missing a third of its pieces.

We spent a good deal of time washing our hands. All the scrubbing with soap and water wasn't doing the trick. They were still a vibrant red.

So we fabricated our own entertainment. We could hear the people in the courtroom above, and, reasoning that if we could hear them, they could hear us, we began to compete with each other for best bird or animal sounds.

"Caw, caw, caw."

"AAAAARRRRRRRRRRRROOOOOOOOOOOO."

Eight of us at once would impersonate everything from howler monkeys to sperm whales. The cacophony lasted only a few minutes at a time, but at each crescendo, a red-faced and furious André would come charging at the bars like a rogue water buffalo.

Exasperated, he would scream, "You will shut up! The judge, he will sentence you to jail if you don't stop."

"Oh," exclaimed Mark Sterk mockingly, "we wouldn't want to go to jail now, would we?"

"Argh, you people, you are crazy, fuck you." And André would storm off again.

"All together now, boys," I'd say.

"GGAAAAAAKKKKKKKK!"

"WhOOOOMMFFF, WWOOOOMMMFF!"

"Get this one, a horny peacock spying a bevy of peahens— GRRRRRRRRRIIIICKKKKKKKKKGAKKKK!"

Although we didn't appreciate it at the time, the safest place for us on the island was right where we were. The apoplectic seal killers were still demonstrating every day in front of the courthouse and still carrying their hangmen's nooses.

Cleveland Amory felt duty bound to come to our rescue. He flew from the ship by helicopter. Journalists Tom Schell and Gene Puskar accompanied him and they had been joined by Russ Hoyle and Marcus Halevi from the Boston weekly, *The Real Paper*.

Cleveland and the Fund's lawyers had appealed to the Canadian government to have us transferred to the mainland to be arraigned, arguing that the Magdalens were much too hostile for a fair hearing. Ottawa and Québec would have none of it. We were told we would be kept in jail until a magistrate could be flown into the islands from the Gaspé.

Cleveland came to the courthouse with Montreal lawyer Jacques Laurin. We were marched upstairs in pairs, with Joe and I the first to be processed in the dock. Judge Yvon Mercier's menacing glare indicated trouble. The room was full of ugly men in black snowmobile outfits and little yellow seal licence buttons on their toques. They yelled and swore until the bailiff told them to quiet down. I am recording my emotions of the time. Technically, I suppose, I broke the stupid law. I was very angry at the Judge and my comments reflect this. Every time I collided with him I was in a rage.

The charges were read.

"You are hereby charged, on the morning of March 9, 1979, with unlawfully approaching a seal hunt closer than one half nautical mile without the permission of the Federal Minister of Fisheries. You are also charged with violating the Seal Protection Act by marking a live seal with dye contrary to the regulations. Furthermore, you are charged with resisting arrest and assaulting an officer."

Stanley Dudka testified that I had assaulted him with a lead pipe.

"Now wait a minute," I blurted out, "I didn't assault anyone. I was assaulted by Dudka and the other officers."

Mercier glared at me, "Another word out of you and you will be charged with contempt of court. Now how do you all plead?"

Joe and I both smiled and raised our hands. With four bright red hands in the air, we said in unison, "Not guilty, your honour."

A few in the courtroom laughed. Cleveland hid his smile behind his hand. The judge just glared.

The other crew followed and made a point of showing their scarlet palms as they pleaded "not guilty."

After we were led away, Mercier set bail at $16,000 and ordered us to stay in jail until the bail was raised. It was Friday afternoon and the courts had timed it just right, setting the bail at the same time the bank closed.

Cleveland returned to the hotel, worried that he would not be able to get the bail money together until Monday at the earliest. He was well aware of what had happened to the crew at the airport. He sat with the reporters in the hotel bar as locals glowered at him. Schell and Puskar resented being there with him. They felt that his presence put them at risk by association—the previous night, a documentary film crew had been attacked in their hotel and their cameras had been smashed. So the reporters loudly criticized Amory and our campaign to let anyone within earshot know they were not part of this anti-sealing crowd.

That night, at 9:45, Puskar agreed to drive Cleveland to the airport to catch the plane. He was able to avoid the sealers, who were busy drinking in the local pubs. It was not until the plane was in the air that the mob realized they could have ambushed Amory at the airport. Having missed the opportunity to savage Cleveland, the mob began to congregate at the hotel where the journalists were staying.

As Puskar returned from the airport, he could see the headlights focused on the hotel room windows. People began to fill the hotel lobby, the loud voices growing steadily in volume. As some fifty bearded brutes rushed into the bar and surrounded their table, the reporters ordered another drink and sat in frenzied anxiety.

A kid with a wispy blond beard and a stocking cap on his head wedged his way between Tom Schell and Russ Hoyle. The other sealers pushed in closer.

The kid slurred out, "You Shee'ea Shepherd?"

"No," said Hoyle, and fumbled for his press pass.

The kid stared at the press pass like it was a winning lottery ticket. "Boston?" He smiled crookedly. "You journalist? No, you Sea Shepherd."

The kid started to pull at the collar of Hoyle's vest. Some other sealers had cornered Halevi. Puskar managed to slip away and reach the lobby. At the front desk, he asked the manager to call the police. The manager picked up the phone and dialed. He spoke French for a minute, nodded a few times, and put the receiver down.

"They say they do not want to hear about it. They want nothing to do with it."

Frightened, Puskar went back into the bar. Inside the noisy pub, a black-bearded sealer spat in Schell's face. "Why were you on that ship?" Blackbeard roared.

"I was on the Sea Shepherd as a member of the press," he said weakly.

"Where is Cleveland Amory?"

Almost apologetically, Schell said softly, "I don't know."

Then Blackbeard turned his attention on Hoyle. Leaning over until his face was inches from Hoyle's face, he said, "Understand one fucking thing. We don't want you here. Get off this island by tomorrow."

At the other end of the table, Puskar was trying to explain himself to seven brutes, repeating over and over again that he was a journalist. As he talked, his voice cracking with fear, one sealer poured coffee over his head. A second sealer butted out his cigarette on his shoulder.

Seeing that Puskar did not retaliate only made the brutes bolder. Three sealers pinned Marcus Halevi against the wall as a fourth spray-painted a red cross on his shirt. Halevi was visibly frightened. Then they dragged him out the front door. Hoyle followed. In the parking lot, the sealers grabbed Hoyle as others spray-painted him with green and brown paint. Then a huge man with a pock-marked face strode up to him and, in a voice tinged with a Glaswegian accent, demanded to know who he was.

"I'm a journalist," answered Hoyle.

"You're a fucking liar," the big man shouted. "You're paid by Cleveland Amory."

"No, I'm not!" Hoyle screamed.

"Liar!"

The big Scotsman turned and shouted in French. The crowd retreated to the door. The Scot shoved Hoyle aside and strode into the lobby.

Hoyle looked around for Halevi. He had disappeared. It turned out Marcus had run down the road and then began to walk toward the airport, intent on getting to the pay phone there to call for help. A car pulled up beside him and two men began to get out. Halevi dashed into a field, and in the blowing snow and the darkness, he quickly became lost. Wandering around without a parka, shivering and fatigued, it took him three hours to find his way back to the road.

Back in the bar, the mob was busy trying to push Puskar and Schell outside for the paint job. Because Puskar resisted, the mob kicked and shoved him. Schell wisely chose to go out meekly, and both men were spray-painted in the parking lot.

Someone told Schell he'd better buy the boys a drink. He, Puskar, and Hoyle were forced to sit in the bar and listen to the drunken sealers rave and rant as Schell bought drinks on ABC's expense account until five in the morning.

The next day, the journalists discovered that an official of the Canadian government had been with the mob all night during what they described as a reign of terror. The big pockmarked man was Jerry Conway, who worked for the Department of Fisheries and Oceans. He never attempted to quell the mob, though he intimidated Schell into letting him read his notes and made him promise not to report on the situation taking place.

Hoyle could not understand why Conway did not call for assistance, or why both the RCMP and the Québec Provincial Police refused to investigate, although they knew something was happening at the Hotel Theriault.

Puskar and Schell figured it was obvious: Canada was punishing them for reporting from the *Sea Shepherd*.

The reporters did not risk another night. They chartered a flight and three Fisheries officers drove them to the airport the next afternoon. They learned that the mob searched until seven in the morning for Cleveland Amory—not to hurt him, laughed one of the officers. "They just wanted to scare him."

Tom Schell looked at them. "I once got caught in the Watts riots with a car that wouldn't start. I covered the civil war in Nicaragua. I've never been as scared as I was here. There's no fucking doubt in my mind that they wanted to kill me."

On March 14, Tina Harrison arrived secretly on the island. Tina was the wife of a dentist in Vancouver and a long-time humane worker. She spoke French, and because she was a woman, Cleveland decided she would not be suspected or targeted by the sealers. She arrived at the court clerk's office with a cashier's cheque for $16,000. After five days in the Magdalen Islands' stinkhole of a jail, we were free.

If we walked out that door, though, we were dead men and we knew it. We scuttled our plans to go straight to the airport when the sealers threatened to blow up any plane that attempted to remove us from the islands. The airlines refused to take us.

Cleveland's assistant, Marion Probst, made some forty-five phone calls before she could find a charter company willing to make the trip that evening. Unfortunately, it could only carry five passengers at a time, so it would have to make two trips.

Matt Herron, Keith Krueger, Tina Harrison, and I decided to be in the second wave. Joe Goodwin, Mark Sterk, David MacKenney, Eddie Smith, and Paul Pezwick headed out first.

The first group made it to the airport, met the plane and took off for Charlottetown without incident. Unfortunately, they were spotted boarding the plane. Word quickly spread that the anti-sealers were leaving the island. A lynch mob was making its way to the jail.

Catching wind of the trouble, and fearing the adverse publicity that would result if we were injured or killed before our trial, the Québec Provincial Police finally decided to act. They hustled us from the building into two police cars; I got into one car with Matt, and Tina and Keith got into the other. The two cars took off in opposite directions. The sky was very dark and the wind was cold. Watching the two police officers monitoring the CB channels, we knew they were tense.

Matt turned to me and said, "This is so familiar, the same unpleasant fear in the pit of your stomach. I've been here before. If it wasn't for the snow and ice, this place could be Mississippi."

Matt had been a nightrider in the early sixties and he was right. This violence and hate were very reminiscent of the lynch mobs of the U.S. south of twenty years earlier—the same backwater hick ignorance and the same irrational ethnic arrogance.

Seeing headlights approaching, our cruiser turned into a deserted boatyard. Some thirty vans, cars, and pickups sped by, heading toward the jail. When it was safe, the police car nosed out of the boatyard, its lights off.

Turning onto the airport road, we saw a Fisheries Ministry Land Rover parked on the shoulder. The CB radio in the cruiser crackled: the Fisheries officers were reporting our location to the mob. As our two police cars met up and headed toward the terminal building, vehicles began pulling into the airport parking lot. Their passengers, sealers holding baseball bats and cans of spray paint, glared at the police cruisers, then began shouting at the police officers.

"*Allons, vite!*" shouted one of the officers in our car, and both cruisers sped off around a fence and onto the runway where our plane was about to touch down. Behind us, the mob burst through the gate, waving their seal clubs and baseball bats and screaming like banshees.

Just before I scrambled into the plane, one of the police officers said, "I hope you enjoyed your stay on our beautiful, friendly island."

Laughing, I shook his hand and glanced back at the mob of idiots tearing across the tarmac. The pilot didn't hesitate. As the snow whirled, the plane's engines roared and we picked up speed until we were finally airborne.

I couldn't help thinking that we would have to return here for the trial. "No bloody way," I muttered to myself.

We made our way to Sydney, Nova Scotia, where the *Sea Shepherd* was waiting for us. Starlet, my father, and the rest of the crew greeted us warmly and we began preparations to return to Boston.

Reflecting on what we had just accomplished, I couldn't help noting that while the self-described "radicals" of Greenpeace had condemned me for being overly aggressive on the ice, Cleveland and the Fund for Animals, who were considered relatively conservative, and the RSPCA, considered ultra conservative, were very pleased with our results. The petty politicking continued. When I called up Bob Cummings to congratulate him on disrupting the fleet in St. John's, I discovered that Bob, a long-time comrade, was now Patrick Moore's man.

"You know, Paul," he said, "Greenpeace has a policy that forbids any Greenpeace activist from talking to you or supporting anything you do. I could lose my job if Patrick finds out that I'm speaking with you."

From Boston, I decided to sail to Bermuda, where it would be warm enough to work on the ship and prepare for our next campaign, although our high-profile presence there stirred up quite a controversy.

The entire island seemed to take sides. It appeared that the large Canadian expatriate and seasonal population were against us, and the more established British residents were for us. Sam and Elizabeth Morse-Brown, resident artists in Bermuda, became our devoted patrons and promptly began introducing us around. When the Catholic priest and Methodist preacher attacked us for our "ungodly" actions against the working men of Newfoundland, we found a champion in Anglican Bishop Anselm Genders, who came down to bless our ship and invited us afterwards to lunch with Governor and Lady Ramsbottom at the governor's mansion.

As we worked on the ship, I found myself being invited to talk about the seal hunt to various groups on the island, including the Rotary Club, the Policeman's Club, the Bermudan SPCA—even the Bermuda Folk Singers' Club. Most remarkable, the British commander of the Royal Navy Dockyard invited us to move from our berth in St. Georges to a free berth in the navy dockyard. He also gave us free access to the navy machine shop and the navy pub, as well as hundreds of gallons of grey paint. Thus our blue hull became battleship grey, though we added rainbow stripes for colour. On weekends, numerous British sailors and members of the police force volunteered to help us overhaul the ship, along with a posse of helpers recruited by Bermuda conservation officer David Wingate.

It was strange to be in the dockyard and to share the small harbour with American, Canadian, and British warships and U.S. nuclear submarines. Even stranger, our radical group of "eco-terrorists," as some Canadian politicians had called us, was being invited to lunch by the captain of a U.S. nuclear submarine; Starlet and I even dined with the captain of a British helicopter assault carrier.

Navy commanders, police officers, a bishop, a governor, and hundreds of Bermudans thought we were doing the right thing. What a morale booster after our recent ordeal on the ice.

The ship was in wonderful shape when it came time for us to depart. We had a new mission: I had convinced Cleveland to fund my quest to search out the pirate whaler *Sierra*. This time against the whalers, not only was I in command of the expedition, I was now in command of my own ship. Joining me was a young and brilliant engineer from Australia named Peter Woof.

Just off the coast of Portugal, we found the pirate whaler and chased her into port. In full view of the shore, I rammed her twice and split her hull to the waterline, forcing her to flee to a dock as her pumps worked frantically to keep her from sinking.

We tried to escape, but the Portuguese navy prevented us. The next morning, in the port captain's office, I was charged with gross negligence. Luckily, I was able to convince the port captain that no negligence was involved—I had struck the ship precisely where I intended to strike her.

The captain laughed. "The real problem," he said, "is that I can't find anyone who admits to owning that ship. Without an owner to file a complaint, I can't proceed with charges. You're free to go."

My ship, however, was detained without an explanation. Without a hearing, a trial, or even consultation with our Portuguese lawyer, a judge ordered that our ship be given to the Sierra Trading Company as reparations for damages to the *Sierra*, estimated at about one million dollars. I found out later that a judge had accepted a $60,000 bribe to turn my ship over to the whalers.

In retaliation, Peter Woof and I returned to Portugal. On New Year's Eve, we scuttled the ship and sent her to the bottom of the harbour.

It had been a hell of a year: Bought a ship, staged a campaign to the seal hunt, hunted down and rammed a pirate whaler, and sank the ship at year's end.

After sinking the *Sea Shepherd*, I flew to London to meet with a special crew. I briefed them on details of a plan to be put into motion the morning of February 6, 1980. I was assured that the plan would be executed professionally, without injuries and on that date.

The full story of our attack against the *Sierra* and the scuttling of the *Sea Shepherd* can be found in my book *Ocean Warrior* (Key Porter, 1994). I included this brief version to explain why in 1980 we no longer had a ship to return to the ice. But there is one interesting sidebar to the *Sierra* saga. The massive international media coverage that resulted led to Greenpeace inviting me back into the fold. Rex Weyler, who was now editing the *Greenpeace Chronicles*, asked me to write a feature on the *Sierra* incident. The same month it ran as the cover story, I, along with some of the other old-time Greenpeacers, attended a meeting to help work out a legal dispute between Greenpeace USA, headed by David McTaggart, and Greenpeace Canada, headed by Pat Moore. At that meeting, we sorted out the differences and formally signed a document to establish Greenpeace International. From having been ousted from the board of directors in 1977, I was now an official founding member of the new Greenpeace International.

Of course the accord was not to last. The McTaggart-Moore personality feud resumed shortly thereafter, and since both men considered me a threat, I was soon persona non grata again.

But by this time I was quite comfortable leading campaigns. With Cleveland Amory's help, I transformed the Earthforce Society into the Sea Shepherd Conservation Society. We would get a ship again, I knew that, but for now, I had a trial coming up.

I was relieved to learn that our lawyers had won a change of venue—we would not be returning to the Magdalens. Instead, the trial, set for February 1980, took place in Percé, on Québec's Gaspé peninsula. We were stuck with the same judge, though—Yvon Mercier.

Peter Woof and Starlet accompanied my crew and I to Percé to stand trial for the 1979 campaign to protect the seals.

As my seven comrades and I stood before Mercier, we discovered that our trial would be in French. None of us spoke French and we protested.

Mercier said that French was the official language of Québec, and if we did not like it, we should not have broken the laws of a foreign country. Since we had, we were now at the mercy of Canadian justice.

"Excuse me, Judge Mercier," I said. "My friends here are American citizens, but I am a Canadian and I request, no, I demand, that I be allowed to stand trial in my own country in my own native language, and that language is English."

The judge sneered. "Not in this province. The trial will be in French."

On the first day of the trial, February 6, I was sitting in the foyer outside the courtroom with a couple of dozen Royal Canadian Mounted Police nearby. A few feet away, a pay telephone began to ring. I picked up the receiver to find a voice asking to speak to me. The man identified himself as Randy Stanfield, a representative of the Department of External Affairs, and he was checking on my whereabouts.

The *Sierra*, he said, had been blown sky-high in Lisbon harbour that day and had sunk to the bottom in ten minutes.

"Really," I answered. "No kidding?"

"Do you know where Peter Woof is?" he asked.

"He's right here, if you would like to talk with him, so you can't blame us," I added. "I'm sitting here with about twenty-five Mounties. You can't get a more ironclad alibi than that, now, can you?"

I hung up, and gave a thumbs-up sign to Peter. We returned to the courtroom to be bored for a few more hours as the lawyers prattled on in French about our actions. No one seemed interested in asking us any questions. After all, we were just foreigners in a foreign land on trial for interfering with a foreign sacrament—the slaughter of the baby harp seal.

Mercier found us all guilty of breaking the Seal Protection Act and fined the crew a total of $3,000 or ten days in prison each, with the exception of me. I was fined $4,000 for violating the Seal Protection Act, $4,000 more for interfering with the seal hunt, and $300 for resisting arrest.

Keith Krueger insisted that he serve the sentence right there prior to returning home to Hawaii. "I'm not going to give those guys the satisfaction of taking the Fund for Animals' money," he said. "It'll cost them to feed me, so let them pay for it. It's a small price to pay for the sake of the seals."

I was ordered to appear in Québec City on March 11 for sentencing on the charge of assaulting fish cop Stanley Dudka.

I dutifully reported on the eleventh and Cleveland came up from New York to support me. The timing was of course political. I was ordered to be imprisoned on March 15. By setting the date for that day, they were able to prevent us from returning to the ice for the 1980 hunt.

I was sentenced to ten days, to begin that day. Immediately, I was handcuffed, pushed into a van and taken to Orsainville prison, outside Québec City.

I felt as though I really was in a foreign country. Although I am a Canadian and this was a Canadian prison, all of the guards refused to speak English and refused to listen to my poor attempts to speak French.

A few days after my incarceration, I was transported back to the courthouse in Québec City and ordered before Judge Mercier to sign a probation order.

"I am sorry, your honour, I can't do that."

The judge looked at me contemptuously and demanded to know why not. "I can see from your attitude," he scolded, "that prison is not having a rehabilitating effect on you. Perhaps you need some time added to your sentence."

"But your Honour, I can't read this. It's in French and I don't read French, and it's never a good idea to sign something you haven't read. Besides, your Honour, even if you gave me ten years, you would never rehabilitate me into accepting that bloody massacre of seals."

Mercier thundered back at me, his Gallic temper rising. "In Québec, you speak French. Sign it or I'll add fifteen more days to your sentence."

"OK, I'll sign it, but I would like the court record to show that I am signing this under protest. You know, your Honour, sir, I mean *vôtre honeur, monsieur*, they did not make people do this sort of thing even at Nuremburg."

Mercier advised me that I was getting very close to being charged with contempt.

So sign it I did, and discovered upon my release from prison that I was now ordered, as Brian Davies had been, to stay away from the seal hunt and the Maritimes for three years. I could not go to the ice legally until 1983. They released me from prison after seven days but did not allow me to make a call to be picked up. They simply opened the massive doors of that Siberian-looking fortress and ushered me outside without a coat into a blizzard.

I returned to Vancouver, where a large media crowd waited at the airport. I seized the opportunity to condemn Canadian justice and Canada's ongoing injustice against the harp and hood seals.

As for the ban on my going to the hunt, I had absolutely no intention of abiding by that convenient piece of political jurisprudence. I told the reporters that I would be on the ice in 1981.

Moira Farrow of the *Vancouver Sun* asked me if I was willing to risk contempt of court by returning to the ice.

"Absolutely," I replied. "I have nothing but contempt for a court that sits in judgment over my compassion."

The Kamikaze Kayak Brigade

(1981)

A crime was committed at Cavendish Beach. I saw a man skin a
baby seal alive. The Fisheries officers and the Mounties saw him do it
also. There were many witnesses. I filmed the cruellest act that I had ever
seen. I was arrested. The crime was that I had filmed a man skin a seal alive.
I was the criminal. The man laughed and walked away.

—Madelaine Burns

The courts had kept both Brian Davies and me away from the hunt in 1980, but a *Sea Shepherd* crew had been able to strike a blow. In January, four of my crew flew to Halifax and boarded the *Martin Karlsen* in the dead of a winter's night. They inflicted some major mechanical damage to the ship, destroyed navigational equipment and ensured that Karl Karlsen would be spending some money to ready his ship for the hunt. They also attempted to sink her, but a watchman discovered the flooding engine room, and a crew with emergency pumps was able to save the wounded ship.

Greenpeace returned to the hunt in 1981, surprise, surprise, this time with a ship, the *Rainbow Warrior*, and with a "brand-new" plan. They intended to dye seals green. Greenpeace, it seemed, couldn't stand to be upstaged by another group. If *Sea Shepherd* sent a ship, they would send a ship. If *Sea Shepherd* dyed seals, they would forget their past misgivings and dye seals. And instead of the Labrador Front, the *Rainbow Warrior* headed to where we had made the news the year before—the Gulf of St. Lawrence.

Still, copycats or not, they were able to make it to the seal hunt where we and IFAW could not. Actually, banning Brian Davies from the ice was a stroke of good luck for the seals and for IFAW. Instead of expending his energies on field campaigns, Brian worked on lobbying the European public and governments to ban seal pelts. In Europe, Brian did more to threaten Canadian sealing interests than he had ever done before within the borders of Canada.

I had no intention of competing with IFAW, and there would be no advantage in duplicating their splendid efforts.

I had sold the movie rights to the *Sierra* story to Warner Brothers, and this gave me enough money to purchase another Hull trawler called the *St. Giles*. I renamed her the *Sea Shepherd II*, but unlike her illustrious predecessor, she would need quite a bit of work. I quickly realized it would be impossible to get her retrofitted in time for the seal hunt in 1981.

I was sitting in the wheelhouse in January reading a book about an old friend of mine when an idea struck me. Ken Brower's book, *The Starship and the Canoe*, told the story of the relationship between physicist Freeman Dyson, a designer of space ships, and his son George Dyson, a designer and builder of kayaks.

The next day, I jumped on a plane back to Vancouver and drove out with Jet and Bob Hunter to visit George at his treehouse home at Belcarra Park. George immediately lent us a three-man ocean-going baidarka of his own design, about twenty-three feet long. We loaded it onto the top of my station wagon, and Jet and I realized that we had our campaign for 1981. If we did not have a ship to get to the ice, I would make good on my promise of a year before that I would get there even if I had to use a canoe.

We did not have much time to organize. I had to get a crew—so far it was Jet and me—and we had to get in some practice with the kayak.

As we were mulling around possible third crew members, the door to our office opened. In walked a visitor from Germany named Joachim Obst.

"Hi," he said shyly. "I would like to join a *Sea Shepherd* campaign."

He was young, fit, and eager. "You know, Joachim," I told him, "you have an incredible sense of timing."

Within a week, the three of us were hosting a press conference at Vancouver's Granville Island. We demonstrated the use of the baidarka and announced that the Sea Shepherd Conservation Society would be returning to the seal hunt to dye seals, this time with a harmless organic blue dye. One reporter asked me how I could return when I was under a court order to stay away from the seal hunt for three years.

"I cannot respect any court order," I answered, "that robs me of my right to oppose an atrocity. I don't think any court orders prevented Gandhi or King from doing what was right, and it won't prevent us either."

We then issued a media release stating that if I was arrested in Prince Edward Island, we would call for a consumer boycott in New England of P.E.I. potatoes. This would actually be easy to do because Maine potato farmers were already angry that cheap Canadian potatoes were being dumped in New England. I did not think that P.E.I. potato farmers would be happy to hear that their crops would be boycotted because the government of P.E.I. felt that appeasing a small handful of P.E.I. seal killers was important.

Joachim and I began the long drive across Canada to Prince Edward Island, picking up Jet in Montreal, where he had just completed some trips for American Airlines.

In Fredericton, New Brunswick, we stopped briefly to have dinner with Aida Flemming and her husband, Sir Hugh John Flemming. Where once as a child I had joined her wonderful group, the Kindness Club, Aida had been one of the first to join my Sea Shepherd Conservation Society.

We carried on to the coast and boarded the ferry for Prince Edward Island. At our hotel, we met up with Lewis Regenstein, who had come up from the Fund for Animals office in Washington, D.C., to join us.

The next day, March 1, we drove over to Stanhope Beach and put our kayak into the water for a media demonstration. As we were paddling, two RCMP cars arrived and four officers quickly strode toward the waterline. One of them was holding some papers. I was pretty sure those papers were a warrant for my arrest.

As the kayak came alongside some shore-fast ice, I got out of the boat and sprang into the woods. Jet and Joachim paddled back down the beach.

I stayed in the woods for two hours and hiked down to the road, where I got a ride from a local fisherman going into town. He did not recognize me. I told him that my grandfather was born in Burien, P.E.I., and that his family had once grown potatoes here. The fisherman liked that and he drove me right to the front door of the hotel, where I made for our room.

The others, who had returned, confirmed that the Mounties had a warrant. When they told the officers that I had taken a hike in the woods, the Mounties said that they had no intention of chasing me. They would get me eventually.

Sure enough, the next morning, they were waiting for me as we left the hotel.

"Last year, in Québec City, you saw the order banning you from the Atlantic provinces," said one of them. "You were given a copy."

"I was shown something in French and given something in French, but I've not had the time to translate it."

"I have a copy of your probation notice right here, Watson."

Some reporters were now gathering, and as is usual when reporters move in, the Mounties were getting nervous. I glanced over the order and handed it back. "Sorry, except for one sentence, it's all in French."

That sentence said that I was not allowed into the area of the Gulf of St. Lawrence—except that the word "allowed" was spelt "allouded."

"It says here that I am not allouded into the Gulf of St. Lawrence. I'm sorry, but I have absolutely no idea what that means."

"It means, Mr. Watson, that you are not allowed in the Gulf of St. Lawrence."

"Oh does it? Do you speak French, officer?"

"No."

"So you don't have any idea what this order says. Do you have a definition of the word 'allouded'? I think a definition will be useful in court, don't you?"

"I haven't got time to debate with you, Watson." The officer frowned. "Hope you've got a fast car. You've got until midnight to be on the other side of the Québec border."

"If you want to knock down our door at midnight, go right ahead. We're going to the hunt."

"So, what now?" said Jet, after the Mounties had pulled out.

"It does seem strange. You would think they would just arrest me and toss me out of the province."

Later that evening, I was tipped off by a reporter that the P.E.I. premier was actually worried about our potato boycott threat and had cautioned the Mounties to be careful not to provoke an incident.

The next day, the Mounties returned. They told us that they would not allow us to launch the kayak and, once again, they were advising me that I was in violation of my probation. If I did not leave by the following day, they would take me into custody.

"Oh, one more thing, Watson," added one officer. "You're ordered to return to Charlottetown on April 27 to answer to your parole violation."

I laughed. "How the hell am I supposed to return to Charlottetown if my probation bars me from being in the Atlantic provinces? Tell me, do you guys ever think these things out?"

The crew and I discussed this latest development. We decided that Jet and I would drive the kayak back to the mainland and store it. Then we would figure

The *Aurora* and *Vanguard,* sealing steamers known as the "Wooden Walls," at Harbour Grace, 1885. (Sea Shepherd—Malibu, CA)

Brigitte Bardot, with Paul Watson on her left, on campaign to save the seals in 1977. (Sea Shepherd—Malibu, CA)

One of the hundreds of demonstrations held worldwide in the 1970s.
(Sea Shepherd—Malibu, CA)

A *Sea Shepherd* crewmember "paints" a seal pup with dye to protect
it in 1979. (Sea Shepherd—Malibu, CA)

Paul and Joe Goodwin are charged under the Seal Protection Act in the Magdalen Islands in 1979. (Marcus Halevi, Sea Shepherd—Malibu, CA)

Charlottetown, PEI, 1981: An RCMP officer orders Paul to leave the province. (Sea Shepherd—Malibu, CA)

The *Sea Shepherd II*, rigged out to blockade the sealing fleet in 1983. (Sea Shepherd—Malibu, CA)

A Coast Guard vessel rams the *Sea Shepherd II* in the Gulf of St. Lawrence in April 1983. (Sea Shepherd—Malibu, CA)

Coast Guard vessels tear gas the *Sea Shepherd II*. (Sea Shepherd—Malibu, CA)

Coast Guard vessels surround the *Sea Shepherd II*. (Sea Shepherd—Malibu, CA)

Paul Watson kneels with a seal in front of the *Sea Shepherd II* in 1983.
(Sea Shepherd—Malibu, CA)

The door that sealers smashed coming after Paul in 1995. (Andre Heger, Sea Shepherd—Malibu, CA)

Martin Sheen, with crewmember Chuck Swift, stands by a sealing boat in 1995. (Andre Heger, Sea Shepherd—Malibu, CA)

Paul, with Martin Sheen, being interviewed in a hotel room in the Magdelens in 1995. (Andre Heger, Sea Shepherd—Malibu, CA)

In 1996, Paul brushes a seal, collecting hair fibers, under the watchful eye of the RCMP. (Sea Shepherd—Malibu, CA)

Paul stands with Farley Mowat in front of the *Sea Shepherd III* in 1998. (Sea Shepherd—Malibu, CA)

Paul holds a baby Harp seal in 1999. (Peter Brown, Sea Shepherd—Malibu, CA)

out some way to return. The seals were moving closer to the coast of P.E.I. and the Department of Fisheries and Ocean was actually recruiting P.E.I. fishermen who had never before killed a seal to try their hand at it. If they intended to walk out onto the ice to kill seals, we could return and walk out onto the ice to spray-dye them.

The next morning, Jet and I departed, leaving Joachim and Lew behind to talk with the media and to watch the situation.

We headed toward the ferry, boarded it and drove off at Cape Tormentine, only to be greeted by an RCMP patrol car that pulled us over a few miles down the road.

Just a routine check, the Mountie said, acting like he didn't know who we were or what was going on. He gave the game away, though, by asking where the third member of our team was.

"Don't know," I replied. "Decided to stay and see Anne of Green Gables, I guess. Anyway, the probation order only applies to me, doesn't it?"

He let us proceed, but the RCMP tailed us all the way northward to Shippigan Island, where we thought we might actually be able to launch the kayak and get out to the seals.

We found a motel for the night, but around ten o'clock, a long-haired fellow in civilian attire came to our door, flashed a badge and announced that he was RCMP.

"Gee, Al," I said, "they're even turning out the narcs for us."

The Mountie had now been joined by his equally unkempt partner. I asked what we could do for them.

"You can pack your bags and get the fuck out of New Brunswick."

"We were planning on getting a good night's sleep and leaving in the morning."

The Mountie actually snarled at me.

"Look, asshole, you've been ordered out of the Atlantic provinces and you will pack your bags and you will get on the road now. Do you understand?"

"Yeah, I understand I'm living in a police state and I'm being expelled from my home province. OK, Jet, I guess we have to leave."

So we packed up and headed south toward Newcastle, a police car constantly on our tail. Around one in the morning, just past Newcastle, a heavy snow began to fall.

As Jet was looking over the road map, I spied a driveway, quickly turned into it, and killed the lights. A few moments later, the police car roared by.

Jet found an alternative route that would keep us off the main highway.

It was an eerie trip. The snow fell thicker and thicker, and the road was not on the plowing schedule. We drove straight down the middle, shearing the snow with our bumper. For 100 miles, we saw nothing but dark forest, snow, and the occasional track of a moose or deer. At least we had lost the RCMP. We weren't worried about being followed, we just didn't like it. I always feel good when I know the Mounties are looking for me and don't know where to find me. It's a small pleasure, but when you're fighting the seal hunt, you take what you can get.

Arriving in Toronto, we discovered that a forty-kilometre strip of ice carrying some 50,000 seal pups had drifted almost to the shores of Cavendish Beach in P.E.I. The DFO had issued 205 licences to forty novice seal hunt teams. Just off of Shippigan Island lay another herd estimated at 50,000 pups. Now we knew why the Mounties were so eager to prevent us from launching our kayak there.

This year the action was happening in P.E.I. and my instinct to use it as a base was dead on. We had to get back there and fast. Back after his three-year exile, Brian Davies had already flown in to join his crew, and Greenpeace had dispatched Peter Dykstra from Boston to set up a media presence in Charlottetown.

Dykstra actually had the gall to tell the media that I had fled the seal hunt and that I was a coward. When the media called me in Toronto about his accusation, I said I would be on the ice and we would spray-dye seals and that was that. In response, Dykstra laughed and said I wouldn't dare because the Mounties would nail me if I did. "I absolutely guarantee," he added, "that Watson will not even see a seal pup this year." Well, I thought, we'll see about that.

Jet and I arranged to meet with Wayne Millard and Madelaine Burns, friends of ours who were producing a film about the seal hunt called *A Hunt Without Pity*. Wayne was also a pilot, and he and Madelaine intended to fly that very evening from Toronto to Charlottetown in Wayne's own plane. They agreed to take both Jet and I and our equipment.

The seal gods were smiling on us. We were going back, and the great thing was that the Mounties did not have the faintest idea where we were.

Wayne landed at Charlottetown airport. We had brought everything we needed for the ice, including a newly acquired inflatable boat. Jet went inside to rent a car, while I climbed the chain link fence to avoid going through the terminal. I stayed low in the bushes until Jet brought the car up close.

We headed straight to Cavendish Beach. It was about seven in the evening and the night was pitch-black and moonless. Although it was still bitterly cold, there was no wind.

Jet dropped me off with the equipment and went to park the car some distance away. I knew that to get to the beach below we had to climb down a sandstone embankment for about twenty feet. I made a couple of trips to the top of the embankment to get everything ready for our climb down. Unfortunately, Jet still had a bag with him—the one with the rope we needed to lower the gear down and assist in our own descent. I would just have to wait for him to get back.

Suddenly, three pairs of headlights rounded the bend and three cars began to move slowly down the road, one of them shining a spotlight along the top of the embankment.

Around me was nothing but open ground. There was nowhere I could hide.

Peering over the edge of the embankment, all I could see was blackness. I knew it was about twenty feet to the bottom and I knew there was sand down there. Without thinking, I began to toss the gear down. The lights were coming closer now, and with only seconds to spare, I made the decision to jump into that black void.

The fall knocked the wind out of me. Because the sand was frozen solid, the landing wasn't as soft as I had anticipated, but at least nothing seemed broken or bruised. I waited on the beach, listening for sounds and watching the beams of light flicker across the top of the embankment and reflect a ghostly white off the ice floes.

I must have waited an hour before I heard Al's voice calling my name.

"Down here," I called.

He lowered the rope and made his way down to the sand.

"I thought they would never go away," he said.

"The Mounties?" I asked.

"No, worse, locals, drunk and armed with clubs. I don't know if they were looking for seals or for seal savers."

We gathered our equipment and made our way out from the shore-fast ice, towing the inflatable boat behind us. About a quarter of a mile out, we came to the shifting, moving floe ice and walked another half a mile until we heard the familiar crying of the seal pups.

We'd made it. We began to go from pup to pup, marking each one on its back with a blue cross. We had marked a few hundred when we realized that we were a fair distance offshore and the ice appeared to be shifting slowly away from the coast. We weren't really concerned. We had been on the ice enough to not be intimidated by it.

One pup I sprayed tried to adopt me. The baby seal began to follow me around on the ice, and, when I stopped to rest, came up and started to suck on the toe of my boot. I had to sit and pet and soothe it for a while until I could quietly sneak away. A few yards away, I could hear Jet whistling as he worked. He seemed to be enjoying himself immensely.

It was eerie out there on the ice in the dark of night—eerie, but strangely peaceful. I always love being with the seals on the ice floes. Alone with them, without the slaughter, I find it very comforting. And the ice, well, it felt like a second home to me.

Around three in the morning, after dyeing hundreds of seals, we decided to head back to shore. First, though, we found a big pan of flat ice and wrote in large blue letters that would be visible from the air:

STOP THE SLAUGHTER
CESSEZ LE MASSACRE

Going back turned out to be much more difficult than going out. The ice was moving offshore and breaking up in places. If not for the small inflatable, which allowed us to cross the widening leads, we would have been in serious trouble. A few times, stuck in icy slush so thick our paddles were useless, we had to slide our legs over the side of the boat and kick to gain propulsion. Our Mustang suits were not waterproof, but they did keep us partially afloat.

Eventually we reached shore, just as the sun began to rise. To our dismay, we saw dozens of seal pups on the ice only a few feet from the beach. We quickly sprayed them, but looking down the beach, we saw hundreds more. All of them would be helpless when the novice Spud Island sealers found them. We stumbled across the sand and scaled the twenty-foot embankment. While Jet went to retrieve the car, I hauled the gear up.

Heading in to Charlottetown, we saw Wayne and Madelaine driving toward Cavendish Beach and alerted them to where the seals were. Once in town, we hosted an impromptu press conference to announce that we had made it to the ice and spray-dyed the seals. One cynical scribe said that we were lying and that it was foolish and impossible to walk out onto the ice floes at night.

"It may be foolish," I answered, "but not impossible. As proof, we left a message out there in big blue letters."

We then excused ourselves from the media to make a quick retreat before the Mounties arrived. I knew they would be furious to see me back. They'd had wind of my return and had placed the airport and the ferry terminal under observation.

While we waited for Madelaine and Wayne to complete their film work, Jet and I hid out at the Kirkland hotel, reading and watching the news. That's how we learned that television cameras managed to locate our sign on the ice and had even filmed a few blue-crossed seals. When they found our frozen horizontal billboard, it was eight miles offshore, having drifted for some ten hours since we had left it. Reporters who had doubted our dead-of-night ice excursion were now silenced. In fact, some of the media were visibly impressed with our feat.

We may not have saved many seals, but we had made a defiant gesture in the face of a government intent on stifling protest to stop needless slaughter. We had made our mark.

Brian Davies was also out on the ice making his mark, along with Wayne and Madelaine, who had set up their tripod on the beach just in time for the arrival of the sealers.

The clubs started falling and the cameras began to roll when the Mounties and the Fisheries officers approached. They promptly arrested the film crew for disobeying the Seal Protection Act by filming the hunt and charged them with assaulting Fisheries officers.

"They confiscated our film," said Madelaine, "so they could see what we filmed." Wayne, understandably, resisted. "They were trying to get the film off Wayne, and they had him on the ground with his clothes all ripped apart and his skin showing. They had his arms twisted behind his back. He yelled for me to take a picture. I did, but they later confiscated my camera as well."

William Murphy, the district manager for the DFO, admitted that his men might have been overly eager to intervene, especially given that, as federal officers, they did not have jurisdiction in a P.E.I. provincial park.

"We will look into this, but that does not let them off the hook for assaulting my officers," he said. "They committed a crime when they resisted."

The same Fisheries officers apologized later that day for seizing film from a Canadian Press photographer who shot the incident. The apology did not include returning the film.

Wayne and Madelaine were told to return to answer to the charges on April 27 and informed that they were now effectively prohibited from witnessing the hunt.

The four of us returned to Toronto in Wayne's plane. Once again, I was forced to scale the fence to get to the runway. Since they had not seen me at all, the Mounties were apparently quite mystified as to how I left the island, and, despite my appearance on television the night before, standing on a Charlottetown street, they reported that the story of my being on the island was unsubstantiated.

The next morning, Peter Dykstra appeared on a Charlottetown radio program, and the radio station called me in Toronto to comment on air about his criticism of me. I don't think Dykstra was expecting me to be sharing the program with him, and he immediately became defensive.

"Greenpeace is not here to make a judgment about the actions of the sealers. Greenpeace is here to bear witness to the world that there are many people who are opposed to this hunt. But you, you come into this province, where you don't belong, like some sort of imperialist telling them that they are wrong to live the lifestyle they are living. You really have some gall, Watson . . ."

I cut him off. "Listen to me, you goddamn Yankee know-it-all. My grandfather was born in P.E.I., my father was born in New Brunswick. My family are eight generations Maritimers. I'm fed up with this bloody government telling me I have no right as a Canadian to have an opinion, and now you, an American, are telling me that as a Maritimer I have no right to an opinion. You know, Peter, these ignorant savages killing these seals are barbarians, plain and simple, and if you would bother to go out and see for yourself instead of being a Greenpeace bureaucrat, sitting on your fat ass, you would agree."

In hindsight, it was a mistake to blast Dykstra—not that he was right and I was wrong, but because he ended up working in the environmental news department at CNN, where he would use his influence twelve years later to prevent *Sea Shepherd* stories from being aired.

I was harshly criticized for calling the sealers savages, but I was vindicated the next day when the P.E.I. landsmen sealers were banned from sealing—only one day after the hunt began—by the federal government. Their ineptitude and blatant acts of cruelty had made worldwide media, and, for the first time, even some Fisheries officers admitted that seals had been skinned alive. With CBC cameras filming it all from the beach, they couldn't exactly deny it.

In fact, hundreds of spectators had stood on the beach and witnessed the carnage,[1] and some Spud Islanders were having second thoughts after seeing those ghastly images. On March 4, the Charlottetown *Evening Patriot* reported that all five citizens randomly interviewed stated that the hunt was inhumane.

After returning to Vancouver, I got a call from the Mounties. An officer informed me that I would not be required to appear in Charlottetown on April 27.

"Why not?" I said. "Look, I know that back in March I said that I wouldn't return, but that was before the sealers went berserk on the beach. I would love to come back and challenge the government as to why men who break humane laws and conservation laws on camera are allowed to get away with it."

"You may not return, Watson, because we have dropped the charges against you for violating your probation. You should consider yourself lucky."

"Well, maybe I should return anyway."

"If you do, you will be in violation of your probation barring you from the Atlantic provinces."

Exasperated, I said, "I tried to tell you that in May—that I could not return because of your ban on my returning, and you said that I had to return to answer to charges of returning. Now you're saying that I can't return because you don't want me to return. If it wasn't a violation for me to have returned in March, and I assume it wasn't a violation because you're dropping the charge despite the fact that I returned twice, then how can it be a violation for me to return a third time but not the two other times?"

The Mountie told me I would risk returning at my own peril, whatever that meant. "Why do you insist on being such a troublemaker?" he added.

"Why do you all insist upon defending the slaughter of innocent seals? If you don't want me to make trouble, then shut down the seal hunt."

"Watson, you're not very loyal to Canada, are you?"

"On the contrary, I'm loyal to those creatures who were here before Canada the political map replaced Canada the real country. My Canada does not include you, or Parliament, or the banks, or the bloody sealers. My Canada includes the seals, the wolves, the bear, the trees, and all that your Canada is attempting to destroy. My Canada is not some damn red maple leaf painted on a piece of cloth. My Canada is that leaf, green and living and attached to a tree."

"You know, Watson, you're fucking crazy." And he slammed down the phone.

As I hung up, I thought to myself, yeah, I guess I am crazy. But I wouldn't have it any other way.

I later found out that the charges against Wayne Millard and Madeline Burns had also been dropped. The government had been embarrassed enough.

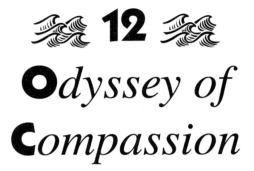

O*dyssey of* **C***ompassion*

(1982–1983)

The root of the matter is a very simple and
old-fashioned thing . . . love or compassion.
If you feel this, you have a motive for existence,
a guide for action, a reason for courage,
an imperative necessity for intellectual honesty.

—Bertrand Russell

I n 1982, we did not go to the ice. After our campaign in P.E.I., I had taken my ship to the North Pacific and the Bering Sea to expose illegal Soviet whaling operations in Siberia. By February 1982, we were en route to Japan to protect dolphins from Iki Island fishermen who were waging a campaign of extermination against the gentle creatures. The fishermen claimed the dolphins ate "their" fish and accused the dolphins of being "bandits"—the same old complaint and tired, bogus arguments of the sealers.

March found me in Iki Island, far from the ice. Though it pained me greatly not to be with the seals, it would have pained me even more to not be in Japan to stop the dolphin slaughter, an objective that we achieved with only one campaign. If only the Canadian government were as reasonable.

The 1983 anti-seal campaign began very early in September 1982. Our ship, recently arrived from Hawaii, was berthed in Vancouver, a long way from the coast of Newfoundland. On top of that, we did not have much money. What we did have were some dedicated volunteers.

My first mate, Cliff Rogers, was working like a Spartan warrior to get the ship ready for the long voyage to the east coast. A month before, in Seattle, we had recruited four young men—Tate Landis, John Miller, Bob Kerns, and Curt Anderson—all of whom were lifeguards. Even though Cliff was treating them like boot camp recruits, they didn't seem to mind and worked fifteen-hour days on preparations to depart. New volunteers joined their ranks and Cliff kept everyone busy.

To raise funds, I had organized a marathon swimathon. Tate, John, and I would attempt to be the first ever to swim the fifty-four kilometres from Nanaimo, on Vancouver Island, to Vancouver. I had been training for it all summer.

The swim was an ordeal that I will not attempt to repeat again. Tate, John, and I dove into the water in Nanaimo Harbour at 0600 hours. As the Nanaimo ferry entered the harbour, it almost ran over us, and we all swam like fiends to avoid the oncoming bow. On the positive side, we had timed the tidal flow perfectly and the rising tide moved us northward toward Powell River.

Finally, after twenty-seven gruellingly cold, wearisome hours, Tate and I reached Jericho Beach in Vancouver. John made it halfway before throwing in the towel. As I felt my feet touch the sand, I painfully hoisted myself from the water and tumbled almost drunkenly toward a small group of reporters. We had done it: Tate and I were the first ever to swim from Nanaimo Harbour to Vancouver Harbour. With the cameras rolling, I opened my mouth to speak. Nothing came out. For the first time ever in front of the media, I was speechless. The salt water had swollen my tongue and all I could do was mumble incoherently. Jet Johnson, who had driven our escort boat, spoke for us.

The *Vancouver Province* newspaper of course reported that the swim was a failure because we had not raised very much for our cause, conveniently forgetting that we had completed the ordeal. The summer before, a fireman attempting to make the crossing got more positive coverage for swimming just a third of the distance, but because we had politicized the event by swimming for the seals, the media belittled our efforts. If nothing else, though, it got me into shape—even if for days I did feel like I had been run over by a truck.

As we raced to get the ship ready and recruit a crew, every day in Vancouver was frantic.

A young man named Bobby David arrived on board to volunteer as second mate. He also worked for OXFAM and asked if I would be interested in taking some medical and agricultural supplies to Nicaragua on our way down to Panama. I didn't see any harm in that and agreed to attend a meeting with him that evening to discuss the idea with the OXFAM relief committee.

Doing a relief trip en route to the Atlantic sounded good. We would be help-ing people, and OXFAM would help with our fuel as far as Central America. I soon found out that the politics of relief agencies could be even more antago-nistic than the politics of the conservation movement.

A fishermen's union organizer named Steve Rankin was chairing the meet-ing, and I quickly discovered that his socialist union was a major participant in Nicaraguan non-governmental aid programs.

Rankin looked at me as if I were a criminal and scowled accusingly as he queried me.

"So what is your motivation for wanting to transport supplies to Managua, Watson?"

"I don't have any motivation. Bobby David asked me and I said why not, since we are going that way anyhow."

Rankin was an old-time pinko who saw counter-revolutionaries under every bed. He was not going to cut me any slack.

"How do we know you aren't working for the CIA?" he said.

"Christ!" I retorted. "What the bloody hell are you talking about?"

"Ha," smiled Rankin. "A little defensive, I see. Perhaps it's because you're a well-known anticommunist. We know about your expedition to Siberia to dis-rupt the Soviet economy there. We know that you're on your way to take the bread from the mouths of the working men in the Newfoundland seal trade. I suppose you're going to deny that also?"

I had had enough. I stood up.

"No, I don't deny protecting whales in Russia or protecting seals in Newfoundland," I shouted at Rankin. "I don't care if the whalers are commies or capitalists. I oppose whaling, period. I don't have time for trivial anthro-pocentric bullshit. I offered my help, free, to assist you in transporting supplies to Nicaragua to help some children, but not now, no sir. I won't allow this piece of shit to accuse me of being a CIA agent because I oppose whaling and sealing. You can all go screw yourselves."

A few days later, Bobby approached me with another offer, this time to take supplies to the library in Grenada. I accepted on the condition that the project was his alone, and I refused to meet with representatives from any relief agency. Bobby agreed, and my second mate filled the hold with medical supplies, agri-cultural equipment, and books for the library.

In late November, we set out down the west coast, straight into the most miserable year of the century for coastal storms. Off Coo's Bay, Oregon, after fifteen hours of trying to batter our way through heavy seas, I decided to turn about and head into the bay to wait out the weather.

Coo's Bay was a diehard logging community where dozens of cars sported bumper stickers proclaiming that the "Sierra Club can kiss my ax," or "Eat a spotted owl for breakfast." So we were not expecting a warm reception and were very surprised to find that when it came to protecting baby harp seals, even the spotted-owl-hating forest-rapers were sympathetic. During our brief forced exile from the weather and the sea, Coo's Bay residents gave us donations of food, material, and money.

Two days later, we set out again, and, although the weather was still rough, we made San Francisco ten days before Christmas and docked at Fort Mason for a few days. It was there that a storm that we named Hurricane Grinch struck.

When the gale careened in from the Pacific and slammed into us, most of the crew were onshore. I was the only officer on board, along with a few volunteers. The ship heaved and bucked, mooring lines snapped, and stout dock piles cracked and splintered. Frantically we paid out the lines, hoping the slack would prevent any further snapping. We were dangerously close to losing all our mooring lines when my chief engineer, Carroll Vogel, and my first engineer, Paul Pezwick, and some local volunteers arrived on the dock.

Carroll tore off and returned a few moments later with the end of a long mooring line. Snaking around the corner came the rest of the line, carried by volunteers from the *Jeramiah O'Brian*, a World War II liberty ship on display at Fort Mason as a maritime museum. Through the deluge and the wind, her crew and ours hauled in the lines and made them fast.

On the dock, Paul Pezwick laughed and yelled up to me. "So much for that wizard with his dumb broom, huh?"

Back in 1981, in Vancouver, just prior to our campaign to protect whales in Siberia, a warlock had presented us with a broom. He asked us to tie it to the top of the foremast. As long as it was there, he had told us, we would be protected from storms.

Although I did not believe in magic, it was comforting to think that, just maybe, there could be something to it. In fact, since that day, we hadn't had any really threatening weather. And now a storm was tossing us about like a rabid dog with a rag doll in its mouth.

I looked up to the foremast. To my surprise, I saw a Christmas tree tied to the broom. I'm not a superstitious person, but I bellowed, "Who the hell put that goddamn thing up there?"

"I did, Captain," said John Miller. "I tied it up there an hour ago."

"Well, get the hell up there and untie it, damn it."

"In this wind?" he asked, sounding both a little frightened and surprised.

"Yes! Be careful, but cut that damn tree down."

A few minutes later, John called down, "Watch out below!"

The Christmas tree dropped like a stone to the deck, and the broom was once again visible on the top of the foremast.

It was as if someone had flipped a switch. A chill went up my back as the wind suddenly died, the rain stopped, The sun poked out through the clouds and a bright rainbow stood between the Golden Gate Bridge and us. The others all looked stunned at this sudden meteorological turn of events.

"I guess that answers your doubts about the dumb broom, eh, Paul," I yelled to Pezwick, who was on the dock

Needless to say, the dumb broom stayed tied to the foremast after that.

Our fund-raising activities in San Francisco gave us the money to reach Los Angeles, where Dan Haggerty, a.k.a. Grizzly Adams, took me off to a New Year's Eve party in Malibu. I rubbed shoulders with Gary Busey, Mick Fleetwood, Eddie Van Halen, and assorted other celebrities while working the floor for support and donations.

We spent a total of two weeks in L.A. soliciting donations of cash, food, and equipment. From the U.S. Department of Agriculture we were able to obtain eight forty-five-gallon drums of various flavours of pie filling.

"We'll never be able to eat all that," said our cook, Marion Stein.

First mate Cliff, her boyfriend and a firefighter by profession, had a brilliant idea. "We can hook up these barrels with a hose feeding into a water monitor," he explained, "and create a pie-throwing cannon."

I immediately recognized the merit of his suggestion. The pie-filling idea could be used to repel unwelcome boarding parties, and at the same time contained an important element of humour.

"Let's do it," I said. And thus the Sea Shepherd acquired her first pie cannons.

It took only two weeks to top off our fuel tanks. We stopped briefly off Laguna Beach to attend a party hosted by Dick Dale, a.k.a. Mr. Surf Guitar, where we met artists Robert Wyland and George Sumner, both famous for their marine life images. Wyland painted a baby seal face on our funnel and George Sumner gave us a donation of one of his incredible whale paintings.

Finally, we headed southward toward the Panama Canal.

Cruising along the coast of Baja, Mexico, I decided one bright sunny day to stop the ship and let the crew go swimming. Carroll Vogel, Carol Bosch, and Paul

Pezwick took out the kayaks and met up with some local fishermen, who agreed to trade some fish and vegetables for a couple of buckets of lemon pie filling.

They were just giving the fishermen the last bucket of filling when an ominous-looking Mexican patrol boat hove into sight. I suddenly realized that I was only half a mile from shore and that we had not cleared Mexican customs or immigration.

The patrol boat pulled up alongside. The half dozen soldiers on deck, armed with automatic rifles, looked both mean and bored. The captain stepped out of his wheelhouse and addressed me in English.

"Captain, good afternoon, sir. Where are you coming from?"

Without even thinking, I responded, "Ensenada. We cleared customs there yesterday. Would you like to see the clearance papers?"

The Mexican officer smiled. "That won't be necessary." He spoke briefly in Spanish to another officer, then turned back and waved. "Have a nice holiday in Mexico, amigos."

With a great sigh of relief, I saw the patrol boat head back to land.

"Let's get the hell out of here," I told the crew, "before they discover that we were never in Ensenada."

Without further incident, we reached Panama, transited the Canal to the Caribbean and prepared for the 1,000-mile voyage on to Grenada. I left the ship in the command of Cliff Rogers and flew up to New York City to debate Jim Winters on the *Today Show*.

Winters, who had been part of the 1978 travelling road show to promote sealing, was a former CBC reporter who had quit radio to take a government position as public relations whore for the sealing industry. He had created this myth that he was a sealer forced out of work by the likes of me. I say "myth" because, first of all, if he was educated enough to be a CBC reporter, he didn't need to kill seals for a living; and, second, I did not know of a single case of us forcing sealers out of work. On the contrary, they seemed to be proliferating like flies.

Brian Gumble and Jane Pauley did not seem very impressed with Winters' defence of the seal slaughter. His obvious dislike for me did not help his case, and I scored some valuable points in the debate.

From New York, I flew to Grenada to rejoin my ship. The tiny island nation had just recently elected a socialist government. The plane landed in a small jungle airport where the décor was nouveau commie revolutionary, and the customs officer confiscated a copy of *Playboy* and *Time*, saying that both were forbidden. Grenada was a very strange communist country. The Queen of England was prominently displayed on stamps and currency, the country had a governor-general, and the Royal Bank of Canada was the dominant bank.

Communist or capitalist, however, it seems bureaucracies never change. When Bobby David and I went to the harbour master's office to see about discharging the cargo, I was confident that the authorities would not give us much trouble. After all, we came bearing gifts.

"Who is your agent here in Grenada?" asked the harbour master.

"We don't have an agent, our ship is registered as a yacht."

The harbour master looked annoyed and said, "All cargo vessels are required by regulations to have an agent."

Bobby David took over. He could see that I was about to lose my patience.

"We don't have cargo in a commercial sense, we have goods that have been donated to Grenada by Canadians sympathetic to your revolution. Your Minister of Agriculture is aware of these goods and has been waiting to receive them."

The harbour master was unimpressed. "The Minister of Agriculture is of little concern to me. I need to know how you will be paying the tonnage tax."

I jumped back in. "Tonnage tax! For chrissakes, we are bringing in materials that have been contributed to Grenada, and you want to tax us to unload this stuff?"

"That is correct, the regulations say you must pay tonnage tax."

I looked at Bobby and said, "If you think I'm going to pay money to this tight-assed bureaucrat to unload gifts for his people, you're mistaken."

"Someone must pay it or the cargo cannot be discharged," mumbled the harbour master.

"Look," I said angrily, "we are going back to the ship and we will wait one hour. If I am not given a place to discharge, and if the tonnage tax is not waived, I intend to unload the entire cargo right in the middle of the harbour. So you get on that phone and call the minister, or the prime minister, for all I care, but I want that damn cargo off my ship."

An hour later, we got a message from the harbour master to bring our ship into the dock for immediate discharge of our cargo.

After that, the authorities gave us a grudging welcome. The local media and the people were much more appreciative and friendly and we stayed a week to rest up before heading north. At the time, Ronald Reagan was claiming that the Cubans were taking over Grenada. We did see a couple of Cubans, but they were supervising construction projects.

Six months later, the U.S. invaded the tiny island. All of my suspicions about the unreliability of the mass media were confirmed when I later saw the network television coverage of the "Grenada Crisis."

According to the networks and the White House, the Cubans were building a secret MIG fighter base on the island. Warehouses were stockpiled with weapons and Cuban soldiers were terrorizing the citizens, especially the 800 Americans who attended the medical school there.

We saw none of that. In fact, some of us had hiked over to where the supposed fighter base was being built, and the workers there were friendly and made no attempt to restrict our access. They told us this would be a new airport, and by the looks of the one where I had landed, they needed it.

We did pull off our own military raid, though, while we were there.

Our task was a hostage-saving mission and our target the St. George's Zoo, a deplorable place. During a tour, we had noticed that the monkeys were being severely mistreated. After giving some American medical students Canadian beer in exchange for sedatives, four of our crew went over the zoo wall in the dead of the night and picked the locks of the monkey cages.

That part was simple compared to drugging the inmates. I was monitoring the radios on board ship in the harbour when the sound of screaming monkeys shattered the quiet night. As the crew managed to inject each little primate ingrate, the cacophony died down, scream by scream. Miraculously, no one in the community, including the zoo security guards, had noticed a thing.

The sleeping monkeys were then loaded into a rented car and driven into the jungle, where they blinked and staggered their way into the greenery. The rescue mission was a complete success.

We left the island quickly, before the monkey caper could come back to haunt us. From sunny Grenada, we sailed due north to the snow and ice of Portland on the Maine coast.

Portland, though a fishing town, was no friend to the Canadian sealers, and we received a ton of donated food and quite a few cash donations there. We were also able to recruit some new crew. One of the women who joined us was a very attractive artist named Josephine Mussomeli, whose contacts in Portland proved very useful in helping us get ready on time for departure. This time, with this campaign, I planned to push the envelope harder. We would not go to the Gulf of St. Lawrence this year. Our destination was the Labrador Front, but first we would go to St. John's, straight to the heart of the sealers. There we would blockade the fleet and prevent them from leaving port.

It was an outrageous, suicidal, foolish, ambitious, arrogant, and wonderful plan, and I felt that although we were risking injury, death, imprisonment, and the loss of another ship, something had to be done to urge this long-running protest forward.

Although Brian Davies was making progress in Europe, and more and more people were becoming aware of Canada's dirty little secret, we were getting impatient to stop the killing.

13

Trial by Ice!

(1983)

Yesterday I didn't know what an environmental
extremist was. Now I is one.

—Josephine Mussomeli

T he morning was frigid, the wind blustery as the *Sea Shepherd II*
approached the harbour entrance to the port of St. John's,
Newfoundland. The mouth of the harbour, known as the Narrows,
emerged from out of the murky fog. As the mist ascended, the
dark, cold bluffs of Signal Hill loomed up before us.

To onlookers on the hill, the *Sea Shepherd II* presented an ominous sight.
Stark black, with a baby seal's face emblazoned on the funnel, her gunwales
wrapped in coiled barbed wire, water cannons plainly visible, she looked
indeed like a dark avenger set upon the defence of the ice pups.

Everything was in position now. Volunteer Scott Trimingham, who had
come from California at his own expense to be our spy, was on shore and had
radioed us from his rented car. His job was to act as our eyes and ears inside
the Narrows and monitor the port for ship movements. His code name would
be "Orca."

As we hove in sight of the Narrows, the Coast Guard contacted us immediately.

160

"*Sea Shepherd*, this is the Canadian Coast Guard base in St. John's. Will you be entering the harbour, Captain?"

"Negative," I replied. "We will be staying outside of the harbour."

After a short pause, the voice on the radio crackled again.

"What are your intentions, sir?"

This was the moment that I would officially announce our game plan, and I knew that the government of Canada would react as if I had declared war.

The CBC camera crew on board our ship signalled that they were in position to film.

"Our intentions are to physically prevent any sealing ships from leaving the harbour of St. John's."

"How do you intend to do that, Captain?"

Lifting the microphone to my lips and looking directly at the camera, I spoke clearly and deliberately.

"If we are forced to ram them to stop them, we will do so."

After a long pause, the voice on the radio spoke. "Captain, we will get back to you soon."

Smiling, I answered, "*Sea Shepherd II* standing by."

After the CBC crew went below, I turned to second mate Marc Busch. "Well, that should start the fireworks."

"You aren't serious about ramming them, are you?"

"No, we won't ram them, but the fact that we may ram them should be sufficient to deter them. They know we have rammed a ship. They know we have sunk whalers. They'll have no problem believing that we mean what we say, even if in this case we don't. It's a case of using a bluff as a tactic."

"So you think they'll take us seriously?"

"I think they will. We have a reputation and they have embellished it to portray us as big, mean, violent, terrorist types."

Josephine was standing by the wheel. "But isn't this lying?" she asked. "We say we will ram them, but we don't have any intention of ramming them."

"True, we are indeed lying. However, it's a tactical lie. Sun Tzu, in his book *The Art of War*, wrote that deception is the strategy of tactical paradox and that all confrontation is based on deception."

Josephine frowned. "But it's still a lie."

"I don't think it is actually a lie if the deception is the primary weapon being utilized. The more important question is, are we deceiving the public over basic truths about the seals and the seal hunt? I don't think we are. The truth of our political and moral position is intact. We're simply being deceptive tactically in this game of confrontation. In this we're no different than any army general in the world, and the world calls that strategy."

"So!" Josephine said. "You mean that the end justifies the means?"

"Well," I laughed, "if the end does not justify the means, what does?"

A few hours later, the marine operator was lining up interviews for us from around the world.

At the same time, meetings were being held by various government departments and enforcement agencies. Words like "crisis" and "situation" were tossed around.

Unbeknownst to me at the time, officials at those meetings discussed sending military commandos to blow the propeller off my ship. This plan got the green light until I made a statement on the local radio station that convinced them to call it off.[1]

VOCM radio had asked what I would do if the government mounted an attack on my ship.

"If they do that, I will immediately scuttle this vessel inside the Narrows."

The prospect of the *Sea Shepherd II* sunk in the Narrows, noted the St. John's *Evening Telegram*, could threaten the jobs of some 4,000 people who depended upon unrestricted commerce into and out of the port. Blocking the harbour for weeks or even months would be an economic disaster. The *Telegram* cited the case of the motor vessel *Bill Crosbie*, a cargo vessel that had rolled onto its side in the east end of the harbour a few years previously. It took a year to clear the wreck, at a cost of $1.5 million.

My threat to scuttle my ship was not a bluff. If forced to choose between armed and violent seizure by the government and scuttling, I would, without hesitation, have carried out the threat.

The Canadian government had not dealt with anyone like us before. We were being outrageously unCanadian. It was not polite to blockade the port and threaten to ram ships, and they could not tell when I was bluffing and when I was not. They knew what I was capable of, and they were convinced that I was crazy, which worked in our favour. They also knew that we had no fear of being arrested or of losing our ship. An opponent without fear is a dangerous opponent, one who cannot be expected to capitulate or compromise.

So, in typical Canadian fashion, they continued to hold meetings and strike interdepartmental committees to brainstorm possible scenarios and solutions.

Federal Justice Minister Mark MacGuigan[2] tried to pass the buck to Newfoundland by suggesting that the Attorney General there could have our ship arrested, while in the House of Commons, Newfoundland MP James McGrath screamed for "justice."

Port manager David Fox took us seriously. He labelled us a "questionable ship" and informed me that I would have to post a million-dollar bond before we entered his harbour. I laughed and told him that I had no intention of entering his port any further than the Narrows.

A few days later, I had to call him up and advise him that we would be entering the port after all.

"You will have to post a million-dollar bond."

"Don't have it," I calmly replied.

"You won't be allowed to enter," he countered.

"Too late, Mr. Fox, I'm already in."

I owed my entry to the CBC. This is what happened.

In Ottawa, Fisheries Minister Pierre De Bane had announced to the Commons that having a CBC crew on board the *Sea Shepherd II* was "totally insensitive and outrageous." He claimed the national broadcaster had no right reporting on a group of protesters whose objectives were counter to the government's and that by so doing, CBC had insulted Newfoundland's seal hunters.

In his attempt to discredit us, De Bane decided to go whole hog and ignore facts. Before the national media, he made this incredible pronouncement:

I hope the CBC will listen to the unanimous point of view of the House and stop giving publicity to a group of people who collect money from the general public to wine and dine and then threaten to ram into the boats of sealers while actually they manage to collide on the first ice and then spend their money on booze or drinks to attract the media.[3]

Listening to De Bane sputter, Marc Busch asked what the difference was between booze and drinks? Cliff Rogers wanted to know where all the booze was being kept, because he sure as hell hadn't gotten any. Pezwick was wondering whom De Bane thought we had collided with on the ice.

On the ship, Bill Donovan, director of the CBC crew, was furious. "Our job is to report the story and you are the story and we are doing our job in covering your side of the issue. We sure as hell cover the government's side of the story."

Yet CBC president Pierre Juneau buckled under. He agreed to yield to the minister's demand and ordered the CBC crew to depart from the *Sea Shepherd II*.

I was not going to be accused of holding the CBC crew against their will. We agreed to have them disembark.

At first, the CBC was going to have a hired boat come outside the Narrows to get them, but they couldn't find a vessel capable of getting through the heavy ice to reach us.

I nixed the suggestion to have the Coast Guard bring their boat alongside. I would cooperate with the CBC's wishes, but I would not allow them to be a Trojan horse for the government.

I radioed the CBC onshore and asked them to bring a pilot boat to the inside of the Narrows. I would then transfer the CBC crew over. Any attempt to smuggle a Mountie onto my ship, I warned them, would result in my immediately scuttling the vessel.

Before anyone in the port knew we were on our way, the *Sea Shepherd* was inside the Narrows. The small pilot boat chugged up alongside. It was in fact carrying an RCMP officer who was doing a poor job of disguising himself as a a pilot, but I would not let him board. When he tried anyway, he found himself looking down the barrel of a pie cannon.

"This gun is loaded for bear with cold chocolate pudding, sir," said Nyles Bauer, who was manning the gun. "I'd advise you not to step any closer."

Apparently fearful of being slimed with chocolate syrup, the Mountie retreated down the ladder, followed by the CBC crew. Then I put the engines full ahead, steamed into the harbour and performed a circular turn before steaming back out of the Narrows.

A fisherman's voice crackled over the VHF.

"I neverrr t'ought I'd see da day that Newfoundland would be brought to its knees by the likes of thees, no sir."

As hundreds of people lined the observation walls on Signal Hill to watch, we emerged from the Narrows and headed seaward. In front of us was a large pan of ice. I struck it at full speed and split it down the middle, our black prow plowing through the white floe without slowing us down. It was an impressive sight.

Back in Ottawa, New Democratic Party member Mark Rose protested that De Bane's decision was "an outright and gross interference in the network's right to report the news," and touched off a small media frenzy. Other media investigated the CBC, and the CBC even investigated itself.

This did not prevent John Power, the director of CBC for Newfoundland, from apologizing to the sealers, which he did on March 13 in a column in the St. John's *Daily News*, for the network's attempts to cover the other side of the story. Power ended his piece by announcing that the CBC would air a special on Captain Abraham Kean the following week. It was to be part of a series called *Yesterday's Heroes*.

On the evening of March 14, we decided to retreat from the harbour entrance. A strong northeastern wind was picking up and the weather reports said that it would be pushing the ice pack hard up on the shores of the Avalon Peninsula.

Turning around and steaming eastward, we quickly discovered that the Coast Guard had dispatched a ship to pursue us, probably assuming we were heading to the Front and the seals.

Fourteen miles from shore, the ice locked up solid and we were held fast. Two miles west of us, the Coast Guard icebreaker also became a prisoner of the ice. It was a worrying situation. The pressure of the ice had actually lifted the 657-ton *Sea Shepherd II* out of the water, and the entire weight of the ship was resting on the tightly packed floe. With the decks inclined at a twenty-degree angle, it was difficult to sleep or even have a decent meal. If the pressure kept up, the ice would literally push both our ships onto the rugged rocks of the shoreline. It is a curious thing how the winds and ice can still conspire to move a ship shoreward through ice that is locked hard against the coastline. Trapped as we were, we would have to go where the ice took us. At the present rate, we estimated that the Coast Guard ship would be on the rocks within a day and we would follow a day or so later.

Luck was with us and the pressure on the ice let up when we were two miles off the coast. The Coast Guard was sweating more than us, for they were only a half a mile off when their ship was released from the icy grip. Freed from the ice, we picked our way through the treacherous floes back to the harbour entrance of St. John's.

On Sunday, March 20, as we settled in for another night on blockade duty, radio VOCM announced that some guy named Howie Hamilton had come up with a plan to bomb the *Sea Shepherd II* with a ton of chicken shit. We laughed uproariously.

"Damn but that's brilliant," chuckled Ben White, the helmsman. "That sounds like one of our tactics."

Howie was vowing to end our blockade. "Those bastards," he said, "are making fools of us. It's got to stop."

The next morning, I called the Mounties to advise them of the threat from the vigilante dung bomber and to ask them what they intended to do about it.

"What do you expect us to do?" said the voice of the officer on the radio.

"It's not legal for a Canadian aircraft to drop any material on a ship, or on people, for that matter. There is a potential for injury here, and as responsible custodians of the law, you should be enforcing the law."

"Why should we?" said the voice. "You have no respect for the law, now, do you?"

I laughed. "Actually I do, contrary to your preconceived notions about me. However, that's irrelevant. You are a police officer and duty sworn to uphold the law. I am not."

The Mountie snickered, "You don't seem to like it when the tide turns and your opposition uses your own tactics against you. Then you come crying to us to save your ass—"

"You don't seem to understand," I interrupted. "I'm not calling you to protect our ass. I'm calling you to protect Howie Hamilton's ass. If he attacks us, we will be forced to defend ourselves, and then someone could indeed be hurt."

The officer interjected angrily, "If you hurt anyone, you will be subject to the law."

"Not if it's self-defence."

The officer cut me off. "You'll be getting no protection from us, Watson."

"The fact is," I replied, "it is now official that we reported a possibility of an attack on our ship and you refused to intervene. Therefore, we will take whatever measures needed to protect ourselves. Have a nice day, Dudley Do-Right."

I then called the radio station and informed them of our intention to defend ourselves from Howie's planned chicken-shit assault. "I wish he were working for us," I added. "Great tactic—hilarious, to the point, media savvy, and possibly effective—but he won't do it."

"Oh," sneered the newsman, "why not?"

"Because he's chickenshit," I said, and hung up.

Howie's initiative certainly revealed the hypocrisy of the government. On the one hand, they were condemning my tactics as violent and illegal and on the other hand they were supporting similar tactics by the pro-sealers. MP George Baker not only supported the chicken-dung raid, he offered to approach the government to provide a water bomber to deliver the payload.

The next morning, a helicopter approached the ship. It was not a government craft, so I assumed it was Howie and his chicken shit.

We were ready for him. During the night, I had ordered all our old expired parachute flares broken out. Armed with four each, the crew were dispersed around the ship. Other volunteers deployed four line-throwing rocket guns, fore and aft, and port and starboard on the bridge deck.

Just to let the pilot know what those little white batons were that the crew were holding, I fired one flare away from the helicopter.

The pilot's eyes widened. He turned and began to argue with a guy we assumed must be Howie. A few moments later, the helicopter, with Howie and his payload of chicken shit, turned and headed back to the beach. The crew cheered and booed Howie on his way. We had successfully repelled the great chicken-shit counteroffensive measure.

We probably could have kept the blockade going for another week, but a call from "Orca," our undercover agent in St. John's, made us change our strategy.

Apparently the sealers *Chester* and *Techno Venture* were in the Gulf of St. Lawrence and had already started to kill seals. We decided to abandon the blockade at nightfall and make haste to the ice floes of the Gulf of St. Lawrence.

As darkness approached, I turned on all the running lights and headed directly north. The observers on the hill would surely notice that we were heading out. We crashed through the floes for some five miles before I ordered the running lights shut down and deadlights closed on all the ports. The *Sea Shepherd II* disappeared, her black hull merging into the inky ebony of the night.

We were bound for the Gulf.

The next morning greeted us with a dense fog that suited our purposes grandly. No overflight would detect us that morning. We were travelling at a respectable fourteen knots and the frigid, ice-free water was an elixir to Behemoth, our main engine.

Still cloaked in a protective mantle of fog, we passed the French islands of St. Pierre and Miquelon and headed into the Cabot Strait, back into the thickening ice floes.

Incredibly, a report from the CBC informed us that the *Sea Shepherd II* continued to lurk outside of St. John's Harbour with the intention of ramming any sealing ship that attempted to leave. The sealers remained in the harbour.

As night fell, we continued to bash through the ice, keeping a watch on the bow to look for seal pups. Stephen Best of IFAW had radioed a position for the sealing ships, and we were making remarkable progress toward them through the ice.

Around midnight, we picked up Norwegian voices from the sealer *Chester*, talking to the ship's owner in Halifax. The *Chester* reported a kill of

1,000 seals for the day and a total of 3,000 since they had begun the slaughter. What excited us, however, was the tone of the voices. They had no idea we were so close.

By 0300 hours, we were into the seals. I stopped the ship's engines for fear of running down the hundreds of fluffy white balls around us. Two miles away, we could just barely make out a sealing ship.

At dawn, we began to slowly advance on the *Chester*.

"*Chester, Chester*, this is the *Sea Shepherd II*."

After a few long moments of silence, they responded.

"*Sea Shepherd*, this is the *Chester*. What do you want?"

I knew that I had to be very careful with my words.

"*Chester*, Captain, it's a great day, I think . . . to go into port in the Magdalen Islands and buy your crew some drinks."

The captain, who had not yet dispatched any sealers onto the ice, did not answer. We saw his engines start up, then the sealing ship slowly began to move away in the direction of the Magdalens. We followed her for about fifteen miles.

The *Chester* never stopped in her full retreat. I turned the *Sea Shepherd II* around and went back to the seals.

This time, it was just us and the animals. An eerie quiet descended, and then we could hear the yelps, cries, and gurgles of the seal pups and the louder, barking responses of their mothers.

I moved the ship into an ice floe and rammed it hard enough to wedge us into it nice and tight.

"All right, boys and girls, you are free to visit the seals for an hour or so."

For the first time in weeks, I felt good. Really good. We had cleared the area of the sealing ships. We had stopped the killing and brought a calming peace to the ice floe nursery.

I stepped off the ship. The sun was warm and pools of fresh water were forming on the white-blue ice. Little bundles of white fur with black noses and watery black eyes cried out as I passed by them. I stopped and petted one of the little guys and to my surprise found that the white hairs of his coat were very loose. Looking closer, I noticed that most of the short white hairs were detached from the skin and were being held in place by the thickness of the new, emerging, grey-black coat underneath. This fella was a little bigger then the others and probably a few days older; he seemed to be molting prematurely. This discovery was the genesis for my idea to practically utilize the molting seal hair as a cruelty-free non-lethal form of sealing that we would promote ten years later.

When I returned to the ship an hour later, I took note of this in my log. I was in the chartroom when Cliff Rogers yelled, "Chopper!"

The crew quickly returned to the ship and were on board by the time the helicopter—a red and white machine from the Canadian Coast Guard—hovered overhead. Then, without any radio contact with us, it turned and flew off.

We had a peaceful evening. The engine crew hosted a birthday party for my father, who was turning fifty-five. Outside, the moonshine radiated over the ghostly ice, accenting the shadows of ice ridges. The seals were all around us, and their soft yelping reminded us that these cold, forbidding ice fields were very much alive.

About midnight, I decided to get some rest. I was deep asleep when the bridge siren sounded. Within seconds, I was in the wheelhouse.

All I could see at first was a blinding light. Slowly I began to make out the outline of a huge bow smashing through the ice like an angry hammer. The bow belonged to a Canadian Coast Guard vessel, a Goliath of a ship. To our horror, she headed for a small patch of seals. I was stunned to see her run them down, crushing a dozen pups as the poor creatures scrambled frantically to get out of the way. I saw one little baby reach safety, only to have a large chunk of flat ice, lifted up by the plunging bow, flip and drop directly upon its fragile body.

The big ship came straight on to us to about 200 feet and then turned to display her 300-foot length. Her name, illuminated in lights above her wheelhouse, was the *Sir John A. Macdonald*, named for the first prime minister of Canada. Macdonald—the man who crushed the Métis and Indian rebellion.

After tearing up the ice in a circle around us, the ship retreated into the darkness. She had not radioed us. She just wanted to let us know that she was there and that the government was now watching our every move.

The morning sun rose to reveal that we were still alone. We discovered from Steve Best of the IFAW in Prince Edward Island that the *Techno Venture* had also left the ice when they heard we were there.

Unfortunately, the peace was not to last. A few hours later, two helicopters chockful of Mounties swooped in low and circled us, then roared away.

The government was mobilizing. The *Johnny Mac* returned, this time escorting the nervous captain of the *Chester*. The helicopters swarmed in for a second attack.

Ben White came running in to yell that a Mountie was preparing to rappel down a rope to our aft deck. I grabbed for the VHF mike.

"This is the *Sea Shepherd* to the helicopter above us. As soon as that officer's foot touches my deck, this ship will be scuttled."

The response was instantaneous. The helicopter veered away.

"Quick, get some ropes," I told Ben, "and construct a netting over that back deck before they return. My threat won't stall them for long."

"Why did they retreat when you threatened to scuttle the boat?" asked Marc.

"It's the bureaucratic mindset. Introduce a factor that they haven't already been briefed on and they'll retreat to get updated orders. No one wants to accept responsibility unless the OK comes from higher up."

Sure enough, the choppers returned, only to confront a new factor, a hastily constructed barrier against a helicopter rappel assault.

"The trick to fending off bureaucrats, Marc, is to constantly inject new tactics and to anticipate what they might do in advance."

"So what's next?"

"If I was in charge, I would bring in the large ship to intimidate us and demand that we surrender. We will of course pretend that we did not hear their message."

And of course that was what they did, except, to impress us all the more, the *Johnny Mac* hit the ice floe beside us at full speed. Beneath the onslaught of that massive bow, the ice shattered and exploded.

Unluckily for the Coast Guard, they wedged themselves in too tight and found themselves held in the vise-like grip of the floe. As the big ship geared into full reverse to pull free, I signalled the telegraph to full speed ahead. We dashed out behind the *Johnny Mac* and made a beeline to the *Chester* a mile beyond.

I could see that the *Chester* had her men spread across the ice, busily clubbing seal pups. Behind us, the *Johnny Mac* was struggling in frustration to break free, but there was absolutely no way she would catch up with us before we caught up to the *Chester*.

"*Chester, Chester*, this is the *Sea Shepherd*. Captain, get your men off the ice. I'm going to ram that floe and I intend to break it in half."

The radio crackled as the captain of the *Chester* replied.

"*Sea Shepherd*, we have the legal right to kill these seals. You have no authority over us, you—"

"*Chester*, this is the *Sea Shepherd*. I have 657 tons of authority under me, being driven by 1,400 horsepower with an ice-strengthened bow. I would advise you to recall those men."

Suddenly, the radio belched out the voice of the commanding officer on the *Johnny Mac*.

"*Sea Shepherd*, you are under arrest. Stop your ship immediately."

I ignored the order and kept on course toward the sealers. I could see the Coast Guard approaching rapidly on my tail.

"Marc, turn on the speakers and let's play some Wagner."

The speakers began to thunder out the apocalyptic strains of "The Ride of the Valkyries." The black-clad sealers looked toward our ship and that monster of a red hull behind us, both coming at them at top speed. They began to run, some of them dropping their seal clubs onto the ice.

They were scurrying up the sides of the *Chester* just as I swung the wheel hard to port. Behind me, the *Sir John A. Macdonald*, because of her superior size and speed, could not turn as quickly. She slammed hard into the floe, splitting it 500 metres across and conveniently separating the crew of the *Chester* from their innocent prey.

With the *Johnny Mac* stuck in the ice again, we moved off toward two small vessels that Ben had spied working their way through the leads.

They were longliners out of the Magdalens, and as we came closer, we could see their men on the ice bashing the skulls of seal pups. As soon as I could read her name on the bow, I called the first vessel.

"*Sadie Charles, Sadie Charles*, this is the seal conservation and protection ship *Sea Shepherd*. Please call your men from the ice and return to the Magdalens."

There was a long silence. Suddenly, an angry voice blasted back, "Fuck you!" followed by a steady stream of indignant French.

Bernard Carlais, a francophone crew member from France, picked up the microphone and ordered the ship, in French, to stop sealing.

"They told me to go to hell and to get out of here or they would beat the shit out of all of us."

Ben was at the helm. I telegraphed the engine room for full speed ahead. "Ben, we are going to pass them at full speed. Make sure you keep that boat at least twenty feet off our starboard side as we go by."

I pulled the airhorn and the sound blasted out. The sealers stopped their killing and looked at us in surprise. Ice pans crashing in front of us, we broke into the open lead and sped toward the *Sadie Charles*.

I walked out onto the starboard bridge wing and watched as our bow wave grew. The sealing boat was midships of me when our bow wave struck, lifting the wooden-hulled craft high and slamming it hard against the ice pack. I could see the angry faces of her crew as they all scrambled knee-deep in scarlet gore. Some 300 seal pelts lay piled, fur side down, on that deck and blood ran in rivulets from the scuppers into the ebony sea. The sealers on the ice dropped their clubs and began running back to protect their boat as it rocked and rolled in our turbulent wake.

"That was perfect, Ben," I said, "absolutely perfect."

As our ship headed down the open lead, Bernard radioed the *Sadie Charles* again and ordered them to leave the area.

The response was a stream of Gallic cursing that went on for two solid minutes. "They said to fuck you," Bernard translated.

I ordered the *Sea Shepherd II* turned about. "Full speed ahead. Ben, this time, make it ten feet."

Accompanied by the ominous strains of Wagner, the *Sea Shepherd II* charged forward.

Marc Busch stood by the radar, humming along with the music. Ben concentrated on keeping the wheel on course. This time, I went out on the port wing and watched the *Sadie Charles* looming closer. A dozen sealers, their little yellow seal button licences pinned to their woollen toques, looked up at us in horror. It must have been a sight. My ship is scary enough just standing still: black and powerful, jagged anti-boarding stakes on her bow, her sides draped with barbed wire, a surging white tsunami bow wave pushing ahead through the inky water, looking like huge white teeth set in the jaws of a black hole.

A mere six feet from the sealing boat, the *Sea Shepherd II* pounced on her prey. Our tremendous bow wave literally picked up the sixty-five footer and tossed it onto the ice floe, jarring the teeth and bones of every crew member on board her. As the boat hit the ice sheet, the ice cracked and broke, dropping the wooden hull through the gap and back into the water, where she rolled and bucked in the chaotic surge. The sealers on the ice were knocked down like tenpins and sent sprawling. After struggling to their feet, they had to run to avoid the growing cracks that chased them across the ice floes.

After making sure that no one had been knocked into the water, I stopped the engines and made to turn about.

This time, not even bothering to retrieve their clubs, the sealers returned to the boat. The *Sadie Charles* and her companion, the *Marie Hélène*, began to move out of the nursery floes toward the Magdalens.

"Well, boys and girls," I said, "I think it's time we split this party. Those boys in red are angry." The *Johnny Mac* was on us again.

As we headed for the Cabot Strait, the *Johnny Mac* followed in close pursuit. I ignored the captain's orders to stop. We assumed we could make it back to the open Atlantic and escape arrest. What we did not know was that another Coast Guard ship, the *Sir William Alexander*, was on its way, carrying more Mounties and Fisheries officers, and that the Canadian Navy warship *Nipegon* had been mobilized and was also approaching.

Unfortunately, the weather was not our friend. The northern wind grew stronger, the temperature plummeted, and the pressure of the pack ice increased dramatically. The *Johnny Mac* stayed glued to our tail, moving without any apparent difficulty through the ice.

As night fell, we found ourselves in an open space of water that was rapidly shrinking as the ice moved in. The *Johnny Mac* held back and watched in amusement as we slowly became entrapped in the congealing ice.

We were so close—only another thirty miles and we would be around Cape North and into the Cabot Strait. But the weather report sounded like a death sentence: extreme pressure from the north wind, ice hard on the shore of Cape Breton. Within hours, we would be locked in tight. There was no escape now and we knew it.

When the *Sir William Alexander* arrived around 2000 hours, there was nothing left to do but wait for the inevitable.

Or was there? Ben White came to me with a cockamamie scheme. "Why don't we," he said, "walk out of here?"

"What do you mean?"

"Well, we know that the government will take the ship in the morning. We also know that they promised in 1979 to kill you if you returned. I suggest that you and I, because it's my dumb idea, and two engineers walk to shore. If we arrive before dawn, we can hide out and travel by night. They will most likely take the ship to Sydney. The idea will be get to Sydney, get on board the ship, fire up the engines and make a getaway to Maine."

I looked at him. Maybe it was a dumb idea, but it was better than no idea at all. Besides, we'd always been good at attempting the impossible.

Carroll Vogel and Cliff Rogers thought we were crazy. Paul Pezwick, however, was up for it, and Bernard Carlais was eager.

I turned the command over to Cliff Rogers. At midnight, with the wind howling and the snow blowing, the four of us draped our orange Mustang suits in white sheets and stepped on the ice. We each carried poles and a small pack with a canteen of water, a thermos of hot chocolate, some chocolate bars, some extra wool socks, a compass, and a small map.

We kept the sheets wrapped until we were too far away enough to be seen by the crews of the Coast Guard ships. Under pressure from the north wind, the ice was hard pack, and we had the lighthouse at Cheticamp to guide us. If we could do two and a half to three miles an hour, we could make it to shore in four to five and a half hours. Once on shore, we would find a place to hide out until evening.

For the first two hours, we made excellent time. And then the wind began to die down and the ice pack began to groan and grind.

"This ain't good, boys," I said. "The pressure is letting up."

We hurried, but to no avail. The pack was moving, actually moving, off the land and up the coast toward the Cabot Strait.

I was the first to fall through the ice. As I stood watching Paul and Ben probe a lead for a footing, the ice beneath me gave way and I plunged chest-deep into thick slush. Chilled to the bone, I clawed my way back onto the pan as another pan moved quickly behind me, threatening to crush me.

When the two pans collided, the bottom of the pursuing pan rode up and over my pan, and three tons of ice came crashing down almost on top of me. My pan cracked and began to split into three pieces. Stumbling across the heaving ice and using my pole as a vault, I cleared four feet of lead to land on a more stable pan beyond.

The other three were having similar problems. Over the next six hours, all of us were immersed numerous times as we inched our way toward the coast. We were no longer thinking escape. Survival was uppermost on our minds now.

As the sun rose, we were devastated to discover the ice breaking up into smaller and smaller pans all around us. Our friends the seals would tease us by popping their heads out of the water to watch our progress. How we envied them their waterproof, freeze-proof bodies!

At one point, we found ourselves in the middle of thousands of churning clumps of ice, each apparently drifting in a different direction, and barely any of them capable of supporting our weight. It was each man for himself, jumping from one chunk of ice to another. We would land, the piece of ice would begin to sink or tip, and we would be forced to jump to another. It took quick thinking and quick reflexes, but it is remarkable how quickly the senses evolve when faced with imminent mortal danger.

Meanwhile, back on the ship, the pressure had eased and the *Sea Shepherd II* was under way again. She did not get very far. The Mounties had launched their assault. The *Sir William Alexander* rammed her starboard stern and fired tear gas and smoke grenades across the deck while her water cannons poured tons of water down our funnel. Cliff Rogers tried to manoeuvre away from the cannons, but the *Sir John A. Macdonald*, rifle-toting Mounties lining her rails, slammed into our ship from the port side.

After ripping away our barbed wire with a special device they'd rigged up, the Coast Guard then dropped boarding platforms into place, allowing unrestricted access to Mounties sporting tear gas masks, flak jackets, and helmets and carrying heavy ordnance, including special cutting tools.

The bridge doors flew open and the Mounties threw Cliff, Jet, and Josephine to the ground and aimed their rifles at them.

Carroll Vogel and his engine room crew had barricaded the engine room, but the Mounties cut through a quarter-inch steel bulkhead and quickly took them prisoners.

In less than ten minutes, all sixteen crew were handcuffed and brought out to the deck, despite some of them being dressed in short-sleeved shirts or coveralls. The police made them stand in the cold for over an hour as they began to search for me and my three companions.

Our absence completely baffled them. They tore open the water hatches and ripped up the engine room deck plates; they searched the anchor locker and every closet on the ship trying to uncover our hiding place.

They crew weren't talking. Their punishment was to be kept outside until some of them began to shiver and their lips turned blue.

The mystery was solved when a report from the Mounted Police headquarters in Cheticamp informed the boarding party that four figures could be seen a mile out on the ice moving toward the shore.

The boarding party, many of whom were from Newfoundland, received this news with visible disappointment. They transported our crew over to the *Alexander* and loaded them into the unheated cargo hold for the trip to Sydney.

Out on the ice, still struggling to reach terra firma, the four of us were oblivious to all these developments. We could see the shore clearly now, and the dozens of cars and spectators lining the bluff. Among the vehicles, we spotted two blue Blazers belonging to the RCMP.

"Ah shit," said Pezwick. "It's the pigs."

Laughing, I said, "Let me do the talking—I'll tell them we're glaciology students or something."

"Yeah, like they'll believe that," said Ben dryly.

We struggled on, hopping from floes to pans to unstable chunks until we reached the shore-fast ice. Defeated, we climbed the bluff and walked over to the crowd.

The people were great. They had hot chocolate and oatmeal cookies for us, and greeted us like long-lost cousins.

A Mountie walked over. Before he could say a thing, I shook his hand and said, "Hi, officer, we're glaciology students from Harvard, out studying the drift of floes. Our helicopter lost sight of us and we were forced to walk ashore."

The Mountie actually looked confused for a second. "Oh, but I think you're all from that ship out there," he finally declared.

"What ship?" said Pezwick. "I don't see any ship out there."

"The *Sea Shepherd*, the seal protection ship. Well, we'll take you down to the station and check your IDs. But as for you, Watson, I think we can safely say we know who you are."

I smiled. "Oh well, it was worth a try."

The Mounties laughed, we laughed and got into the Blazers.

The officer driving looked back and said, "I can see it now in the headlines. Watson walks on water to save seals." Ben remarked, "That isn't far off from the truth."

At the station, the jailer wheeled a television set into our cell so we could see our crewmates paraded down the gangplank of the *Sir William Alexander*.

Our ship was under tow to Charlottetown, in Prince Edward Island.

"Look, Ben," I said, "even if we had made it to Sydney, the ship wouldn't have been there. But it was a good idea anyway."

"No it wasn't. It was a very dumb idea, in fact the dumbest idea I've ever had."

I laughed. "You're right. It was a dumb idea, but damn it, it was like climbing Everest or going over Niagara Falls in a barrel. We walked across more than thirteen miles of chaotic ice floes and survived. Now, that was worth doing."

"Perhaps you're right and it's a story worth telling my grandkids." Ben yawned. We were exhausted; all we wanted to do was sleep. Every muscle in my body ached.

Suddenly, the door to the hallway of the lock-up flew open and two Fisheries officers stormed in, screaming, swearing, and threatening to lynch us. One of them actually tried to grab me through the bars.

"What the hell is your problem?" I yelled.

"You son of a bitch, you stinking asshole, I'll have your balls, you shithead!"

"If you can't behave like a civilized person," shouted one of the Mounties, "then get the hell of here!"

The two fish cops were escorted out of the hallway. The Mountie smiled at us. "Sorry about that," he said. "Some people are born assholes."

Bernard looked up from his pillow. "Those guys really take this personally."

I shrugged. "That's what you get when you work for the government and don't have much of a life. See you in the morning, boys."

The Québec Inquisition

(1983–1984)

Truth fears no trial.

—Thomas Fuller, *Gnomologica*

The morning after the day of our arrest, we awoke to a hearty breakfast in the Cheticamp jail before being escorted to two police cars. After a scenic drive up the Cabot Trail to Sydney, we joined the rest of our crew in the local jail.

The crew were in excellent spirits.

That afternoon, we were taken to the courthouse to appear before a federal Crown prosecutor and a judge. There we discovered that although the entire crew had been arrested and jailed, the only person charged had been me. The others, we were informed, were being "detained."

The prosecutor informed me that I had violated Canada's Seal Protection Act by approaching within half a nautical mile of a seal hunt. He said that the Mounties had also charged me with extortion, conspiracy, intimidation, and resisting arrest.

He then surprised us by saying that there was insufficient evidence to prosecute, and the charges against me were dismissed.

Our elation was short-lived. Apparently the Mounties were furious that all the money and energy they had spent pursuing us had been for naught. We were informed within an hour of the charges being dismissed that instead of being released, we would be turned over to the custody of the Royal Canadian Mounted Police for transportation to the province of Québec, where the charges would be prosecuted by a Québec judge.

Additionally, John Crosbie, the federal Minister of Justice, had been quoted in the Newfoundland press as saying that he would personally see that our scalps were taken for interfering with the great and holy Newfoundland tradition of sealing. John Crosbie of the Crosbie sealing family could certainly not be considered an impartial justice when it came to deciding our fate.

That evening, all twenty of us were taken from the holding cells at Sydney and driven to the airport. There we were handcuffed to Mounties boarding a flight to Percé.

The Mounties were very annoyed that we laughed and joked during the flight and told us that we should be taking our situation more seriously. Saralee James, the eldest member of my crew, looked at the officer in charge and said, "You people really should lighten up, it's not like we robbed a bank or killed anyone." Saralee was from Vancouver and came on board to do a photographic project on *Sea Shepherd*. She was not very happy that all of her film had been confiscated.

I joked with Pezwick that we might get a friendlier judge this time. I mean, what were the odds that we would draw the same bastard of a judge the second time around? But then I thought to myself, "This is bloody Canada."

From the Percé airport, we were driven by bus to the jail. The jail is usually closed during the winter, but it was opened just for us. The guards were actually happy to see us—they were all smiles, and very friendly.

It was to be our home for the next fourteen days. We had to find lawyers, then wait four days for an arraignment and for bail to be set because we had been booked the day before Good Friday and the Easter weekend.

On Monday, the Québec prosecutor brought us before a woman judge, Madame Jeanne-Roch Roy. Both Pezwick and I felt a great weight fall from our shoulders.

"Thank God, maybe we can have a fair trial this time," Pezwick said, although things had not gotten off to a promising start: Unlike the rest of the crew, I was forced to enter the courtroom with my hands cuffed and my feet shackled. Our lawyer, a Mr. Gilles Gaul from the nearby town of Chandler, accused the police of attempting to prejudice the judge by making me appear a desperate criminal.

We were formally charged with two counts of conspiracy to commit mischief, two counts of conspiracy to commit extortion, three counts of intimidation, one count of mischief, one count of conspiracy to disobey the Seal Protection Act, and one count of disobeying the Seal Protection Act by approaching closer than a half a nautical mile of a seal without the permission of the Minister of Fisheries. I was additionally charged with the dangerous operation of a vessel.

The Crown said the combined charges would put me and Pezwick in prison for the rest of our lives and that was where we belonged to protect the public safety.

I swear that justice in Canada was designed by fans of Kafka. It was hard to believe these people could take themselves so seriously.

The judge set my bail at $10,000 and each of the crew were given a bond of $3,000 except for Paul Pezwick, who, because he was a second offender, received bail set at $7,000.

In addition to the monetary conditions, Judge Roy ordered us to leave eastern Canada and not to return until June 13, 1983, unless called to court. We were ordered to not talk about or publicize our case, and we were not to protest, demonstrate, speak out against or write articles opposed to the seal hunt.

The Crown attempted to appeal the decision, stating that all bails should be raised considerably and that Paul Pezwick and I should be denied bail because we were second offenders and incapable of rehabilitation.

The judge asked me if I would I still express opposition to the seal hunt if I were released.

"Of course, your Honour."

"As you can see, your Honour," said the Crown prosecutor, "he displays absolutely no remorse."

The judge, however, let the original bail conditions stand, much to the disappointment of the Crown, who then set the trial date for the month of June. If we could not raise the bail, in cash, we would not be allowed to leave the jail until then. In the meantime, the judge ordered my ship to be moved to Halifax to be held as evidence.

A sum of $71,000 dollars in bail was an incredibly high amount for the Sea Shepherd organization. We simply did not have that kind of money, let alone the funds to hire a lawyer.

In Vancouver, Starlet Lum immediately began to solicit support for us. People from all over North America offered to put up funds to bail us out. Mike Farrell, one of the stars of *M*A*S*H*, covered my bond. Saralee's son bailed out his mom. Some people, like Jet Johnson, covered their own bail.

Starlet also arranged for Hébert and Picard in Montreal to represent us. She had originally located the first lawyer by contacting another firm in Montreal, both of whom shall remain nameless, but after the bail hearing, we decided to change representation. The problem was that the firm charged us $15,000 for the lawyer to appear at the bail hearing and then the lawyer charged us another $15,000. Later, this matter ended up in a lawsuit when I objected to being double billed. To challenge this, I had to hire a third lawyer in Vancouver, who advised me that we would win the case on the double billing but it would cost about $20,000 to do so.

The two weeks in the Percé jail were actually quite pleasant. A friendlier bunch of prison guards I have never seen or heard of. The women were put on one side, the guys on the other, but we were quite spread out over the three-floor facility because we were all allowed to choose our own cells. Except for me—I was given a "special" cell. It didn't look any different, but as Roger, one of the guards, explained, "We thought you should have the celebrity cell."

"So who was the celebrity here before?" I asked.

"Well, there were two of them. One was a very famous bank robber who was killed not long ago in a shootout with police in Paris. The other was Paul Rose."

Rose, a Québec nationalist and member of the Front de Libération de Québec, had been convicted of the kidnapping and murder of a prominent Québec politician in 1971, and it only goes to prove that one man's terrorist is another man's freedom fighter. These guards had nothing but praise for Rose and seemed to be quite proud that he had been jailed in their facility.

Within a few days, we were running the place. The guards opened the cells and we could walk the halls. I was able to use the phones and watch television in the prison office.

One afternoon, the phone rang. I answered it.

"Hello, Percé jail."

"May I speak with Paul Watson?"

"You're speaking to him."

There was a pause on the other end. "I am calling the Percé jail, am I not?"

"Yes, and I am Paul Watson."

Bewildered, the *Los Angeles Times* reporter asked how I could be answering the phone.

"Oh well, the guard on duty stepped out to the men's room."

"So, Paul, how is the jail there?"

Half-mockingly, I said, "It's brutal, the food stinks, the beds are hard, the place is freezing, and the guards are pretty tough."

"It couldn't be all that bad if you're able to talk on the phone," he said.

I laughed. "That's just it, you'd think I could get away from talking to reporters for a few days, but I suppose they had to punish me somehow."

Then I went on to expound on the real crime, the ongoing slaughter on the ice and how the seal hunt was making criminals of decent people just because they were opposing a bloody, cruel hunt.

After I hung up, there was a loud knocking on the door. I got up and opened it to let in one of our crew, Peter Hartley. He had been across the street having a beer at the pub.

The guards didn't bother keeping the front door locked. We wouldn't try to escape, they reasoned, because Percé was at the tip of the Gaspé Peninsula and on a lonely single road 100 miles from the nearest town.

The only times, in fact, that we were hustled into our cells was when the jailers were informed that RCMP officers would be arriving to interrogate us. The Mounties would find us sitting in our cells, looking appropriately miserable. Once they left, however, the cells were opened and we had the run of the place again. Finally, one by one, we raised our bail and after two weeks found ourselves free again. Once out of jail, though, we were stuck in Percé. There was no public transportation in or out of the town.

Leaving the rest of the crew in a pleasant *auberge* outside Gaspé, Ben White and I drove a rental car down to New York. A friend there had offered to lend us a van to transport the crew out of Québec. I also needed to do a couple of network shows out of New York City, and consult with Cleveland Amory. The rental agency told us that we could not leave the province and that it would cost ten cents per mile. We assured them that we would drive to Québec City and back. Instead we crossed into New Brunswick and over the border for the long trip to the Big Apple. Carroll Vogel disconnected the odometer and we just had to judge our speed for the 2,000-mile return trip.

Back in Percé, we loaded up the van and headed south to drop off crew in Portland and Boston before returning to New York.

In June, we all had to make the trek back to the Gaspé and it turned out to be a major expedition to get us there. I started out with Marc Busch and Bernard Carlais in a long Ram van. From Vancouver we drove down to Seattle to pick up

Carroll Vogel, Bob Kerns, Lori Sorenson, and John Miller. Then we went on to Portland, Oregon, to pick up Carroll Bosch, over to Idaho to get Cliff Rogers and Marion Stein, across to Boston to pick up Paul Pezwick, and up to Portland, Maine, to collect Josephine Mussomeli. By the time we pulled into Percé a week later, we had twelve people crammed into the van.

The others made their way on their own—Ben White up from Virginia, Bill Bruinn from New York, my father, Tony, from Toronto, Miles Goldstick from Sweden, and Jet Johnson from San Francisco.

We found rooms at the local motels and settled down to prepare for our trial. The little town was filling up with government witnesses, reporters, lawyers, and our supporters, and the atmosphere was almost festive. We made a point of visiting our friendly guards, and Jet and I even got invited to dinner with some of them.

We had two good lawyers this time, Jean-Claude Hébert and Francois Picard from Montreal, but the trial was going to be another French-language-only fiasco for us.

Our spirits were further dampened when we discovered that our judge was not to be Madame Roy. Instead, sitting there on the bench, with the look of a toad suffering from hemorrhoids, was the dreaded Judge Yvon Mercier himself.

Our first move was to try to have the judge disqualify himself on account of personal bias because I had written disparaging things about his character in my book *Sea Shepherd*.

The judge refused, citing that the passage in question did not bother him and would not affect his judgment. He would try the case, he said, sounding very defensive, impartially and without prejudice.

His attitude during the rest of the trial, in the opinion of the crew and our lawyers, was one of blatant hostility to our side. He actually interrupted a couple of my crew and me and accused us of lying on the stand when we said that we had seen whitecoats being taken and that we had seen cruelty. He then dismissed both observations as irrelevant to the charges.

Since he had refused to allow us to have a jury trial, the outcome was predictable from the first day this legal circus began.

I discussed a strategy with our lawyers, and we agreed that if Mercier was going to be hostile to us, we would then be hostile to him, with the hope that he would overreact when it came time for sentencing and give us grounds for appeal.

So we became very uncooperative, answering questions as briefly as possible and using mostly "yes," "no," or "I can't recall." Ignoring his order not to speak with the media, we blasted the judge to the press, and at lunch, in the only restaurant in town, we made jokes about him in his hearing. We were quite convinced that we were pissing him off.

After ten days, the trial ended and Pezwick and I were ordered to return to Québec City on December 20, 1983. The crew all departed and I returned to Vancouver.

It looked like a ship campaign for 1984 would be out of the question unless we could get the *Sea Shepherd* back out in January. I wanted to think there was still a possibility.

But it was not to be.

In December, Paul and I went back to Québec City for our appearance before Judge Mercier. Walking into the courthouse, I asked the receptionist for the number of Mercier's courtroom. He grunted without looking up from reading his copy of *Le Devoir*.

"Excuse me, please," I repeated, "could you tell me which room Judge Yvon Mercier is in?"

Looking up in disgust, he said, *"Je ne parle pas anglais,"* and resumed his reading.

Patiently, I inquired again. *"Excusez moi, monsieur. Quelle salle pour Juge Mercier?"*

Without taking his eyes from his paper, he muttered, *"Ne parle pas anglais."*

Pezwick looked at me and said, "How in hell are we going to find out where to go if this guy can't speak English and doesn't understand your French?"

"Oh, he understands all right. My mistake was in being polite. I was just using the wrong approach." I raised my voice and said, "Hey asshole, I'm talking to you, what room is Mercier in?"

"Two-oh-five."

"Thanks or *merci* or whatever." In room 205, we took our seat and waited for our lawyer. Jean-Claude Hébert was looking hopeful. "I can't see him giving you anything more than a small fine," he said.

Mercier came in and spoke with Hébert for a few moments before ordering Paul and me to stand up.

I could tell from the tone and a few of the words I picked up that Mercier was reading his decision. I remember thinking how strange it was to be a citizen on trial without the right to an interpreter. I thought I made out the words *"quinze mois"*—fifteen months. My heart sank. Surely I could not have heard that right. For an hour and a half, the judge read in French while Paul and I stood, wondering what the hell he was being so long-winded about.

Suddenly, Mercier stood up and turned to leave the bench. Paul and I looked at each other. The judge did not look at us as he made haste to exit.

I shouted across the room. "Hey, Judge Mercier!"

The judge turned, a smile beginning to appear on his face. "You bastard," I thought. He was so eager to nail me on a contempt charge. I could read it in his face.

Before he could say anything, I smiled. "Merry Christmas, your Honour," I said.

Mercier's face turned red and he stormed out angrily.

Four court officers swiftly escorted Paul and me through a side door and into a holding cell. Half an hour later, Hébert entered the cell.

"You almost got some extra time for shouting at the judge like that," he said.

"I was only wishing him a Merry Christmas," I said, all innocence.

"Well," Hébert remarked, "it was really the only thing you could have said to avoid a contempt charge."

"Yeah, can you imagine getting sentenced for contempt for saying Merry Christmas? Even Canada would have a hard time justifying that. So," I continued, "what's the verdict?"

"Not good."

My sentence was indeed fifteen months for conspiracy to obstruct the seal hunt, plus an extra six months for mischief. In addition, I was fined $5,000 and the *Sea Shepherd II* was ordered confiscated. Paul was given three months in jail and a $1,000 fine. The rest of my crew were all fined $3,000 for three violations of the Seal Protection Act.

It was clear now too that Mercier had scheduled our trial for December 20 on purpose because he knew that we would appeal and that the Christmas holidays would make it impossible for us to be granted release on appeal until after the holidays. This guaranteed Paul and me a nine-day stay in Orsainville prison during the festivities.

It was tough being in prison over Christmas. My daughter, born to Starlet in 1980, was only two and a half years old, and Mercier had chosen to separate us for the holidays for no other reason than it pleased him to do it.

But we knew that to take a stand to defend non-humans is to court reprisals from the anthropocentric forces of the status quo. We were not about to let such reprisals dampen our resolve to protect the seals.

I spent Christmas Day 1983 writing letters. One of the letters was published in the St. John's *Evening Telegram* on January 14, 1984:

To the Sealers of Newfoundland,

I am writing to you from my cell in Orsainville prison near Québec City. I am sure that many of you are happy to hear of my fifteen month jail sentence, of my $5,000 fine, the loss of my ship and the fines against my crew totalling $64,000. Many of you will be glad to hear of my internment just prior to Christmas. I am sure it will be a source of enjoyment to know that my little daughter will not have her Daddy with her on the special day.

You probably think that I have been taught a needed lesson and that my punishment will serve to "rehabilitate" me.

If so, I am sorry to disappoint you. Dissent may be temporarily halted by internment, but only temporarily. It has been my lifelong objective to shut down the barbaric practices of whaling and sealing and this jail sentence is serving to renew my dedication towards th[at] end.

So you took my ship. This is not the first ship that I have lost, nor will it be the last. The public outrage at my internment will enable me to raise the needed funds to obtain another. Wars are not won without cost and I am fully prepared to pay the cost to defeat the seal hunt.

It matters very little how many battles are lost if, in the final outcome, the war is won.

The tactics of the Sea Shepherd Conservation Society will now change. We will now focus our attention on economic targets.

Our energies will be directed at the boycott of fish products from Newfoundland and towards discouraging tourism to Newfoundland. This is a campaign that I can direct in prison.

Feel free to gloat over the fact that the courts have handed you a minor victory. History will be my judge, and history will absolve me and condemn thee.

I will never rest until this bloody blight, this clubbing of defenseless creatures, is ended forever. Jail will not deter me.

In reality, the victory was ours. Paul and I were released on December 29. We were told that as a condition for our release we could not enter the Atlantic provinces for three years and that we were not to correspond, speak with, or discuss any subject with any journalist, anywhere in the world, for three years and we were not allowed to speak with any person about the seal hunt for three years.

I arrived back in Vancouver on New Year's Eve to be greeted by my daughter and her mother, Starlet, and dozens of media people. As you can see I was infuriated and my comments were full of rhetoric.

"I've been ordered not to speak with any reporters on any subject for three years," I told them. "However, I believe in freedom of speech and I don't believe that any judge or any politician has the right to deprive any citizen of the freedom to express themselves and the freedom to speak out against injustice. The seal hunt is a wasteful, cruel, barbaric burden to the taxpayers of this nation. Judge Mercier did his political duty in sentencing me, but he did not exercise justice, nor did he appear to have much respect for the law. Justice Minister John Crosbie said he wanted our scalps and Mercier delivered upon that request. If Mercier wants to throw me back in jail for speaking my mind, well, he can do so. I do not intend to keep quiet and I do not intend to stop fighting the barbarism of sealing in Canada."

The Truce

(1984–1994)

There is no rest on planetary duty.

—Captain Al "Jet" Johnson

N ew Year's Day 1984 marked a new era for me. I had just been released from a Québec prison pending an appeal of my conviction for saving seals. Although I was confident that I would eventually win my legal battles, it was frustrating to not have possession of my ship. It was, however, gratifying to see that the Canadian media, usually subservient to the government, were responding to the harsh sentence I'd been given. The January 11, 1984, editorial in the *Globe and Mail* said it best.

> Canada's annual seal hunt still has the capacity to arouse intense emotions . . . . [H]ere at home, we are accustomed to the rhetorical excesses and drastic actions of those who traditionally rely for income on the hunt and those who feel compelled to bring it to an end.
>
> Few of the excesses, however, could match that of the court which recently called Paul Watson to account for attempting to block the 1983 east coast hunt. Mr. Watson, a Vancouver environmentalist charged with

conspiring to obstruct the hunt and causing mischief, was sentenced to fifteen months in jail and fined $5,000. The ship he sailed to the hunt, the *Sea Shepherd II*, was ordered confiscated.

We do not doubt that in areas where criticism of the hunt is most strongly resented and where there is deep irritation with attempts to disrupt it, there will be a feeling of satisfaction that Québec Provincial Court Judge Yvon Mercier threw the book at Mr. Watson and stung his supporters by confiscation of their ship. Where the issues of the hunt seem a little less clear-cut and the emotions more low key, however, the severity of the sentence will be less easily understood.

New Democratic Party MP Ian Waddell has raised with Justice Minister Mark MacGuigan the matter of what he called an "unduly harsh" sentence—though it seems more likely that an appeal court judge will be the first to assess the fairness of the sentence.

There may not be too many seagoing misdemeanors with which to make comparison, but one might consider the episode last spring in which eight Nova Scotia fishermen were involved in chasing fisheries officers from two patrol boats, which they then towed out to sea and burned. The eight were given suspended sentences and ordered to perform community service.

The seal hunt did not end in 1984. It had merely been struck a severe economic blow. The ban on harp seal pelts in the United States in 1972 had not hit the sealers hard, because the demand had never been great there anyway. The ban on imports of harp seal pelts into Europe was another story. Europe represented the lion's share of the market.

The big ships had been effectively, albeit temporarily, stopped. The landsmen's hunt, however, continued.

The violence continued too. An IFAW helicopter that set down in the Magdalen Islands to refuel en route to observing the seal herds was violently attacked by sealers. As members of the Québec Provincial Police and the RCMP looked on, the sealers tore down the security fence at the airport and assaulted the machine with clubs, bottles, and chains. One of the crewmembers, Dan Morast, was told that the IFAW people would be allowed to fly out on a chartered plane on condition that they turn film of the killing of whitecoats over to the sealers, who had been telling the media they were no longer killing whitecoats.

Despite what amounted to a hostage-taking and the write-off of a very expensive helicopter, the police refused to charge any of the sealers. A sealer named Langford had organized the assault. "We had to wake up the world," he said. "No one is going to tell us we can't club seals."

The airport manager, Daniel Paiemont, defended the police. "The police play hockey and baseball with these guys," he noted.

Sergeant Jules Perreault of the Québec Provincial Police added, "It's like a big happy family here."

Dan Morast retreated from the island, leaving his badly damaged chopper on the tarmac. "Law and order do not exist on the Magdalen Islands," he said.[1]

Despite the violence and the continued killing of whitecoats, it was widely reported on television and echoed in the newspapers that the hunt was over. Greenpeace declared a victory. The landsmen's hunt was swept under the carpet and ignored. No one in North America wanted to hear about it, and without my ship, which remained impounded, I could not return to oppose it.

Sea Shepherd did, however, manage to publicize in the European press the kill of 60,000 seals in 1983. And instead of going to the ice in the spring of 1984, the Shepherd turned the tables on the authorities by championing the cause of the wolf. Since I'd been banned for three years from the Atlantic provinces, I decided I'd simply turn to raising hell in the west by opposing the British Columbian government's wolf extermination project in the Peace River valley.

The wolves were being killed in a remote location, hundreds of miles from any town or road. The conditions were frigid and the terrain treacherous. Not much different from the seal hunt. The reason for the kill was vague. It was called a wolf control program, but the objective was 100 percent extermination. We found out later that the North American Wild Sheep Foundation had been lobbying for the kill. B.C. Environment Minister Tony Brummett was a member of the same foundation and had received a substantial campaign contribution from them.

February and March 1984 saw me leading a coordinated land and air assault on the government aerial wolf campaign. We mobilized a crew, an airplane, and a helicopter, then headed into the bush on snowshoes to confront rednecks at a town meeting. In the process, we succeeded in making the wolf issue an international media event, and Project Wolf evolved into Friends of the Wolf.

I went back into the bush in the spring of 1985 though I knew when I took on the project that I could not let myself get distracted from protecting marine wildlife—not because I cared for marine animals more than any other species, but because to be successful we had to focus our energies rather than spread ourselves too thin.

But I also felt personally obligated to enter the fray on the wolf issue. Back in 1973, as recognition of my services as a medic for the American Indian

Movement during the battle at Wounded Knee, the Oglala Lakota Nation had given me the warrior name of Grey Wolf Clear Water. Ever since, the wolf had been my totem animal.

Ironically, it had been the spirit of the wolf that guided and protected the shepherd. I owed the wolves, and it was gratifying to return the favour.

In the end, I was very satisfied with the wolf campaign. My crew, notably David Garrick and the three women I called my wolf girls, took command. Myra Finkelstein, Susanna Rodriguez-Pastor, and Renée Grandi took the British Columbian government to court in 1987 and won a restraining order. That, coupled with their skydiving into the subarctic bush in the winter to directly protect the wolves, brought the aerial shooting to a halt.

It took me two years to recover my confiscated ship from the Department of Fisheries and Oceans. It took until 1987 to win my appeals on the convictions from the trial of 1983, which were overturned on a technicality. Because the federal prosecutor had charged me in Nova Scotia and then dropped the charges, the Québec Court of Appeal ruled that the province of Québec could not charge me under federal regulations after the feds had refused to do so. Paul Pezwick's sentence they simply dropped without explanation.

The ironic thing was that the government spent millions and pulled out all the stops to get me, including going after my whole crew. In the end, I was acquitted on all charges. It took me another ten years to successfully sue the federal government for damages to my ship. Actually, the suit never went to court. On the Friday preceding the scheduled Monday court date, my lawyer received a call from the government attorney with an offer of $50,000. The money wasn't half as gratifying as the satisfaction of seeing the Department of Fisheries and Oceans hand me the cheque.

I was learning that the might of a government could be overcome by a combination of patience, stubbornness, and a never-say-die attitude, but it was the seal hunt that I really wanted to beat, and that remained a formidable, if not impossible, task. I knew one thing for certain, though—I would oppose the killing of the seals until my dying day.

In 1984 and 1985, the Canadian government set up a royal commission to investigate the seal hunt. From the very beginning, I did not have much confidence in it. I suspected it was just another group of government appointees who would give a report heavily favoured as the government position.

I delivered my testimony before the royal commission on February 4, 1985, in Vancouver.

The executive director of the commission, Gilles Poirier, had set the terms of reference for all briefs submitted. The terms of reference addressed included the effect of seal populations on fish, the transmission of parasites, the economic and regulatory costs, trade in seal products, management, etc. I started by pointing out that all the subjects to be addressed were of relevance *to the fishing industry and the interests of the Department of Fisheries, and that none addressed issues relevant to conservation or animal welfare interests.*

After reviewing the population history of seals, which I have already covered in this book, I took the government to task on the issue of the impact of the hunt on the fisheries. I was especially proud of this inclusion because my position was vindicated twelve years later by the government's own scientists when the myth of the cod-destroying seals was finally laid to rest.

I told the commission:

Those who support the theory that seals are destroying the fish are only exposing their ignorance of ecological systems. The reasoning that less seals will result in more fish or that more seals will deplete existing fish populations is an unscientific belief because it is a belief not backed by observation or data.

Seals are an essential element in maintaining a state of ecological stability.

The ocean is a complex, living environment that has evolved since the beginning of the planet. In our present state of evolution, the natural world we live in has found a key role for marine mammals in marine habitats. The issue of harp seals cannot be separated from the issue of the long-term future health of the oceans.

The seal slaughter is a contributing factor to the overall ecological crisis now taking place. Other major factors directly damaging the marine environment are destruction of spawning areas; over-fishing by commercial trawlers, especially vessels of foreign registry; waste dumping of oil, chemicals, and sewage; and the slaughter of other marine mammals such as whales and dolphins. The synergistic, or combined, effects of all these different sources of ecological disruption are having a catastrophic impact.

The life that thrives in the oceans has a critical influence on the overall health of the ocean system. The great herds of seals are a life force whose influence on the health of the ocean can be recognized once the complexities of the food chain are investigated and understood.

When harp seals eat in herds, they return massive amounts of nutrients in the form of fecal material, which feeds the plankton, which feed the fish, which in turn feed the seals. The removal of this nutrient base would be critical to the health of plankton and fish populations.

The migrating seal herds, and other marine mammals, move nutrient wealth in a way no other force can: in giant north-south loops and from great depths to the surface. By going through regular periods of gorging and feasting, seals provide large amounts of nutrients at key times of the year. The combination of the seal-supplied nutrients in the area where the Labrador Current meets the Gulf Stream of Mexico is responsible for the great fish grounds of the Grand Banks. Reference to the logs of Captain Jacques Cartier, Samuel de Champlain, and John Cabot illustrate that at the time of the greatest number of seals prior to European exploitation, the fish were so abundant that Cabot described the Grand Banks as "so swarming with fish that they could be taken but in baskets let down with a stone."

I could tell that the commissioners were not in the mood for a history or biology lesson, but I continued nonetheless.

Plankton, the smallest animals in the ocean, require organic matter and sunlight to grow. Once the sun reaches a high enough point in the sky in the northern latitudes so that sufficient sunlight is available to the plankton, the seals arrive and begin to eat and defecate, releasing the needed supply of nutrients. Plankton cannot eat fish, but they can consume fecal material as it is broken down into nutrients. The plankton then provides for krill and up the food chain through the fish and back to the seal.

The commission had already been briefed on the fact that harp seals do not even eat in the Gulf or along the coast of Newfoundland during the pupping and breeding season. They had also been presented with evidence that harp seals were not large consumers of cod but that they did eat fish species that preyed upon young cod. But of course this was not information that they had been organized to hear. They had obviously reached a conclusion prior to beginning the inquiry and they seemed to only want to hear data that would support that foregone conclusion.

Despite this, I completed my brief.

An analogy that helps to understand the role of the seal herds in the
ocean is that of trees in a forest. A healthy forest can be viewed as being
dependent on a healthy soil. The soil is made up of minerals that come
from rock, and organic material from trees. Without the rocks or the
trees, there would be no soil and no forest. The impact of clear-cuts is
well known. Once the trees are taken away, a desert is left behind. In a
similar manner, taking seals out of the ocean environment takes away
an important source of organic material to the plankton, and thus leaves
a relatively sterile environment behind.

To suggest that seals threaten the ocean is to suggest that trees
threaten the forest.

I then went on to recount our experiences on the ice, including the cruelty
we had witnessed and our mistreatment by the police and fisheries officers. I
also expressed my concern that the government was not very objective in dealing with the issue.

During my testimony, Justice Albert Malouf interrupted me and ordered me
to withdraw comments I had made about two federal politicians. He also
ordered reporters not to repeat the allegations "in any newspaper, any journal,
any media in this country."

Despite that order, the *Globe and Mail,* I was quite gratified to see, referred
to the two politicians I named, in defiance of the judge.

The *Globe* wrote:

Mr. Watson had referred to John Crosbie's seconding of a motion in
Parliament in 1977 requesting that military action be used against
seal hunt protesters. He called Mr. Crosbie "a man without obvious
prejudice if one chooses to ignore that Mr. Crosbie's family fortune,
the money that gave him his élite private school education, was a fortune earned from exploiting both seals and sealers in Newfoundland."[2]

At the end of my testimony, the commission lauded me for proposing an
alternative industry based on tourism for the Gulf of St. Lawrence. Even though
IFAW had proposed this idea in the early seventies, they acted as if they had
never heard of it before.

Some of the leaders of the sealers were travelling across the country at tax-payers' expense to attend all the meetings as they convened in Canadian cities. I ran into Mark Small, president of the Canadian Sealers Association.

Because I had attended in uniform, Small commented as I walked by, "What gives you the right to wear that uniform, Watson?"

I turned and looked at him, wearing his sealskin jacket and sealskin hat.

"Mr. Small, I came to this commission hearing wearing my uniform because I am entitled to wear it as a master of a British-registered ship. I see that you have come attired in the clothing of a barbarian, yet I did not deem it necessary to insult your attire, that is until now, considering this rudeness was initiated by you."

Small did not know what to say in response, so I turned on my heels and walked away.

Mark Small was not very bright. In an interview with the *Vancouver Sun* right after the meeting, he said, "Sealing is part of our daily life. You take, for instance, a hangman," said Small. "He's got to do his job."[3]

I chuckled as I read the analogy.

The Royal Commission on Seals and Sealing was, in my opinion, nothing more than an expensive whitewashing of a barbarous industry. In the end, all that came out of it was a three-volume report telling the public that the hunt was humane, well-regulated, and economically practical. The commission actually reported that they had not heard any evidence of observed cruelty, in spite of lengthy testimony to the contrary by me and others.

The report did, however, bring up the concerns of the Inuit and attempted to portray anti-sealers as racists with no regard for Native culture. In fact, not one member of the anti-sealing movement had made a comment or criticism about Inuit sealing. We had focused on the Norwegian and Newfoundland hunts, and I was actually quite astounded at the audacity of Newfoundlanders crying crocodile tears for Native culture. Whereas I had actually put my life and freedom on the line in 1973 at Wounded Knee, I was now being labelled a racist by a people who had delivered the Final Solution to the indigenous Beothuks.

In fact, not all Inuit supported the hunt. Back in 1982, Arnaituk M. Tarkirk from Kuujjuak, in northern Québec, wrote this letter that was published in the March 27 edition of the *Ottawa Citizen*.

We have been hearing all about the European vote to ban the importation of seal products from the so-called seal hunt. I am an Inuk and I would like to say what I think about this.

Peter Ittinuar, Northwest Territory MP, has been saying that this vote will put a lot of Inuit on welfare. This is stupid. The money from the hunt goes to Norway mostly and it has nothing to do with the Inuit.

We are skillful hunters who hunt adult animals for food; that is not the same as bashing a pup, which can't move, over the head.

In fact, if the hunt were stopped, we would benefit most. There would be 180,000 more seals left for us to eat, when they are a few years older, and also people would not have such an aversion to sealskin products as they have after seeing the way they kill the pups, so craft work made with adult skins would be more popular.

The Hudson's Bay Company and the government are just using the Inuit to further their own purposes. I am surprised Peter Ittinuar, whom I know, could allow himself to be used like that. I know people who are against the seal hunt, and they are not against the Inuit.

I am an Inuk, and I oppose the seal hunt.

Tactically, though, the racism ploy was working. Being masters of media manipulation ourselves, we were not surprised at the deployment of this new spin. We merely marvelled at the fact that the sealers had learned so quickly from us.

To make matters worse, our side began to weaken.

By August 1985, Greenpeace was being run by bureaucrats who had not been a part of the original seal campaigns and they made an embarrassing announcement: They actually apologized for ending the hunt. First of all, this was an incredibly arrogant position. They assumed that Greenpeace, and Greenpeace alone, had stopped the commercial hunt, when in fact the primary credit belonged to IFAW and their work in Europe.

Greenpeace went on to explain that they had not realized that damaging the market for seal pelts would hurt the Inuit and Native American cultures.

Personally, I had no reason to apologize for what we had begun with Greenpeace. We had been very much aware that a ban on seal pelts could, and probably would, have an economic impact on the Inuit, both in Canada and in Greenland.

I believed then, as now, that consideration for the economics of a culture should not influence actions that protect species or alleviate suffering, and past chauvinistic practices should not be allowed to influence moral decisions in the present. The Inuit had absolutely no pre-Columbian historical cultural right to sell seal pelts to the Europeans. The Europeans drafted the Inuit and Native

Americans into this economic union and, by the same token, could take responsibility to end it. (Analogously, Africans could argue they have a cultural right to sell slaves to Europe, since Europeans recruited them into capturing and selling slaves to them in the first place.)

The killing of seals by the Inuit is a cultural right within Inuit society and no one had interfered with that right. The wholesale slaughter of a quarter of a million seals a year, however, had never been an Inuit practice. This was the obscenity that we opposed and continue to oppose. It was the Greenpeace apology that was not thought out, not our initial decision to protest the slaughter.

Fortunately, groups like IFAW, the Fund for Animals, and the International Wildlife Coalition did not back down when faced with cries of "cultural necessity." But in the spring of 1986, Greenpeace followed up on its apology when Vivia Boe of Greenpeace Seattle told Barbara Yaffe of the *Globe and Mail* that "Greenpeace has no problem with a 15,000-pelt subsistence hunt."[4] The kill was of course four times that number, but Greenpeace put on blinkers and only looked at the kill taken by the small co-op set up by the Canadian Sealers Association. What struck me as immoral was that Greenpeace, as the best-known opponent of the seal hunt, was raising the most money from people wanting to end it, yet had changed their policies to actually support the hunt.

The year 1986 saw a revolution at the Toronto Humane Society when my friend Victoria Miller was elected as president. Vicki was the founder and president of Ark II, an animal rights organization. The status quo was worried that Vicki would radicalize the Humane Society and would incorporate an animal rights objective. They were right. Vicki intended to do just that.

I met with the board of directors of the Toronto Humane Society to request funding for an icebreaker to patrol and protect seals. The new board was very sympathetic and it looked as if they would support this idea. I was to find out, though, as did Vicki and other board members, that being elected democratically to the government of a non-profit society does not necessarily mean you have control of the society. Nervous of the board's new radicalism, the *Toronto Sun* allied itself with the Ontario Humane Society, still run by our old enemy and seal-hunt defender Tom Hughes, the Canadian government, and the fur industry in a protracted effort to permanently tie the hands of all the THS board members.

It did not look like I would be able to replace my ship after all—at least not for the moment.

There is a truism about conservation work that victories are always temporary while defeats are generally permanent. Our so-called victory over the sealers was tested in 1987 with the announcement that the commercial offshore hunt would resume. Some animal rights groups flew to Halifax to protest.

The International Wildlife Coalition under Dan Morast took the lead. They had distributed 30,000 copies of a poster warning tourists not to go to Prince Edward Island for fear of being accidentally shot on the beaches by out-of-control seal hunters. Their strategy had the desired effect: Premier John Buchanan responded with a sputtering, angry retort that only served to publicize the hunt more.

Buchanan complained that the anti-sealing forces were fabricating facts and figures and distorting the truth. I agreed. The problem is that when the media are your conduits for educating the general public, you are forced to simplify, even if simplification sometimes results in exaggeration. Newspapers and television will not tolerate complex explanations that employ science, history, sociology, and statistical arguments. With the media there is one simple rule. KEEP IT SIMPLE, STUPID. Even more important, CREATE VISUALS.

The creation of visuals is not restricted to capturing images on camera. What you need is a visual image that captures the public's imagination, like spray-painting seals, for example. By creating a visual image of tourists wearing red caps and jackets on the beaches of Prince Edward Island, Dan Morast had done a similar thing. Never mind that very few tourists would be on those beaches in March or April—the absurdity of the image guaranteed that it would provoke a response. Premier Buchanan fell for it and the sealers fell for it. It was not a believable lie, it was a tactic—it's as simple as that.

By the same token, the government and the sealers used their own tactics. Equally absurdly, they conjured up an image in the public's mind of the seal hunt as a Native hunt and of Inuit starving because of the protests. The sealers used their own tactical deceptions, such as denying that Brigitte Bardot had ever really posed cheek-to-cheek with a seal because a seal was a wild animal and would tear your face off. On second thought, perhaps they actually believed this to be true, having restricted their relationship to seal pups to bashing them on the heads.

In 1987, they came up with another falsehood to use as a tactic. The government began to disseminate the tired old propaganda that the decline of the cod populations was the fault of the seals.

It was a brilliant tactic. The media reported it and people began to believe it. Hell, even the fishermen of the east coast began to believe it, and they of all people knew the truth. Over-fishing, not the seals, was wiping out the cod. In fact, a paper released by Fisheries and Oceans scientists that same year concurred, and stated quite clearly that "the harp seal does much of its heavy feeding in the Arctic, where it consumes crustacea and fishes of no commercial value."

> Whether or not a socially acceptable industry can be redeveloped remains in doubt. Thus concern has been widely expressed about the impact of an increasing herd on fishery interests. 1) Food capacity (consumption) of individuals has been inflated, although not generally by scientists, a number of whom inside and outside the department have addressed this aspect. 2) Food consumption levels, whether exaggerated or not, have been translated directly into commercial fish losses. In fact, the harp seal does much of its heavy feeding in the Arctic, where it consumes crustacea and fishes of no commercial value.[5]

This false accusation that the seals were responsible for destroying the fish began a debate that would last for another decade and prove to be very embarrassing to the Department of Fisheries and Oceans. In fact, it is this debate that I believe exposes the DFO for the hypocrites they are. Their accusations that conservationists distort facts pales in comparison to a government agency that deliberately distorts facts and nurtures a lie.

The difference is that conservationists do not use tactical deceptions that are long term, nor do they manipulate scientists to prop up their deceptions. Every deception utilized by anti-seal hunt forces that I am aware of—such as Dan Morast's poster or my own threat to ram sealers in 1983—was merely tactical.

But the one exception to these short-term tactics was the government's big lie—the seal as destroyer of the cod.

This was more than tactical. This was a protracted lie, and to make it work, the government of Canada intimidated its own scientists, stifled their reports, and misled the public. And since they spread the lie with the help of tax dollars, the government implicated the citizens of Canada in its lie.

I, and the members of Sea Shepherd, IFAW or IWC, have no obligation to the public. The sealers have no obligation to the public. The government, however, has a duty to the people to conduct itself with integrity and without deceit.

Instead, it began a systematic campaign against the seal. Newfoundland writer Calvin Coish was put to work writing articles that talked of "correcting nature's imbalance. This time the killing would be done humanely,"[6] and by 1990, the DFO lie that seals were destroying the cod had gone international. An article in the *Sunday Express* in Britain on January 7 started out by saying,

"More than a million seals are eating into the dwindling stocks of fish which provide a living for thousands of people in Nova Scotia" and went on to quote a fisherman, Fred Monroe, as saying, "Put the last seal in the world on the back of my boat and I'd happily cut its throat. People are more important than seals. Tell that to Greenpeace, because hundreds are going to starve here in Canso."[7]

All right, it was tactical. No one would believe that hundreds of people would be allowed to starve in Canso, although someone should have informed Mr. Monroe that, at the time, Greenpeace was on his side.

As the sealing industry struggled to regain its former stature on the east coast of Canada, I found myself embroiled in a controversy over sealing in my home province of British Columbia.

Fisheries Minister Tom Siddon had appeared on Jack Webster's talk show in the first week of January 1987. A sports fisherman called in and bragged that he shot seals on sight. Siddon should have pointed out that the man was breaking the law. Instead he said that he understood why the fishermen were killing seals, because the populations were out of control.

With one thoughtless comment, the federal Minister of Fisheries tossed out the rule of law, ignored science, and lowered himself to the level of the rabble. To make matters worse, the seals referred to were actually seal lions, although the fishermen were screaming for the heads of harbour seals too.

Urged on by Siddon's unofficial "seal" of approval, fishermen were buying ammunition and preparing for a massacre, and Bill Procopion of the United Fishermen and Allied Workers' Union called for a pet food industry using sea lions.[8]

A good many fishermen sobered up when I announced that we would sink any fishing boat involved in the illegal slaughter of sea lions.

"We'll be taking down the names of boats," I said on television. They knew what I meant.

Only two months before, my crew had scuttled half of Iceland's outlaw whaling fleet and destroyed the whale-processing plant in that country. The fishermen were well aware that we had sunk ships and did so quite effectively. They took my threat seriously.

The confusion and sheer incompetence of the Department of Fisheries and Oceans was apparent by the close of the decade following the last great protest in 1983. The eighties were the best years of the century for the seals, not counting the relative peace they enjoyed during the Second World War, when the sealers did not dare venture out for fear of the German submarine wolf packs.

Brian Tobin, the Newfoundland-born federal Minister of Fisheries and Oceans, told the *Ottawa Citizen* on July 8, 1994, that he would not consider a return to seal culling on the east coast despite fishermen's claims that the seals threaten Newfoundland's endangered northern cod. Evidence of the impact of seals in the destruction of cod was not clear, he said. "There is no doubt in my mind that man has been a far greater predator."

I remember reading that and saying, "Oh, oh, the bastard is going to start the seal hunt up again."

One of my crew read the story and said, "He says here that he won't."

"The last time I heard a Canadian Fisheries minister say he was going to ban the hunt was in 1975. A month later, Romeo LeBlanc raised the quota. Tobin probably believes what he's saying right now, but he's got ambitions to be prime minister. In a few days, he'll have the political feedback from Newfoundland and he'll reverse himself. In the long run, you can always count on a politician to sacrifice the truth if it threatens his political future."

But before Tobin reignited the seal hunt controversy, I was invited, in 1989, to Newfoundland to debate former Newfoundland premier Brian Peckford at Memorial University.

The best way to describe this debate is to picture Winston Churchill debating Adolph Hitler in Germany in 1941. The crowd of over 1,000 were not only opposed to me but were openly hostile in their vitriolic rantings from the floor. Mark Small was there, wearing his sealskin coat, and telling me to go back home to Russia.

"Mark," I said, "I don't speak Russian. But I have been there, and they are far more civilized than you, and certainly more intelligent."

I opened the debate by pointing out that I was not a foreigner, that I was a twelfth-generation Canadian and an eighth-generation Maritimer. I pointed out that my father had been born in New Brunswick, his father had been born in Prince Edward Island, and his father before him had been born in Nova Scotia.

Peckford responded, "So you're an eighth-generation Maritimer, are ye, Paul. Well, I'm a ninth-generation Newfoundlander, so how de ya like them apples, b'ye."

The crowd roared its approval.

I retorted, "Gee, Brian, I didn't think this was to be a pissing contest, I was just establishing that the opposition to the seal hunt is not foreign. The opposition originated in the Maritimes and is led by Maritimers like Brian Davies and myself."

Looking at the audience, I could see that the front row had been reserved for people with disabilities. Some were in wheelchairs, and some had the distinctive look of victims of Down Syndrome.

One of these people, a man with a speech impediment, stood up and read from a note.

"We're handicapped and we make products out of seal skin. Do you support what we're doing?"

So, I thought, they wanted to play dirty.

I looked the man in the eye and said, "Just because you are handicapped, this does not give you the right to benefit from the cruelty inflicted upon these seals. No, I do not support what you do."

The audience, as I expected, booed and hissed.

Peckford spent the debate making one predictable accusation after another. He accused Bardot of staging the famous photo of her and the seal in a studio. He accused us of killing seals ourselves for the films.

Since I knew that I was not going to win over any of the locals—after all, it was the home team's court—I decided to speak to the media.

"The only difference between the sealers of Newfoundland and the cocaine farmers of Colombia is that the peasants in Colombia need the money more. Sealskins are just as immoral as cocaine and sealers are trafficking in obscenity and cruelty."

That, of course, was the statement that made the national news, and that is the statement that I knew would make the national news.

16

Ice Shepherds

(1993–1997)

"Brian, as one pirate to another, what's the difference between
what I did on the Grand Banks and what you did?"

"The difference is, Paul, that I had the support of Parliament and you did not."

"Well tell me, Brian, how can Parliament give
you any authority beyond 200 miles?"

"It's a question of saving the fish, Paul, and sometimes you
have to be ahead of the law to make a difference."

"Brian, I was two years ahead of you doing the
same thing. So what's the difference?"

"There's a big difference and I won't waste any
more time debating this with you."

—Debate between Captain Paul Watson and
Fisheries Minister Brian Tobin for CTV, 1995

An amazing thing happened in the summer of 1993. I actually became a hero to the sealers.

I had purchased a ship in Halifax, a retired Canadian Coast Guard buoy tender called the *Thomas Carleton*. I renamed the vessel *Cleveland Amory* after my long-time friend and patron, the president of the Fund for Animals.

We had departed Halifax and headed to the Grand Banks, where I intended to evict foreign draggers from the Nose and the Tail, those two parts of the Banks outside the Canadian territorial limit.

Despite a small armada of Canadian government vessels intent on stopping me from stopping the foreign draggers, I was able to chase the Cuban fleet off

202

the Nose of the Banks. The Mounties, however, attacked and arrested me after we had begun the same eviction tactics against the Spanish.

I was taken on board a Canadian Coast Guard ship and held by the Mounties. They commandeered my ship, and the Canadian flotilla of Coast Guard and Fisheries Department ships took us under guard to St. John's.

I was flattered. All this money and effort to arrest little old me, and to prevent my crew and me from protecting the cod.

As the ship approached St. John's, I was helicoptered off the vessel and taken to the St. John's lock-up to await a court appearance.

I've always liked the St. John's slammer; it's a jail right out of the old school. Set in the basement of the courthouse, it resembles something out of *The Count of Monte Christo* with its dank, damp, stone-walled, dungeon-like appearance. I think a jail should have a romantic, medieval quality about it. It's hard to be inspired by stainless steel sinks and toilets.

It was a short stay. Farley Mowat, whose books had so inspired me as a child, now came to my aid and he posted the bail of $10,000. I was released after spending the weekend in jail.

The amazing thing was that during my weekend rest in the cell, a number of Newfoundland fishermen had been organized to demonstrate in front of the jail. These were the very same fishermen who had despised me for my years of opposing the seal hunt, yet this time they were carrying signs that said "Free Paul Watson" and demanding I be released and the charges against me dropped.

For championing the cod, I was now a hero. Upon release, I was invited to the Fishermen's Co-op in Petty Harbour for dinner and drinks. Newfoundlanders, it seems, despise "criminals" who protect seals but love "criminals" charged with protecting fish from foreigners.

Despite this support from the fishermen, Canada wanted to use me to set an example. Although I had not damaged any property nor caused any injury, I did intimidate the bandit fishermen, and for this Canada charged me with three counts of criminal mischief.

I took the opportunity of my new status in Newfoundland to try a different approach to saving seals.

During the autumn of 1993, I contacted the Department of Fisheries. In my dealings with them this time, I opted for cooperation and communication rather than confrontation. But, as I said to the media, "Things were much easier before. Attempting to work with the Canadian government is much more frustrating than our past efforts at confrontation."

I had a proposal for them. With this idea, people could still make money from seals, but they would not have to kill them. This idea complemented my previous suggestion, once dismissed as impractical, to promote tourism based on seal-watching. Nearly ten years after my presentation to the Royal Commission on Seals and Sealing, trips to see the baby seals now provided an economic boost to Prince Edward Island and the Magdalens.

I had even received encouragement for my proposal at the Fishermen's Co-op dinner. In return for our campaign against foreign draggers, some fishermen were willing to listen to new ideas. We were now temporary "allies," although I knew it would not last: Their interest was in protecting the fishery, and my interest was in protecting the fish. But in the meantime, perhaps we could agree on something that would benefit both the fishermen and the seals.

With Tobin rumbling about running for premier of Newfoundland, we knew we only had a window of a year or two to work with these fishermen. Once the seal hunt was opened up again, it would be full-scale war between us once more.

My idea was simple but revolutionary. I had met a woman who had spun the hair her Newfoundland dog shed and knitted it into a sweater, and I recalled the incident I'd noted in 1983 when I'd petted a molting seal pup. The white hair had been completely detached, yet remained anchored in the new glossy pelt beneath and would gradually fall out as the pup, known at that stage as a "raggedy jacket," rubbed against the ice. I wanted to collect the seal hair, have it spun into fibre, then use that fibre to make garments that could sell as high-end, cruelty-free products. Instead of sealskin coats, we could produce seal-hair sweaters.

In September 1993, I contacted the Department of Fisheries and Oceans. After two frustrating months of wading through its bureaucratic morass, I was finally given a name to contact.

On November 29, I wrote to director general Alphonse Cormier, the man in charge of Fisheries for the Gulf of St. Lawrence. I sent him a research proposal with a request for a research permit.

Two months later, on January 28, 1994, I received a letter from Cormier requesting additional information. I replied the same day and told him that we wanted to collect enough material to experiment with knitting a sweater or to produce felt. We also wanted to produce a sleeping bag using the hairs as an insulating material, because microscopic analysis of the seal pup hair I had collected revealed that the hair was not white, but transparent, and each individual hair follicle was hollow. These transparent, hollow hairs trapped and retained heat, creating, in effect, a solar-powered coat to keep the pups warm. On February 18, we were finally issued a permit, valid from March 12 to April 3, 1994, to brush seals.

I had to deliver a lecture at Brock University in St. Catharines, Ontario, on March 12, so our crew went ahead to the Magdalens, where they recruited two sealers from the English community on the islands to assist us in brushing the seals for ten dollars an hour. One sealer was reluctant but willing to do it for the money, while the other was very open-minded about the idea. The French sealers, by contrast, scoffed at the idea and said they wanted nothing to do with it.

Joining us was photojournalist Marc Cleriot, representing a German magazine called *Focus* and *L'Express* in France, and a television crew from Switzerland. I thought it ironic that the Canadian media were ignoring this novel story.

When I arrived on the thirteenth, the crew had already collected a few bags of seal hair. It had been a decade since I had last been on the ice and it was with profound anticipation that I flew to meet the seal pups once again.

Looking into those huge, dark, innocent eyes reminded me again of why we had to champion these creatures. The seals were indeed the little lambs of God, their vulnerable innocence in such contrast to the raw, mindless cruelty of the ice floes, a cruelty dwarfed only by the merciless, mindful cruelty of man.

I loved them every one. And what we love we defend.

The pups seemed to enjoy it when we brushed them. They did not struggle or protest. They were much too young and inexperienced to have cause to fear us, and we moved quickly, to reduce potential stress.

Our collecting time was cut short because I was scheduled to appear in court in St. John's on the charges stemming from our campaign to protect the codfish on the Grand Banks in August 1993. Once again, the government had scheduled my court appearances to coincide with the seal hunt in an effort to hinder any possible actions that I might have been considering.

In the meantime, Marc Cleriot offered to take our seal-hair samples to Prince Edward Island for us, where he would have the chance to photograph the secondary stage of our seal-brushing plan.

He turned the bags of seal hair over to Lynne Douglas, a designer and owner of a company called Sheep's Clothing, who would investigate the possibility of producing sweaters from the hair.

In Newfoundland, I was acquitted. The Coast Guard had charged me for not having the proper charts for the Grand Banks during the cod campaign. I'd had the charts, but the Mounties had confiscated them for evidence, which they then denied doing. The only thing that saved me was that I had kept the receipt for the purchase of the charts with the chart numbers written upon it. Reluctantly, the judge agreed that this constituted "reasonable doubt," and I was remanded until September 1995 for trial on the other charges. The judge also banned me from bringing a ship into Maritime waters until the resolution of the case.

I returned to Los Angeles, where the Sea Shepherd Conservation Society had been based since 1988. (People often ask why we had moved there, of all places. I always replied that if you have a message you want to deliver globally, then go where you can do that most effectively. LA was, simply, the media capital of the world.) Soon after, I received a letter from Lynne Douglas. In it, she explained that although she had spun a variety of fibres over the years, she did not think the seal hair was spinnable. "It is too short," she wrote, "but more importantly, it does not seem to have the right microscopic structure, i.e., it is smooth, like hair rather than wool. For the same reason, I doubt if it could be felted, although it is worth an experiment." I was, of course, very disappointed. Fortunately, Marc Cleriot's article was published in *Focus* and in publications in France and Britain, and the Swiss TV program was also shown in Germany.

As a result, we received a fax from a man named Tobias Kirchhoff, who owns Kirchhoff Bettwarenfabrik in Munster, Germany:

Dear Paul,
Please let us introduce ourselves as one of the leading bedding goods manufacturers in Europe, producing quilts filled with cashmere, camel fibre, or alpaca.

In the German news magazine *Focus* we have seen an article about your project to use seal hair and produces fibres out of them, instead of killing the poor animals.

We think, judging from the picture, that we could use these fibres for filling purposes for winter comforters. As we are used to dealing with cashmere, we also know that seal fibre has not the price of a synthetic fibre, but will be much more expensive. We could use the fibre in washed form, it has not to be spinned into yarn. Please advise us if we can obtain fibre samples. I would like to come to California in June to meet with you to discuss this idea.

With best regards
Tobias Kirchhoff

We met with Tobias and he was delighted to receive the samples, which he took back to Germany for analysis.

Kirchhoff's research revealed that the hollow, transparent hairs made an excellent insulating fibre, superior even to eiderdown. Using a special technology, the company could crimp each individual follicle to increase the bulk of the hairs for use in quilts or clothing.

In Tobias's opinion, seal hair could become a very valuable resource, but our announcement in the Canadian media received a predictably skeptical response.

Tina Fagan, the executive director of the Canadian Sealers Association, said, "It's a good idea if it came from anyone but Watson."

Mark Small, president of the same organization, was "worried" that brushing seals would be inhumane and cause the pups stress. He argued that clubbing the seals was more humane than brushing them. I responded by asking Small what he would prefer: to have a hair brush run through his hair or to have someone bash his skull in with a baseball bat?

The government felt, however, that with a large European company interested in the idea, the matter should be investigated further. They agreed to issue us another research permit to brush seals for March 1995.

A year later, we returned, this time with actor Martin Sheen to help us publicize the merits of the idea. Among those joining us were Bob Hunter and Todd Southgate for Citytv in Toronto, photographer Marc Gaede, and a television crew from Germany. Tobias Kirchhoff would arrive a week later to speak with interested parties in the Magdalen Islands.

Tobias never made it. He was forced to cancel his trip after the mob attacked us in our hotel and I was beaten and forcibly evicted from the island, as I related in Chapter 1, all for advancing the "faggoty idea," in the words of sealer Gilles Theriault, of seal brushing.

Of course, no charges were laid against my attackers. Police chief Pierre Dufort informed me that after a thorough investigation, the police had found no evidence that I had been assaulted.

I can't say that I was shocked or even surprised. The cops had witnessed the assault, as had my crew. Martin Sheen had related the attack in an interview on the program *A Current Affair* and throughout the international media. Citytv and the German reporters had witnessed and documented the attack. We had photos of the attackers and I identified my assailants by name.

It was hard to feel like a citizen in a nation that allowed violence directed at me to escape punishment, yet forced me to appear before a judge and jury in September 1995 to face charges of mischief to save fish.

I had not hurt any or damaged any property, yet I was facing the trial of my life. The Crown was seeking maximum prison sentences for our campaign to chase drag trawlers off the Grand Banks. In fact, I was facing two times life plus ten years.

Even worse, I was to be tried by a jury of Newfoundlanders in a province where I was one of the most despised individuals in their history. One reporter even asked me on the first day of the trial, "What's it like to be the most hated man in Newfoundland?"

I smiled and answered, "I thought Brian Davies had that honour."

Colin Flynn, the chief prosecutor for the province of Newfoundland and a man who hated to lose, was appointed as the attorney for the Crown. Fortunately, our efforts to save cod had won us some support and there were two men on the jury who were clearly not in the government's corner.

My defence was that I had acted in accordance with the United Nations Charter for Nature and that it was necessary for us to intervene to protect the fish.

In summing up his case, Flynn delivered a fiery speech stating that the authorities had to send the message that "citizen interference with over-fishing must not be tolerated; it is the responsibility of the government and not Watson to protect the fish."

The jury saw me smile at that remark. A couple of jurists smiled back. They knew, as I knew, that the government had done nothing to oppose foreign draggers until I embarrassed the authorities in 1993.

Flynn went on to say that my actions were "akin to those of skinheads and neo-Nazis painting swastikas on the walls of synagogues. It is vandalism and interference in the rights of others."

Now that was a jump, equating the saving of fish to anti-Semitism. But by now, twenty years of fighting the seal hunt had inured me to the extreme prejudices of the governments of Canada and Newfoundland and the fishing and sealing industry.

The jury deliberated for seventeen hours. My champions on that panel of twelve smiled at me when they returned.

I was acquitted of all serious charges and convicted of the minor offence of being an accessory. The two older men who had stood up for me were stubborn and only agreed to that charge near the end of the seventeen hours. My excellent attorney, Brian Casey, told me that a charge like that would only bring a maximum fine of $100.

I knew better.

The next day, I appeared before the judge and received a fine of thirty-five dollars. Because the judge felt the fine was insufficient, given that the Cubans had lost millions of dollars because of my interference, he ordered that I be sent to prison for thirty days as a lesson.

Nine days later, Brian appealed the sentence and secured my release. I was released on condition that I continue to post $10,000 bail and receive property bonds by two citizens of Newfoundland. I also had to report to the RCMP every Friday.

After weathering the riot in the Magdalens, the 1996 season presented us with entirely different problems—primarily political. First we needed to secure another research permit for March 1996. The prior two years, the DFO would simply issue a permit, but after the recent release of a video showing two fishermen torturing newborn seal pups for hours, the department had received a great deal of unwanted media attention, and they became less than cooperative.

Despite our persistent efforts, repeated phone calls and faxes to officials went unanswered up to the week of our scheduled departure. After more calls, we were told that new regulations had been put in place in March 1995 and that we had not filled out the proper forms. It was the first mention of the existence of such "forms." In addition, if our permit was issued, the only people besides me who would be allowed to brush seals were full-time commercial fishermen from the Magdalen Islands, and none of my crew could accompany me.

This was very strange. Did the government really believe it was safe for me to allow Magdalen Island sealers to accompany me to the ice without my crew? I could see that becoming a one-way trip, with a full accident report made out in triplicate explaining the unfortunate problems that led to my being lost under the ice.

Given that the Canadian government had denied anything happened in March 1995 when we had been mobbed, these new regulations were totally unacceptable.

We asked why we were not told of these new regulations and forms in any of the detailed conversations we had been having with DFO representatives for almost six months. Nobody could answer that question, although the DFO did inform us that the new regulations were put into effect because of the conflict that had arisen in March 1995 on the Magdalen Islands.

It seemed absurd that because we were attacked unlawfully, the government would retaliate against us, the victims, by imposing restrictions on our activities.

I spoke for hours with numerous DFO bureaucrats in Ottawa and the Maritimes. I repeatedly told them that our 1996 Seal-Brushing Project proposal specifically stated we were going to be based out of Prince Edward Island, not the Magdalen Islands, and that it was necessary for the crew to accompany me to the ice as observers. If we couldn't watch to make sure no one was killing seals, how could we guarantee that the seal-hair product would be cruelty-free?

The stipulation that only full-time commercial fishermen be allowed to brush seals presented another ridiculous hurdle: The province's only remaining legally sanctioned, full-time commercial fishermen were lobster or ground fishermen making over $100,000 a year! The average inshore, non-commercial fisherman in the Maritimes is unemployed—forbidden by law to fish as a result of the cod-fishing moratorium of 1992. By allowing only the rich fishermen to participate, the government was attempting to sabotage our project, because those men had no incentive to stop their lucrative fishing in order to brush seals. At the same time, the people we wanted to hire were being deprived of work. We countercharged that this was favouritism and discrimination.

We finally managed to convince the government to allow my crew to go to the ice, but they were prohibited from touching or brushing any seals. This left us at a major disadvantage. Only I could brush seals to obtain samples of molted seal hair. The fishermen, as expected, boycotted our project.

On the first trip to the ice, I was accompanied by Tobias Kirchhoff and Reinhard Olle of ORIGO, one of Europe's largest natural products retailers. The company was also interested in the project and had contributed $10,000 toward the research. Both men, who pride themselves on the cruelty-free quality of their products, were very impressed with our method of brushing the seals and felt that the seal hairs had excellent commercial possibilities.

The *Sea Shepherd* crew was able to make three trips to the ice, but weather and ice conditions prevented the gathering of a substantial amount of seal hair. However, the fabric experts noted its potential, and both Kirchhoff and ORIGO were willing to pursue further research.

The government, ever "vigilant," made a point of dispatching a Mounted Police officer and a Fisheries officer to monitor our adherence to the permit. What they really wanted was to make sure that I brushed seals and did not witness a killing. In an effort to hide the baby seal slaughter, the government has made it a criminal offence to witness or photograph the seal hunt without a permit from the Minister of Fisheries. The penalty for filming, photographing, or even seeing a seal being slaughtered in Canadian waters carries a maximum sentence of up to two years in prison and a substantial fine. This law, which amounts to a kind of censorship, is disguised as DFO "fishing" regulations.

Yet DFO regulations seem to be selectively enforced. During this campaign, we were informed that on their way to monitor our activities on the ice, the RCMP and a DFO "conservation officer" had requested that a sealing boat stop so they could board it. The vessel ignored the official request. The officers let it go and proceeded quickly to the ice to monitor the notorious seal-brushers instead. Meanwhile, the government-sponsored slaughter of seals continued unabated. Not a single sealer that year was arrested or charged for cruelty or for exceeding quotas.

And the quotas were indeed exceeded. The hood seal kill was more than double the quota of 8,000 and finally numbered about 25,754, a figure that DFO spokesperson Lorne Humphries brushed off by saying, "It will have no impact on conservation. They could have killed more without any adverse affect."

When it was pointed out by seal hunt opponents that the legal kill quota was illegally exceeded, the government of Canada dismissed that as unimportant.

The harp seal quota of 250,000 animals was also apparently exceeded. The unofficial figure from the Department of Fisheries and Oceans as of July 1, 1996, was 242,262 animals reported. This figure does not reflect the seals shot and lost and not landed. Thousands of bodies have washed up on the shores of eastern Canada since April 1996. Again, Canada had made no apologies. Humphries stated that a "million seals should have been killed."

Officially, the harp seals taken by Canada are classified as adults, but the fact is that Canada classifies any weaned seal as an adult. A four-week-old pup is thus listed as an adult.

While Norway did not release any official kill figures for that year, what we do know is that the Norwegian government paid eight million kroner (eight kroner = US$1) in subsidies to the sealers. In return for the subsidies, the hunt returned the following: 550,000 kroner for blubber, 225,000 kroner for meat, and 110,000 kroner for seal penises.

It is obvious that the Norwegian seal hunt, like the Canadian hunt, is a glorified welfare program for fishermen, but the public in Norway and Canada is being sold the lie that the seals must be killed to bring back the codfish. It is this lie that is being used to justify the overkill. The fact is, as mentioned elsewhere in this book, that harp and hood seals do not prey on cod, although they *do* prey upon fish that eat young cod. The governments of Canada and Norway have a horrendous record of managing fish and continue to search for scapegoats to justify their incompetence.

Meanwhile, Canada gave absolutely no encouragement to the Sea Shepherd initiative to provide real jobs by creating a product that two German companies are willing to invest in. Canada made its choice: Instead of a creative, non-lethal, cruelty-free industry that will attract foreign investment, Canadians would rather have a glorified welfare project that kills more than a quarter of a million seals each year and returns nothing to the Canadian economy. Nevertheless, we continued to push for this new, harmonious approach to working with the seals. Unfortunately, we have not been able to make any progress on the seal-brushing idea due to the refusal of Department of Fisheries bureaucrats to allow us to continue to explore the possibilities of implementing a practical seal-brushing industry.

The government announced in a DFO news release on July 12, 1996, that the Canadian seal hunt had yielded a value of $13 million to $15 million. The government was continuing to pick profit and population figures out of a hat. A request under the Access to Information Act elicited an answer from Scott Crosby of DFO on October 19 that said "all records dealing with the data calculations and studies underlining the estimate of the processed value of this year's seal fishery $13-15 million as outlined in the DFO News Release of July 12th cannot be found."[1]

The president of the Canadian Sealers Association (CSA) was setting a good example for his trade when he was charged along with 101 other sealers with illegally selling seal pup pelts. The Department of Fisheries and Oceans laid the charges in mid-November 1996 after investigators seized more than 25,000 pelts earlier in the year from the Carino Company's processing plant in South Dildo, Newfoundland.

Small had been caught selling 102 blueback or baby hood seal pelts. Despite this, Tina Fagan, the executive director of the CSA, stood by Small and issued a release saying that he would remain president.[2]

The investigation that led to Small's arrest revealed a growing illegal trade in blueback hooded seal pups. The Canadian public had been repeatedly told by the government that the sealing industry does not kill baby hoods for commercial sale. The investigation demonstrated that this was not true. Bluebacks were found at Newfoundland's Carino Company being prepared for shipment to the Reiber Company in Norway under the name "hopper hood" to disguise the newborn pelts as being those of adults. The term "hopper hood" was created to replace the term "blueback" so as to deliberately mislead. These baby pelts could then slip into the European market to bypass the ban on pup pelts.

This flouting of the law did not make the Canadian government very happy. The government wanted the seals killed, but the hunt had to be seen as legitimate and above board. John Crosbie, then federal Minister of Fisheries and Oceans, wrote to the CSA, saying "a departure from the sealing policy approved in 1987 would draw a negative reaction and may affect the markets that are based primarily on the harp seals."

I was amused to read in September 1996 that a seven-month-old hooded seal had swum 2,000 miles south to the U.S. Virgin Islands, apparently trying to put as many miles as possible between him and those slaughtering his brethren in the north. It was also interesting to read that the U.S. Coast Guard had transported the little fellow to Puerto Rico for a flight back north. As the Newfoundlanders slew tens of thousands of baby hoods for $28 per pelt, the United States was spending a few thousand dollars to rescue one lone hood seal from the warm waters and friendly tourists of the Caribbean.[3]

Canada's new commitment to re-energize the seal hunt was also demonstrated on December 18, 1995, when the Canadian Department of Fisheries had announced the new quota for the 1996 season. The total allowable catch rose from 186,000 seals to 250,000. This was accompanied by another taxpayer-funded public relations blitz to blame the seals for the decline of the cod.

Only days before the announcement, Canada's High Commissioner in London, Royce Frith, wrote in a letter to the *Financial Times* that "the real problem with harp seals in the North Atlantic goes on—a massive, increasing herd with an appetite which is disastrous for the regeneration of depleted cod and other white fish stocks. . . . If the herd carries on unchecked," he continued, "there will be no fish left for anyone."

The Canadian government was playing quite a juggling feat with the facts. On the one hand, they were insisting that the cod were not endangered and promising the fishermen that they would return. On the other hand, the bureaucrats were saying that the cod were endangered because of consumption by seals.

A real look at the facts is in order here.

In October 1996, the International Union for the Conservation of Nature (IUCN) added the Atlantic cod, *Gadus morhua*, to its *Red List of Threatened Animals*. The species was classified as vulnerable, meaning that it faced a high risk of extinction.[4]

The next year, in 1997, Dr. Kim Bell prepared a confidential report for the Committee on the Status of Endangered Wildlife in Canada (COSEWIC). Dr. Bell recommended that the Northern Atlantic cod be given the designation of "endangered." This was not a report that sat well with the current Canadian Minister of Fisheries and Oceans. Brian Tobin was promising fishermen that he would lift the codfish ban in 1997. To admit that the species was not recovering would be to expose governmental posturing since 1992. Tobin was promising something he knew he could not deliver, and he was using the harp seal as his escape route.

"There is only one major player still fishing the cod stock," Mr. Tobin told a news conference. "His first name is harp and his second name is seal."

In Canada, science must give way to politics. True to form, the Department of Fisheries and Oceans attacked the IUCN report, claiming there were "hundreds of millions" of cod and that it was "ludicrous" to call them endangered.

Fisheries and Oceans were also not happy with COSEWIC's findings. In 1998, the *Ottawa Citizen* reported that plans were in place to replace COSEWIC, which made decisions based on objective scientific criteria, with a Canadian Endangered Species Conservation Council, to be made up of provincial, federal, and territorial wildlife ministers who would make decisions based on both science and political consensus.

Also in 1998, Dr. David Lavigne, in a technical briefing to the International Marine Mammal Association, wrote:

So, are Canadian cod stocks really endangered?

In a word, yes. They are endangered by the biological criterion-that their numbers have been dramatically reduced, largely by over-fishing . . . [M]ost depleted cod stocks have yet to show any signs of recovery despite moratoria on commercial exploitation. They are endangered by the fact that even if they were to be designated by COSEWIC as threatened or endangered . . . Canada has no federal endangered species legislation and, unlike some developed countries, there is no legal requirement for the government to do anything to offer increased protection to endangered species or to promote their recovery. And finally, cod and other commercial stocks, including seals, remain endangered in Canada by the continuing arrogance of senior DFO bureaucrats and politicians, by their disregard for the lessons of history, and by their capacity for self-deception when the truth is unpalatable."

In the mid-nineties, I was heartened to see that there was a new generation of seal hunt opponents emerging.

In 1995, I had met a twenty-two-year-old, straight-A student from the University of Victoria, Frank Arnold, who was very concerned about the welfare of the seals. He wanted to do something on his own to inflict economic damage on the hunt, and I encouraged him to follow his heart in this matter. I told him, though, that I could not give him any material support because I could not risk Sea Shepherd being involved in a conspiracy to commit economic sabotage.

Although Frank was unable to carry out his plan, I consider his attempt to be heroic nonetheless.[5]

Frank knew that the Carino seal-processing plant had been the lynchpin of the sealing industry in Newfoundland for thirty years. The plant is used only for seal processing and is closed from July to March every year. This was the place where the seal penises were processed and packaged for the Far East. Millions of innocent seals had been "processed" there over the years. Frank believed that destroying the Carino plant would cause severe economic damage to the hunt. This was especially important in 1996, on the eve of the biggest buildup in sealing in twelve years.

In late February, Frank arrived in Newfoundland. He had arranged to obtain false identification and carried a bag of tools with him. After carefully surveying the six buildings to ensure that there were no people on the premises, he planned to torch the buildings.

As he drove up to the Carino plant, a parked police car suddenly turned on its flashing lights and pulled him over. Frank was stunned. He knew if the police searched his car, they would find all the tools of an arsonist. When a police officer made him get out of his car, Frank decided to make a break for it and ran into the bushes. The bushes were actually a bog, and in the abnormally warm February weather, he found himself up to his waist in freezing water. He stayed low as the officer played his spotlight on the bog and numerous police vehicles began to arrive.

With his legs getting increasingly numb, Frank made his way through the bog and headed for the town of Whitbourne, reasoning that the police would expect him to go toward St. John's. He covered ten more miles and spent a cold night sleeping in a greenhouse that had been closed for the winter.

In the morning, he hitched a ride to the town of Colinet, but the driver recognized him from a police description. Within a few hours, he was apprehended.

The police had been at the Carino plant because the previous year someone had attempted to sabotage it. They were expecting further attacks and Frank had walked into their stakeout.

Charged with conspiracy to commit arson, Frank was kept in jail until June to await trial. He refused to talk with police or make a deal to implicate other individuals or groups in return for leniency. He pleaded guilty and was given six to twelve months. In October 1996, he was released and returned home to Vancouver Island.

Frank has no regrets for attempting what he did. "I had to do something," he told me a few years later. "This slaughter compelled me as a Canadian to do whatever I could do to stop it. My biggest regret is that I failed to take out that damn bloody plant."

I found it interesting that, during the entire time of Frank's arrest and imprisonment, there was not a single mention of the incident in the local or national media. It seems that the mainstream Canadian media have an unwritten agreement with the government not to report attempts by citizens to attack environmentally destructive or inhumane industries. If the attempts are blatant and highly visible, then the media have no choice, but if the public can be kept in the dark, so much the better. The last thing the government wants is to encourage similar activities or create martyrs.

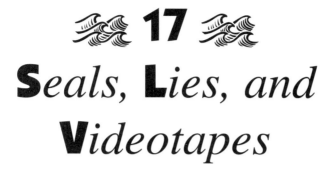

17

Seals, Lies, and Videotapes

(1998–1999)

I can remember when the bison were so many that they could not be counted, but more and more Wasichus came to kill them until there were only heaps of bones scattered where they used to be. The Wasichus did not kill them to eat . . . they took only the hides to sell. Sometimes they did not even take the hides, only the tongues; and I have heard that fireboats came down the Missouri River loaded with dried bison tongues. You can see that the men who did this were crazy.

—Black Elk, Lakota Nation

In 1998, the *Sea Shepherd III* was the first ship to return to the newly escalated seal wars. It had been fifteen long years since those bitter and angry showdowns with the sealers and their government bully boys. Would this bloody awful hunt ever be shut down?

Expecting me to be confrontational, the government had begun to mobilize the appropriate policing and intelligence apparatus. This was fine with me, because I wanted them to spend as much money as possible. But they would be in for a surprise this time around. I had absolutely no intention of getting anyone arrested this year, or my ship seized. The strategy would be to let them do the work for us and to create the story by responding to what they thought I would do.

I was overjoyed to see a new and energetic IFAW initiative to oppose the hunt. Under Rick Smith, the Canadian branch of IFAW was building a strong campaign. Prominent Canadian artists and activists had been incited to join the

IFAW-sponsored Canadians Against the Seal Hunt group: Farley Mowat, William Shatner, Loreena McKennit, Bob Hunter, and many more.

I had not been invited, but that was because, as Rick Smith told me later, "IFAW is conservative in its approach and it would be inflammatory to have you listed."

I had to laugh. "Jesus, Rick, in an unpopularity contest in Newfoundland, you guys beat us hands down. Maybe *I* should be concerned about being associated with *you*."

The fact is that neither IFAW, Sea Shepherd, nor any organization opposed to sealing was very popular among east coast fishing communities or Canadian politicians. It was back to the old days of us against the entire Canadian establishment.

In March 1998, an all-party parliamentary committee announced that the Department of Fisheries and Oceans should loosen all restrictions on the seal hunt. Despite all the scientific evidence to the contrary, the seventeen members of Parliament, from all five federal parties, charged that expanding seal populations were threatening the disappearing cod and diminished capelin stocks. The politicians, ignoring population studies, flatly stated that there were between six and eight million harp seals on Canada's Atlantic coast, when in reality the numbers were probably half that or less.[1]

The panel claimed to have heard from 500 witnesses in communities across the Maritimes. Of course, no one from the conservation or animal welfare interests were invited or allowed to testify, nor were scientists consulted, even though respected government and non-governmental scientists had repeatedly stated that the harp seal was never the cause for the destruction of the cod. The age-old fisherman's claim that seals were destroying the fish was all that the politicians wanted to hear.

Peter Meisenheimer, representing the International Marine Mammal Association, wrote a paper entitled "Seal, Cod, Ecology and Mythology." His summary illustrates the problem very clearly:

> ... published reports in scientific journals, including those authorized by DFO biologists, unequivocally conclude that seals are having no demonstrable impact on cod recovery.
>
> "Common sense" arguments that culling seals will "obviously" benefit the fishery are premised on a mythological view of predators that is unsubstantiated by most scientific evidence.

Research conducted in other fisheries has indicated that the complexity of marine food webs, and the diversity of seal diets, mean increased seal numbers can sometimes lead to positive effects on commercial fish stocks.

Consistently, recent research in terrestrial systems indicates that top predators can have a significant positive impact on numbers of herbivores by reducing smaller predators.

The Canadian political agenda for dealing with the collapse of the cod stocks has evolved to include a subsidized seal cull, and suppression of internal reports contradicting the "common sense" position adopted by the political leadership.

Ecology is not as simple as the minds of government bureaucrats. The laws of ecology dictate that impact on ecosystems is due to complex interactions based on the three main ecological laws of interdependence, biodiversity, and finite resources. The ecosystems of the western North Atlantic are not simply seals vs. cod. These are only two of hundreds of interacting species.

Pre-European populations of harp and hood seals were in excess of thirty million, yet the wealth of fish in those centuries is legendary. Nature balances itself. Human greed upsets that balance. It was the fishermen who destroyed the cod, and the cod will be further damaged by continued destruction of the seals. But the government doesn't get it.

What the Department of Fisheries and Oceans needs is fewer biologists and more ecologists.

The problem is not, and never has been, between fish and seals. The problem is between politics and science, greed and ecology. But in 1998, after a quarter of a century of opposing the seal hunt, I was beginning to finally realize that "the seals are killing our cod" myth could not be debunked by any amount of scientific observation. Nor, I realized, could anyone or anything convince a Canadian government bureaucrat that there was cruelty on the ice.

In 1995, IFAW went to the ice and deployed, for the first time, their latest high-tech cameras, gyro-mounted from helicopters that could hover some two miles from a seal hunt. Sealers were being documented without any knowledge that they were being filmed. Veterinarian Dr. Mary Richardson, the chair of the Animal Care Review Board for the Solicitor-General of Ontario, reviewed videotapes supplied by IFAW. In her report, she wrote:

In 1995 the Canadian government pledged that the renewed seal hunt would be humane. After viewing the videotapes that IFAW collected, it is clear that a large proportion of the seals taken by the sealing industry are suffering long and painful deaths. Throughout my career as a veterinarian, I have seen animals die in slaughterhouses, research labs and animal shelters, and I can assure you that the cruelty existing in the seal hunt would not be tolerated in these institutions . . .

The events depicted in the videotapes of the 1996 seal hunt demonstrate that the provisions outlined by the VMA [Canadian Veterinary Medical Association] have not been met: Quotas were not adhered to, all seals hunted were not killed (some that were wounded by gunshot escaped), and the killing methods are not recognized as humane.

As chair of the Animal Care Review Board for the Solicitor-General of Ontario, I am required to assess whether an animal is in fact in "distress." This is often a difficult task. However, when asked by IFAW if the seals on the videotape were suffering and in distress, I could quite easily answer yes in many cases. The fear and pain they endure before being killed is both unnecessary and unacceptable.

Video evidence provided by IFAW in 1996 resulted in the conviction of six sealers for a variety of abuses, including skinning a seal alive. In February of 1997, IFAW released footage of a second investigation that resulted in seventeen cruelty related charges against seven different sealers. Two sealers actually entered pleas of guilty. One of the sealers charged had previously been praised by the national media as a prime example of the Canadian professional sealer.

The courts of Newfoundland could not deny the depictions of cruelty and of sealers blatantly violating sealing regulations, but on CBC radio, on February 11, 1997, Newfoundland Fisheries Minister John Efford dismissed the actions of the sealers as an "isolated incident."

The federal politicians were more defensive. Minister of Fisheries Fred Mifflin told the House of Commons that the 1997 "seal fishery . . . will be monitored like it has never been monitored before."[2] His bureaucratic spokesperson, David Beven, insisted that the "hunt can be managed in a humane manner" and that "this year [1997] the hunt will be the most tightly monitored ever."[3]

A year later, Beven told the media that the 1998 hunt would be monitored even better than the previous year's. "As always," he said, "regulations to ensure a humane and responsible harvest will continue to be strictly enforced."[4]

We would see for ourselves.

In March 1998, my ship and crew set sail for the ice fields of the Gulf of St. Lawrence.

Only a few of my new crew had been to the ice before. As we entered the Cabot Strait prior to stopping at the port of Sydney, Nova Scotia, a large raft of jagged ice, a mile across and eerie white in the moonlight, suddenly loomed before the bow.

It had been fifteen years since I had last navigated a ship into the formidable ice packs of the Gulf of St. Lawrence. I had almost forgotten what it was like. For a moment I hesitated and my hand reached for the pitch controls to slow our speed. This new ship, *Sea Shepherd III*, was built as strongly as her predecessors, but ice is an unpredictable element.

At the helm, crew member Holly Gray was staring wide-eyed at the rapidly approaching ice. "Shouldn't we slow down?" she asked.

I raised the binoculars and scanned the ice ahead. It was clear. No seals or pups were in harm's way.

"Just keep it on course, Holly. We need the speed to push us through."

We struck the first pan and split it in two, moving into the second and then the third. The crew watched as a jagged crack rapidly shot across each large pan and opened up to let us through. The crew below deck were startled to hear the ice grinding against the hull.

Within ten minutes, we were on the other side—the ice had not slowed us down at all. But I knew this was just a teaser, and I also knew now that this ship would do the job.

We rounded the cape and headed down into the bay into a raging seventy-mile-per-hour wind, taking it full on the bow. Rain and sleet flew by the bridge windows in horizontal sheets and it was bitterly cold. So severe was the weather that the pilot boat would not come out to meet us, choosing instead to keep in contact by radio from the shore.

The crew found the experience frightening. All they could see was an oncoming blast of sleet and hail speeding toward us out of utter blackness and reflected by our searchlights. We were like a starship hurtling at light speed through the galaxy, with every hailstone a star.

The wind helped us slip into our berth in Sydney, where we picked up crew and, most important, our international chairman, Farley Mowat. Two television crews, one from Germany, the other from Austria, also joined us.

Heading into the Gulf, I was struck by the fact that, despite the ice rafts that had teased us, there was not one speck of ice to be seen anywhere. Usually, the

Strait is filled with solid fields of ice at this time of the year. The reports that we had been hearing were true: The ice pack was dramatically reduced—by almost 80 percent—this year. Except for the Prince Edward Island and New Brunswick coastlines, most of the Gulf of St. Lawrence was ice-free. This was an occurrence without recorded precedence, and certainly a herald of the reality of global warming.

Lack of ice presented a great problem for the sealers. They would not be able to walk across the ice from the shores of the Magdalens to kill seals. To reach their prey, they would have to take their boats and travel some seventy miles.

Unfortunately, the reduced ice pack presented a far greater problem for the seals. The mothers needed to be able to haul out onto the solid ice packs to give birth and to raise their helpless pups, but solid pack ice was in short supply.

A day out from Sydney, we reached the ice around Prince Edward Island and immediately began to see seals—hundreds of them, but all adults. Never before had I seen so many adults at this time of year without pups.

Finally, in the late afternoon, with our helicopter support preparing to land on the ship, we spotted our first whitecoat. We had found them.

The helicopter dropped off an Australian television crew and several European journalists, including one of the world's foremost photojournalists, Bernard Sidler. Famed Montreal talk show host Howard Galganov also came on board to broadcast his show directly from the seal nurseries.

As we entered the Gulf, it was evident that the Canadian government had not forgotten us. Predictably, officials overreacted. Hot on our tail were two large Canadian Coast Guard icebreakers, the *Terry Fox* and the *George R. Pearkes*. On board the two ships were a detachment of Royal Canadian Mounted Police and another unit of armed Canadian Fisheries officers. The surveillance force deployed against us also included numerous helicopters, jet and prop aircraft, and a backup unit of Mounties on the Magdalen Islands. I estimated the cost of this overkill response at about $200,000 per day for the ten days they were with us. Thus, simply by making our presence known, we succeeded in increasing the expense of supporting the hunt—already subsidized to the tune of some seven million dollars annually—by an additional two million dollars.

At one point, with the journalists' cameras and documentary crews focused on me, I radioed the *George R. Pearkes*, which we could see running down defenceless seal pups as it plowed through the ice, and I advised the captain to be careful and avoid the seals. He replied that he did not see any seals. When I told him that we had just filmed him running down a pup, he repeated that he saw no pups.

"Perhaps you are running down pups also," he added, sarcastically.

In all the years that I have taken ships to the ice, we have never run down a seal.

"I don't think so, Captain," I said. "We take precautions, and I can see that you do not."

Finally, just to see what he would reply and for the benefit of our documentary crews, I asked, "Sir, what are you doing here in the ice?"

"We are protecting the sealers from people like you, Mr. Watson," he answered.

"I see," I replied. "I wonder who is protecting Mother Nature and the seals from the sealers and your government?"

There was a pause. "To cut the conversation short, sir, I believe that is what you are doing."

"Interesting," I said to the television crews. "The Coast Guard has admitted that it is our job to protect the seals and not theirs."

The campaign's main emphasis for 1998 was public relations. We needed to re-educate the international public to be aware of the seal hunt again. In 1998, the Canadian hunt, after three decades of opposition, was still the largest government-subsidized wildlife slaughter in the world, a glorified welfare scheme that produced nothing that was either valuable or necessary. Over one million seal pelts lay in Rieber's warehouses in Bergen, Norway, that year, because there simply was, and continues to be, no market for sealskin. The only part of the seal with any commercial value was the penis. For some strange and perverse reason, the seal penis, because it has a bone in it, is considered by some cultures a cure for impotence. Sealers were getting between C$20 and C$50 per penis, and in Asia, the dried, shrivelled little phalluses were selling retail for around $400 each.

In addition to this highly controversial product, the Canadian Sealing Association (CSA) was trying to stimulate markets for canned seal meat and omega-3 seal oil. They were having trouble, though. Fans of the blackish, fishy-tasting meat were in short supply, and the people who tended to buy health food supplements were not the sort who would buy products potentially laden with PCBs and derived from cruelly slaughtered baby seals.

So that year our purpose was to continue to press the alternative of a non-lethal seal-hair harvest and to draw international media attention to the cruel and wasteful slaughter of the hunt—a hunt that had been forgotten by the world since 1983.

To that end, Farley Mowat walked out onto the ice to pose for a picture with a baby seal. As one of Canada's most famous writers, Farley guaranteed that the media would consider this a story, and it gave him a forum to once again denounce the hunt.

The same day, John Paul DeJoria and his daughter Alexis arrived by helicopter. John Paul is the CEO of John Paul Mitchell Systems, a well-known manufacturer of hair care products renowned for being cruelty-free, meaning they are produced without animal testing or animal research, as well as containing no animal products. As a long-time supporter of Sea Shepherd, John Paul had an idea for helping us get the word out.

Along with his daughter and me, he planned to pose with the baby seals and to have the photos distributed worldwide to his hair salon clients.

"Everyone talks to their hair stylists," said John Paul. "What better way to reach so many people?"

DeJoria later had the photos published in two full-page ads in *In Style* magazine, which helped our cause greatly.

The arrival of Canadian actress Bronwen Booth, the sister-in-law of British prime minister Tony Blair, afforded yet another photo opportunity, and we eagerly awaited the arrival of Brigitte Bardot, who had agreed to join up with us again. This would have made a great story, as it would have marked her return to the ice after twenty years, but her Air France plane broke down on the runway just prior to departure, and our window of opportunity with the baby seals was too slim for her to reschedule. However, she did write an excellent article on our campaign for *Paris Match* a few weeks later.

We also succeeded in recruited another famous actor. Pierce Brosnan was in nearby Québec, filming *Grey Owl*. Looking very much like Archie Belaney, the legendary Canadian protector of beavers, Brosnan spoke to the media:

"The seals are being ground up by an industry based on human vanity in exactly the same way the buffalo were," he said, "and with precisely the same excuse—that there will always be plenty of them."

When asked about brushing seals, Brosnan replied, "The idea of an industry based on brushing the molt of baby seals instead of slaughtering them wholesale is so clearly superior to the present practice, so obviously sane, right, and practical, that Canada should license it immediately and tender an apology to Captain Watson and the people of the Atlantic provinces for having dragged its feet for so long and blocked Sea Shepherd's efforts to put this idea into practice."

Back in the Gulf of St. Lawrence, the *Sea Shepherd III*, her crew, and I were in the seal nurseries on the opening day of the hunt. We were surrounded by seals, and the Coast Guard and the Mounties were keeping us under constant surveillance.

Despite this, the sealers did not show. Perhaps it was the distance from shore, or the unusual ice conditions, or the fact that we were there. Or perhaps it was a combination of all these factors.

In the midafternoon, we spotted one sealing boat in the ice. As we slowly headed for it through the ice, the *George R. Pearkes* manoeuvred rapidly toward us, running down seal pups all the way.

Something was not right, though I could not put my finger on it. I stopped the engine just at the half-mile legal distance to the "sealing" boat. It was frustrating—we heard gunshots and we could see men on the boat shooting at seals.

A hundred yards more and the Mounties would order our arrest for the crime of approaching a sealer.

Consulting the charts, I saw that the area was defined as a protection zone and sealers were prohibited from operating in that area.

It was slowly dawning on me that this might well be a trap. As difficult a decision as it was, I could make no other. I gave the order to not advance.

Some of the crew volunteered to walk across the ice to the seals—while they would be arrested, our ship would be spared—but the unstable ice and open leads forced them to turn back.

The "sealing" ship disappeared at dusk and we did not see it again for the rest of the week. It seemed odd—but odder still, the news media reported that not a single sealing ship had made it to the ice for the opening of the hunt.

My suspicions were confirmed. The small blue and white boat that we had come so close to confronting was not a sealing boat at all. It was simply a decoy positioned by the Mounties to lure us into breaking the so-called seal protection regulations.

We spent the next four days in the ice. The second day of the official sealing season brought in a storm of driven snow and biting cold. The third day was pleasant, but still no sealers approached, though the Canadian authorities continued to lurk nearby. We went on filming, and Howard Galganov did his broadcast from the ice floes. The CBC, Global TV, and several Maritime newspapers came out to visit the ship. We used every opportunity to blast the government for irresponsibly announcing a kill quota of 285,000 seals without taking into account the increased mortality caused by the unnatural ice and weather conditions.

At one point, I put on a dry suit and jumped into the water with the adult seals. They swam around me curiously, bobbing their heads only a few feet from me.

With just my head out of the water, I had a seal's-eye view of the world. It was fascinating. The cries of the whitecoats were louder and more distinct at this level. The view was so severely restricted that it occurred to me that seals would never see their human predators until they were only a few feet away.

As I swam in the black waters of the lead, I reflected on the many years that I had been opposing this obscene hunt.

Why did the government continue to insist on subsidizing such a perverse culture of waste and cruelty? Unsubsidized, this horror would diminish. But with taxpayers rewarding this sadism, the hunters had no reason to lay down their clubs and knives. It is a difficult thing to love your country and to despise its government and dislike its people—my people. I revere these fields of ice, as I hold sacred the once-proud forests and once-pristine lakes and rivers of Canada. Yet to my government and to many of the people of Canada, the forests, the lakes, the wildlife, and the beauty of nature are nothing more than sacrificial offerings to the economic theology of human overlordship.

The ancestors of the sealers are my ancestors. But I have risen above this cult of violence and disrespect for nature and other life forms.

I know that I am not alone. Yet the government of Canada promotes the fallacy that the opposition to the seal hunt originates from outside the Canadian Maritimes. We are depicted as foreigners, as outsiders, or, as they say in Newfoundland, "from away."

It is just another lie, like the lie that the seals destroyed the cod fishery, or the lie that sealing is economically essential to the Maritimes.

The fact is, my family roots are in the Maritimes and I was raised and educated in New Brunswick. Brian Davies, IFAW's founder, began his crusade in New Brunswick after witnessing the seal slaughter in his capacity as a field agent for the New Brunswick Humane Society. Rebecca Aldsworth, the former president of Montreal's Concordia University Student Union and one of the most active in-their-face anti-sealing activists in Canada, is a Newfoundlander. The current Canadian leader of IFAW, Rick Smith, has a grandmother from Newfoundland.

And there are many, many other Maritimers who have opposed this hunt.

This outrageous and hideous annual massacre is built upon lies and perpetuated by wasting millions of tax dollars. The question is, why? Why this violent, irrational, and stubborn defence of the indefensible? I have an opinion as to why:

Because the government and the fishing companies need a scapegoat to divert attention away from the incompetence and greed that destroyed the fishing industry. Because politicians gain politically by creating enemies from without so that people will not discover or dwell upon the fact that the enemy is within. Because the hunt has been supported for so long, by so many politicians and bureaucrats, that it has become a matter of pride to defend it for the sake of defending it.

As I swam through the icy slush and dark waters, I thought of the walrus that once swam here, now extirpated from the Atlantic completely. Looking upward, I saw in my mind's eye the migratory formations of the beautiful white and black Labrador duck, blasted into extinction by the guns of the Newfoundlanders. Beneath me was the ghost of the Atlantic grey whale. The white bear, eliminated. The beluga, gone from these waters. So much lost, and yet we have not learned a thing.

The *Sea Shepherd III* left the ice after a week. The sealers had not arrived and the wind had driven the ice well into the protection zone north of Prince Edward Island. Our finances would not permit us to stay much longer. We could do nothing more, and so I reluctantly turned the bow of our ship toward the Cabot Strait and the Atlantic Ocean, believing that the sealers would not be able to hunt in the protected zone.

I was wrong. A week later, the Canadian government lifted the protection zone and allowed the Magdalen Islanders and the Newfoundlanders to bring their boats to Prince Edward Island's northern waters for a bloody orgy of extraordinary cruelty.

Fortunately, a helicopter deployed by IFAW was able to expose the lies of the Canadian government again. With those special long-range cameras, IFAW filmed the sealers from outside the exclusion zone. Their faces were visible from three-quarters of a mile away. While covering only a small part of the overall hunt area in a three-day period, the sky cameras caught 146 offences and nineteen abuses. Included in the video footage were thirty-eight cases of skinning or bleeding a seal alive, twenty-four cases of hooking a live seal, five cases of abandoning dead seals on the ice, fifteen cases of clubbing seals with a boat hook or other illegal weapon, and one case of toying with a live seal pup on the ice, eighteen incidents of dumping unwanted pelts, and one case of a seal struck and lost.

IFAW released the tape to the media and police and demanded an investigation. Without even seeing the footage, the Canadian Sealers Association dismissed the tape as a fraud and accused IFAW of staging the killing.

This accusation was consistent with every response the sealers had ever made about evidence presented against them. In the film, the sealers and the ships can be clearly identified.

Of course, there were no arrests.

Despite the continued denials of atrocities by people like Tina Fagan, further evidence appeared that year with the publication of *Over the Side, Mickey*. This firsthand account by sealer Michael Dwyer directly contradicts the sealing industry claims of a humane and well-regulated hunt:

> One beater among the pile lifted its head and started to scratch his way around, his eyeballs two swirling pools of blood. His lower jaw was hanging down from his mouth by a thread of skin. "Darrell, kill that, will you?!" Gerard said.
>
> Grabbing the hakipik, he did not kill it immediately. Instead he pressed the wooden handle up against the top teeth of the suffering creature. "Bite that if you can." The poor thing had no bottom teeth and all it could do was crawl around in the swath.[6]

Dwyer even agreed with the hunt opponents' charges of barbaric cruelty:

> I had heard the anti-sealing protesters say that sealers were barbarians. They were right. You have to be a barbarian to survive it! . . . How barbaric one became depended on how long one was subjected to it. Once, after only a short time into the Hunt, I had saved up ten heads that we used for two hours to play "head-ball." It was like hockey but instead of using sticks, we used our hakipiks to try to shoot the head between two twitching carcasses we used as goal posts. We all took turns in the net. By the time the game was over, eyeballs, teeth, fragments of skull bone and lower jawbones were scattered all over the rink. Darrell won but we all had a great bit of fun.[7]

The slaughter after we left that spring was horrendous. The quota of 285,000 was reached and surpassed by mid-April, and the sealers actually demonstrated before the offices of the Department of Fisheries and Oceans to demand that the quota be raised immediately. In their zeal to kill, the sealers off Newfoundland lost three sealing boats, sunk after grinding ice damaged their hulls. Another seventeen vessels were damaged.

Not included in the quota were the thousands of pelts on the sunken boats, or the tens of thousands of seals shot that sank and died beneath the hard ice. Over 700 baby seal bodies were counted on one beach in Prince Edward Island, many bearing the marks of castration. In my opinion, the overkill was equal to the quota, meaning that more than half a million seals were ruthlessly slain by the sealers of eastern Canada in the spring of 1998.

Only in Canada can the laws of mathematics be so contemptuously ignored. The population size of the harp seal is not definitely known, but on the high end it may have been four million in 1998, on the low end, under two million. But with a half million seals killed in 1997 and another half million in 1998, Newfoundland Fisheries Minister John Efford climbed onto his soapbox to scream that "six million seals were eating up the cod."

Efford's ignorant accusation came a half a year after the scandal that had erupted when the federal government was caught suppressing data that demonstrated that the harp seal was not a factor in the decline of the cod. But Efford needed a scapegoat to rally the unemployed fishermen, and the seal is the most convenient scapegoat available. If only the seals could be wiped out, according to Efford, the cod would (mysteriously) return.

I was surprised he did not recommend sacrificing a few virgins.

Toward his stated end, Efford announced that, despite reaching the set quota, the slaughter must continue and that Newfoundland should send ships northward to follow the seals into the Davis Straits. For Efford, it was no longer a hunt but a search and destroy mission.

I responded in the media to Efford by saying that if such an idea became the policy of the Newfoundland government—to kill outside the laws of the Canadian government and to escalate the slaughter as a "final solution" to their perceived seal problem—I would not hesitate to view these Newfoundland ships in the Davis Strait as pirates, poachers, and advocates of specicide.

The only solution to this kind of ecological lunacy would be to stop it—aggressively and physically. For there was no doubt that Canada's war against the seal was entering a new phase.

On April 25, 1998, Max Short, senior advisor to the federal Minister of Fisheries and Oceans, delivered a speech to a deep-sea fisheries conference in Marystown, Newfoundland. Short noted that "it took a crazy man" to ignite the conflicts in each of the two World Wars and declared that he longed for someone "with similar nerve" (as the Newfoundland *Evening Telegram* discreetly reported it) to put into motion a solution to the seal question.

In answer to Short's call, Newfoundland Fisheries Minister John Efford declared himself the man with the solution to the "seal problem."

On May 4, as recorded in *Hansard*, Efford had this to say to the Newfoundland House of Assembly:

"Mr. Speaker, I would like to see the six million seals, or whatever number is out there, killed and sold, or destroyed or burned. I do not care what happens to them. The fact is that the markets are not there to sell more seals; 286,000 were hunted and sold. If there was a market for more seals the commercial sealers would be hunting and selling seals . . . . What they wanted was to have the right to go out and kill the seals. They have that right, and the more they kill the better I will love it."

This was Short's crazy man indeed.

On Monday, April 12, 1999, Efford, in a conference with Federal Fisheries Minister David Anderson, presented "evidence" that seals were not only eating up all the cod, but only eating the stomachs, wasting the fish, and costing the fishermen of Newfoundland over $20 billion a year!

His evidence was an underwater film taken in Bonavista Bay showing thousands of rotting cod corpses. Divers examining the dead fish in the film observed that only the stomachs had been eaten out. The video did not show any seals actually eating the cod, nor did it explain just how the divers, equipped with underwater video cameras, stumbled upon the dead fish at the bottom of the bay in wintertime.

Efford demanded increased quotas, and when Anderson replied that increasing the kill would reflect badly on the exports of the other provinces, Efford stormed out of the meeting and told reporters that he was concerned with Canada's program of "ethnic cleansing and cultural genocide of our fishing communities."

In response to Efford's video, I told the Newfoundland media that in my opinion the minister was lying and that the video was faked. In fact, I said that the Sea Shepherd Conservation Society would pay anyone $25,000 to produce video documentation of a harp seal eating the stomach out of a codfish.

I also compared Efford to Nazi propaganda minister Joseph Goebbels and said that, like Goebbels, Efford believed that if you tell a lie often enough, people will begin to believe it is the truth.

This was met by a flurry of outraged Newfoundland editorials attacking me for calling Efford a Nazi. How, they demanded, could I dare to compare the slaughter of seals to the slaughter of Jews? I responded that it was ironic that Efford was calling for a "final solution" by killing "six million" seals. These were his words and not mine.

Efford further displayed his ignorance at Dalhousie University when asked why he did not call for the extermination of sharks for eating codfish. He answered that there were no sharks in Newfoundland waters—this to an audience of astounded marine scientists who knew very well that white and Greenland sharks feed on seals and cod and are caught by Newfoundland fishermen.

And as if to prove his ignorance had no limits, Efford came up with the ridiculous idea to kill two million seals to feed refugees in Kosovo. A spokesperson for the refugees politely said no thanks.

In March 1999, I challenged John Efford to a debate at Memorial University. He responded in the St. John's *Evening Telegram* that he would accept my challenge. "I've been waiting for four years, God damn it, bring him in today."[8] However, my attempts to nail down a date with him through his office never went anywhere. Efford is a blowhard and will go the way of all the politicians— he will move on, he will be replaced, and he will be forgotten.

Sea Shepherd could not oppose the hunt by ship in 1999 because our vessel was engaged in protecting whales in the North Pacific.

Tina Fagan, the executive director of the Canadian Sealing Association, was quick to say that our absence was proof that the seal hunt opposition was dead. She conveniently ignored the IFAW trips to the ice, and the mounting global opposition that culminated in the forming of Global Action Against Seal Hunts (GAASH) in 2000. GAASH is an international grassroots coalition opposed to seal hunting whose primary organizing force originated in Canada.

She also ignored the fact that one of the emerging leading opponents to the seal hunt, Rebecca Aldsworth, was on the ice in the Gulf in 1999, representing IFAW.

In 1998, Rebecca and another woman, Alix Alison, had made international headlines by skating nude down the Rideau Canal in Ottawa, attracting some sixty media cameras in their "I'd rather go naked than wear fur" protest. Later that year, Rebecca was one of the primary organizers for the Rally for the Seals in Ottawa—the largest protest for animals in Canadian history, whose partici-pants came from as far away as Newfoundland and Nova Scotia.

As Fagan was attempting to show opposition to the hunt waning in 1999, Rebecca was working behind the scenes to shut down the domestic market for seal oil capsules. By the end of 2000, the vast majority of pharmaceutical chains in Canada had either dropped the product or pledged never to carry it, and today there are few Canadian stores offering seal oil. Rebecca is living proof that there is hope for change. She is a dedicated vegan and animal rights champion of seals and she is a Newfoundlander. The sealers and the government will be hearing much more from her in the future.

Fagan also ignored people like seal protector Patricia Gray from Prince Edward Island. "People are getting tired of the whole thing," she said. "But I am more determined than ever. The seal hunt has to stop."

And Tina Fagan was wrong about us. I was on the ice in March 1999 to film seals as part of a preparation for a major motion picture about Sea Shepherd. We were not there with a ship, but we were there with cameras, and Fagan still did not understand that the sealers have more to fear from cameras than from our ships.

Epilogue

The Sea Shepherd Legacy for the New Millennium

I have been to heaven.

It is cold, clean, and pure. It is formed out of the air and it floats and drifts, constantly moving, at once solid and at the same time ephemeral. In its powdery clefts and bluish-white radiance, it gives birth to angelic lambs. It cradles them, sustaining them in their innocence and purity. It is a place where cathedral mirages formed from crystal ice particles hang in the frosted air, and where the blazing whiteness, stretching farther than the eye can see, can easily blind any mortal who gazes on it overly long. It is a place where you can actually feel life as an eternal beginning; you can sense the turning of the world, and believe in the rightness of all there is.

It is a place where ice-sculpted castles hang suspended upside down in a surreal dimension of green, black and aquamarine, as flippered angels with harps on their backs rival Nureyev and Isadora Duncan in movement and grace.

I have been to Cocytus, the ninth circle and lowest level of hell. It is a place of ebony water and red ice, ruled over by demons conscripted by Lucifer whose faces and hands drip red with the blood of the innocent and whose blackened hearts are harder than the ice upon which they tread in their hobnailed boots. These demons transform heaven into a perdition of unimaginable pain and suffering, where heaven's lambs are mutilated and murdered with remorseless cruelty.

I have stood on the heaving ice of that glacial Hades, and I have sworn by all the righteous passion in my heart that the madness would be vanquished. But the enemy is all-powerful—it is the anthropocentric will of primates who have the arrogance and audacity to believe themselves to be gods. Armoured by the philosophy of dominion, all killing is sanctioned, and all morality is bartered away for denial.

The slaughter of the seals is an annual baptism of blood, where the killers, according to Magdalen Island sealer Pol Chantraine,[1] often drink the blood from the heart of their first victim and paint their faces with the hot, salty liquid of life, mumbling chants of becoming one with the ice as blood drips down onto their silver and gold crucifixes.

I have trod the darkened killing fields as the north wind howled in my ear. I have stumbled over small, bloodied bodies as the Milky Way illuminated the shadows of grieving mothers standing guard over the violated corpses of their young.

"That doesn't happen!" say the defenders of the slaughter. *"It's a lie; the mothers ignore their dead!"* Yet I have seen it.

I have seen newborn seal pups skinned alive as the killer laughed and government officers looked on and grinned. *"Another lie!"* they say. Yet many times I have seen this too.

I have seen a motherless infant try to suckle on the toe of my boot, searching for nourishment that I could not provide, the body of its mother nearby, blood oozing from a bullet hole in her skull pooling blackly on the ice in the moonlight.

The horror lives within me. I've seen it, and because I have seen it, I must live it every day. Yes, I have been to hell and it is the Canadian and Norwegian seal hunts. Today they constitute, as they have for centuries, the largest and most brutally horrific slaughter of wild animals on the planet.

What sensitive, sane soul can stand in the presence of such insanity and do nothing? Yet to expose the slaughter of seals in Canada is to deliver oneself into the hands of a bureaucratic inquisition. To witness the killing of a seal is a crime. To film or photograph the slaughter is a felony. To oppose the massacre is to subject oneself to jail time, beatings, heavy fines, and officially sanctioned harassment.

The war against the Canadian seal hunt is more than a protest. It is a crusade to bring about harmony between the natural world and humanity. All of us who oppose it are dedicated to the protection of life and the abolition of cruelty.

The war against the seal hunt is also a war against lies.

And what are these lies?

I have mentioned many, but there are many more.

As well as the lie about seals destroying the cod, and the lie that the seal hunt is humane, there is the lie that seal defenders only care about baby seals because of their beauty, innocence, and vulnerability. As if this is a sin. The fact is, if we cannot protect a species so beautiful, so helpless, so innocent, then how can we ever hope to save sharks or crocodiles, beetles or frogs?

And let us remember that those in the media who accuse us of protecting seals only because of their "cuteness" are the same people who avidly make use of images of seal pups, but, when we protect fish, who don't look as "cute," are not interested in the story.

Hypocrisy, lies, persecution . . . we should not be surprised. People who can condone the battering of baby seals before the eyes of their nursing mothers are capable of any evil.

Most of my visits to the ice have been incursions into hell, but in March of 1999, I returned to the ice fields—this time to the heavenly side. I was with a motion picture crew to shoot second-unit footage for the production of a movie based on my life story. Ironically, I was playing a sealer, and the camera caught me jumping from floe to floe with a club in my hand approaching a group of baby seals. It was an opportunity to put myself in the shoes of a sealer, and it was all I could do to prevent myself from vomiting.

After the filming, I sat down on an ice floe and called my girlfriend, now my wife, Allison Lance, in Los Angeles. Technology had certainly advanced since our first campaigns. Communications from the ice were once difficult and very costly, but now I could sit on a chunk of ice in the middle of the Gulf of St. Lawrence and make a phone call.

As I spoke to Allison, a mother seal popped her head out of an air hole in the ice at my feet and looked me in the eye.

"Allison, right at this moment I have a mother seal only inches from my foot and she's looking up at me right now."

Allison was excited. "Tell her I love her and her baby."

"Tell her yourself," I answered and lowered the phone down.

The eyes of the seal seemed to widen as she heard Allison's voice. Then she slid back into the water and disappeared.

"Allie, I wish you were here. I can't begin to tell you just how fantastically beautiful this place is. It's a paradise sculpted from ice, full of the sounds of life and so peaceful. For millions of years, it's been like this, until our kind came here. How I wish it could be like that again."

For I knew that somewhere on this vast, white expanse, there were men with clubs and murder in their eyes, and my greatest wish was for them to come no more.

After talking with Allison, I walked across the ice and was surprised to find a little pup born later than the others. Instead of being white and plump, this little guy was slim and blond and obviously under a week old. I held him in my arms and my friend Peter Brown took some photographs of the two of us.

As we walked back to the helicopter, I knew that I would be coming back here until the day I die because these ice fields, these wondrous nursery floes, are like heaven to me, and in the baby harp seal I see the innocence and the suffering of every other species on this planet.

When I first took up the challenge of fighting the seal hunt, I was twenty-four and full of optimism that we could shut it down and bring an end to the killing. Now, at fifty-one, I am beginning to accept that the killing will most likely not end in my lifetime. The massacre of the seals had been renewed with a vengeance. The slaughter of the whales has escalated. Fish populations are crashing worldwide. It is the revelation of my own helplessness that hurts me now. What difference did it all make? Perhaps I should have just become like the people I've been fighting all my life—the uncaring, materialistic, what's-in-it-for-me types.

But then, closing my eyes, I hear the words I heard in a vision so many years before: "You do what you must because it is the only thing you can do. It is the right thing to do, the just thing to do. You are a warrior for the Earth. You will live the life of a warrior and you will die a warrior's death."

This cause is bigger and more important than any of its participants. It is in fact an epic struggle—a classic clash between right and wrong, between good and evil. It is a crusade to defend *kotik*, the Lamb of God.

And thus I have been a shepherd, and I have tried to be a good shepherd and to defend as many of my flock as I can.

Notes

Chapter 1

1   Dufort's nod to the mob was witnessed by Marc Gaede.

2   From Thomas B. Macauley, "Horatius at the Bridge."

Chapter 2

Some material for this chapter was drawn from George Allen England, *Vikings of the Ice* (Doubleday, Page & Co., 1924); Captain Robert A. Bartlett, "The Sealing Saga of Newfoundland," *National Geographic* (July 1929); James E. Candow, *Of Men and Seals: A History of the Newfoundland Seal Hunt* (Environment Canada, 1989).

1   Farley Mowat, *Sea of Slaughter* (Toronto: McClelland and Stewart, 1984).

2   Ibid.

3   Ibid.

4   From Cassie Brown with George Horwood, *Death on the Ice*, (Toronto: Doubleday, 1972).

5   Mowat, *Sea of Slaughter*.

6   Brown, *Death on the Ice*.

7   Originally quoted in the *New York Times*. Reprinted in England, *Vikings of the Ice*.

Chapter 4

Some material for this chapter was drawn from Brian Davies, *Savage Luxury: The Slaughter of the Baby Seals* (Toronto: Ryerson Press, 1970).

1   Peter Lust, *The Last Seal Pup* (Montreal: Harvard House, 1967).

2   Position of Dr. David Sergeant reported by the *New York Times*. Quote from Paddy Milligan from Edward Cowan, "Baby Seal Hunt Is on Again and So Is Dispute," *New York Times* (March 18, 1971).

3   Elsie Carper, "Legislation to Protect Seals from Slaughter Introduced," *Washington Post* (March 25, 1971).

4   Lewis Regenstein, "The Slaughter of the Baby Seals," *Washington Post* (March 13, 1972) and "Ax Is about to Fall Again on the Canadian Fur Seal," *Washington Post* (March 7, 1971).

5   Quote from an unknown American tourist in Fred Bruemmer, "Look But Don't Touch. Live Seals Could Be Worth as Much as Dead Seals," *Weekend Magazine* (June 15, 1974).

Chapter 9

1   Mr. Mark Raines, MP Burnaby-Seymour, "A Question of Privilege," House of Commons, Debates, March 12, 1979.

Chapter 10

The conversations and details of the incident in the Theriault Hotel were drawn from Russ Hoyle, "Confrontations at the Seal Hunt," *The Real Paper* (March 24, 1979). Confirmation received from Mr. Jerry Conway on the accuracy of his portrayal in *The Real Paper* article. Experiences attributed to Keith Krueger are taken, with permission, from his journal, written during the March 1979 campaign.

Chapter 11

1   "Fisheries Officials Impound Animal Welfare Fund 'Copter. Watson Still Plans to Sail," *Charlottetown Guardian* (March 4, 1981).

Chapter 13

1   Court-subpoenaed records from the RCMP document the plan to use commandos against the *Sea Shepherd II*, including the use of tactical explosions to disable the propeller.

2   Quotes from Federal Justice Minister Mark MacGuigan and Newfoundland MP James McGrath, reported by the Canadian Press, March 22, 1983.

3   Pierre De Bane, quoted in "CBC-TV's Film Crew Leaves *Sea Shepherd*," *St. John's Daily News* (March 14, 1983).

Chapter 15

1   Quotes from Dan Morast and Langford reported by the Canadian Press.

2   Brian Gory, "Probe Lauds Tourist Plan for Seal Area," *Globe and Mail* (February 5, 1985).

3   Mark Small, quoted in Tom Barrett, "Sealing Grounds as Tourist Trap Urged," *Vancouver Sun* (February 5, 1985).

4   "Sealers Innocent after Trade Killed," *Vancouver Province*, editorial (September 5, 1985).

5   Tom Siddon and Bill Procoption, quoted in Matthew Fisher, "Inuit Hunters Angered, Perplexed by Campaign against Seal Hunting," *Globe and Mail* (July 17, 1986).

6   Vivia Boe, quoted in Barbara Yaffe, "Fishermen's Future Tied to Sealing" *Globe and Mail* (April 26, 1986).

7   Alan Story, "Seal Hunt May Be a Pretty Tame Affair," *Toronto Star* (March 27, 1987).

8   *Seal Research in Canada*, Report of the Fisheries and Oceans Research Advisory Council to the Minister of Fisheries and Oceans, September 1987.

9   Calvin Coish, "Newfoundland's Hunt for Seals Must Resume," *Kitchener-Waterloo Record* (March 19, 1986).

10   Fred Monroe, quoted in "The Culling Fields," *Sunday Express* (January 7, 1990).

11   Tom Siddon and Bill Procoption, quoted in Greg Middleton, "Seal Hunt Scrap," *Vancouver Province* (January 11, 1987).

Chapter 16

1   DFO Scott Crosby, letter to Sally Hamilton, October 21, 1996.

2   Reported by the Canadian Press, November 26, 1996.

3   Reported in the *Milwaukee Journal Sentinel* (September 17, 1996).

4   IUCN, *IUCN Red List of Threatened Animals*, 1996; "Confidential Report Calls Atlantic Cod Endangered," *Canadian Geographic* (July/August 1997); "Put Cod on Endangered List. Scientists Say Once Abundant Fish Faces Extinction, and DFO Won't Admit It," *Ottawa Citizen* (April 18, 1997); "Canada Working to Keep Cod, Other Fish off Endangered Species List," *Globe and Mail* (April 16, 1997).

5   This account of Mr. Frank Arnold's activities is taken, with his permission, from www.nocompromise.org/features/8franka.html.

Chapter 17

1   Reported by the Canadian Press, March 23, 1998.

2   Fred Mifflin, House of Commons, Debates, February 11, 1997.

3   David Bevan's statement was reported by the Canadian Press, February 11, 1997.

4   David Bevan, quoted in DFO new release, December 30, 1997.

5   IFAW investigation report, 1998.

6   Michael J. Dwyer, *Over the Side, Mickey: A Sealer's First-hand Account of the Newfoundland Seal Hunt* (Halifax: Nimbus, 1998), 140.

7   Ibid., 74.

8   John Efford, quoted in the *St. John's Evening Telegram* (March 31, 1999).

Epilogue

1   Pol Chantraine, *The Living Ice: The Story of the Seals and the Men Who Hunt Them in the Gulf of St. Lawrence* (Toronto: McClelland & Stewart, 1981). Chantraine describes in detail the ritual of drinking the blood from the first seal killed.

Index

For information on opposing the Canadian seal slaughter, contact
The Sea Shepherd Conservation Society:

In Canada
  P.O. Box 48446
  Vancouver, BC
  V7X 1A2

In the U.S.
  22774 Pacific Coast Highway
  Malibu, CA
  90265

Web site: **www.seashepherd.org**